DOWN WE GO

LIVING INTO THE WILD WAYS OF JESUS

KATHY ESCOBAR

Down We Go

Living Into the Wild Ways of Jesus

by Kathy Escobar

*Inspiration and challenge for ecclesial dreamers,
church burn-outs, missional practitioners and ordinary people
who want to live the ways of Jesus in practice.*

CivitasPress

Publishing inspiring and redemptive ideas.[sm]

Copyright Notice

ISBN #13: 978-0615467900 (Civitas Press)
Published by Civitas Press, LLC
Folsom, CA.
www.civitaspress.com

LCCN # 2011928811

Contents

Introduction   13

SECTION ONE - DOWNWARD MOBILITY   17

Chapter 1 - It Stinks Down Here but I Really Love the Smell   19

Chapter 2 - Dreams are Much Prettier When They Are Just Dreams   33

Chapter 3 - There is No "Them or Us"...Only Us   50

Chapter 4 - "The Kingdom Isn't Just Going to Drop Out of the Sky"   67

SECTION TWO - CREATING LIFE DOWN HERE   91

Chapter 5 - Extending Love, Mercy and Compassion   94

Chapter 6 - Welcoming Pain   109

Chapter 7 - Honoring Doubt   130

Chapter 8 - Diffusing Power   150

Chapter 9 - Practicing Equality   168

Chapter 10 - Pursuing Justice   182

Chapter 11 - Cultivating Creativity   199

Chapter 12 - Celebrating Freedom   212

SECTION THREE - STAYING THE COURSE   227

Chapter 13 - Beautiful and Hazardous   229

Chapter 14 - We May Look Like Losers   239

Chapter 15 - We May Be Crazy But We're Not Alone   251

Chapter 16 - Born Again and Again   263

Suggested Resources   272

References   274

Dedication

For The Refuge, you are beautiful.

For all the dreamers, it's possible.

Endorsements

"Like Kathy Escobar, and like a lot of Christians, I've spent a huge chunk of time and energy trying to climb the ladders of religious success. Ascend to higher knowledge. Rise to loftier faith. Climb to a position of more influence. You know the drill. But like Kathy, I keep discovering that this upwardly-mobile program is about 180 degrees off course. The way of Jesus, the way of the Kingdom of God, celebrates descent. It's about solidarity with the needy, not isolation with the elite. It's about being the friend of sinners on the margins, not of the hot shots in the inner circle. And it's about abandoning 'Christian witness' to 'the unsaved' down below us and moving instead towards 'Christian with-ness' where we join God with those who are considered outcasts, losers and lost causes. Page after page in *Down We Go*, I feel the crazy sanity of the kingdom of God seeping back into me. I'm so thankful for Kathy Escobar, The Refuge, the TransFORM Network and everyone who dares to switch directions and become more profane — in the holiest sense of the word." **- Brian D. McLaren, Author of *Naked Spirituality* and *A New Kind of Christianity***

"In *Down We Go*, Kathy Escobar explores how to move from 'doing' ministry for others into creating sacred spaces where all can be a part of the Kingdom of God. Those desiring something beyond 'comfy church' will find inspiration in Kathy's downwardly mobile journey that puts human skin on Jesus' radically inclusive parables that redeems those the world rejects." **- Becky Garrison, Author of *Jesus Died for This?***

"In *Down We Go*, **Kathy Escobar leads us on a guided tour of the wild ways** of Jesus. Traditionally, leaders who intentionally choose to work among **the poor, disadvantaged and mentally ill come from upper middle class** backgrounds (think St. Francis and Mother Teresa). Unlike them Kathy came from a background of economic deprivation and struggle. Wanting to escape that fate, she pursued the American (and Christian) dream with laser focus **and became a star both outside and inside the church, rising to the status** of mega-church staff pastor. Her love for Jesus however would not let her rest. She voluntarily walked away from predictability and professional comfort, knowing the cost. Today she finds herself leading a community of people Jesus loves and together with them has invented a whole new way of understanding what it means to be the church. She is one of my favorite leaders. I hope to continue to learn from her example for years to come." - **Jim Henderson, D. Min, Author of** *Jim and Casper Go To Church* **and** *The Resignation of Eve*

"In *Down We Go*, Kathy Escobar takes us down into the trenches where ordinary hurting people live and where we, too, need to live out our faith. Her personal faith journey from mega-church pastor to ministry with the destitute and marginalized is a compelling and convicting read. An important book for all who want a deeper walk with Jesus." - **Christine Sine, Author and Executive Director of Mustard Seed Associates**

"Through her bold, beautiful blog and now this book, Kathy Escobar shares her story and shows us how to live into the way of Jesus in the midst of our swirling, confusing communities that tell us everyday that 'bigger is better' and more is better than less. From her nearly two decades of life experience, Kathy redefines success in an accessible way. I may not be able to sew my own clothes like Shane Claiborne, but I can follow Kathy Escobar where she is going — down into the mess of our real lives where it's dark and smelly but beautiful things grow. I don't have to go there alone, either. I can go in community and with Kathy Escobar's wisdom along the way. And there's no better guide to have on this journey of discovering that the last will be first and the weak will ultimately punk the strong." - **Steve Knight, Community Architect for TransFORM Network (www.transformnetwork.org) and Leadership Development Consultant for the Hope Partnership for Missional Transformation**

"In the flowing rhythmic style of the prophets of old, Kathy speaks on issues that the church needs to hear. By shedding light on what the realities of the Kingdom of God truly are, she exposes the underbelly of the counter-kingdoms of power, division and exclusion for all to see. This is a must-read for anyone considering the notion of planting a church and anyone currently taking on a leadership role in an existing community of Jesus. Likewise, this book is mandatory for anyone choosing to follow Jesus into the weird, wild, realities of Kingdom living that take them to places and people that no one has gone to before." - **John Martinez, Co-Pastor of The Distillery Church, Albany, NY**

"In a time when we are inundated with books about re-thinking church and rediscovering Jesus, Pastor Kathy Escobar describes for us a refreshing and unpretentious alternative as it is lived out in her own church community — The Refuge. Her focus is not about new structures, forms or cool ideas but the church itself, the real people living in both their human dignity and broken disarray. With the tender eye of a good shepherd, what Escobar describes is not merely a new spin on the therapeutic model of church in which people are cared for and ministered to. Instead, she proffers what it means to create a community in which people are gathered together in true communion as a 'we.' People are free then to live in their imperfect and authentic selves, and free to grow, create and work together to redeem and restore the brokenness in the world around us. This book is a beautiful theology of descent into the depths of real human lives, where Jesus lives and heals and creates the Kingdom right here in our midst." - **Ellen Haroutunian, Therapist, Pastor at Urban Skye and Co-Author of *A New Kind of Conversation*, with Brian McLaren**

"As I read this book I am reminded of the question from poet Mary Oliver, 'Tell me, what is it you plan to do with your one wild and precious life?' Kathy is persuaded by beauty and grace and she has followed that beauty and grace into some unlikely places. When she can't follow she falls into that same beauty and grace. Either way, she occupies those places with such generosity. It makes me want to do the same. What a gift!" - **Kris Rocke, D. Min., Executive Director at Center for Transforming Mission**

"I wish everyone who picks up a copy of *Down We Go: Living Into the Wild Ways of Jesus*, could spend a few days at the elbow of its author, Kathy Escobar. If you did, you would discover what I already know — that Kathy is the real deal. She speaks, not from her head, not from a lofty theory, but from her actual practice. The wisdom she shares in these pages is the fruit of cultivated, intentional and courageous community, lived in the company of souls who have the most to teach us about the ways of Jesus. In *Down We Go*, Kathy confronts our safe ideas with exuberance and love for the ones Jesus loves, with the beauty and the pain, the hope and the tragedy of real kingdom living. She invites us to lay aside our comfortable fortresses and dare to follow Jesus where he died to lead us — into the trenches of messy humanity. I wholeheartedly endorse this book. May it light a fire in the hearts of those who long to spend their lives following that wildest of wild men, Jesus of Nazareth." - **Phyllis Mathis, M.A, Professional Counselor and Life Coach**

"Many of us have been sort of forced to embrace downward mobility by virtue of a collapsing economy. Kathy Escobar thinks it's a good idea to choose it intentionally, and by it she means something far more costly than just living on less money. This is a disturbing (in a good way), vulnerable, gritty field **guide to places and people that many of us have avoided in our quest for** happiness and security. It's an eye-opening glimpse into what the downward journey looks like at a place called The Refuge, and a rather compelling and passionate case that calls us to consider what it might look like to lose our lives so we might find them. Read at your own risk. Kathy will likely win you over, and you may find yourself choosing to make the great descent, too." - **Randy Siever, Executive Director of Doable Evangelism**

"Kathy takes the reader on a trip down the rabbit hole with this challenge: 'If **we are really living out the gospels the way that Jesus modeled for us, then** we should be known as the weirdest, craziest risk takers and lovers of people in town.' She prophetically calls out the ethos for the church of the future with these sage bits of wisdom — learn to experience neediness; learn to receive from others, as well as give; wholeness is accepting our own brokenness. **Kathy Escobar has forged her wisdom in the crucible of everyday experience,** enabling her to cut to the heart of Kingdom living, which is 'let the greatest among you become the servant.' It is a dangerous read for the complacent!" - **Deborah Koehn Loyd, D.Min, Church Planter and Adjunct Faculty at George Fox Seminary**

"Kathy has given readers a playbook on how to flip the script when it comes to being a faith community of Jesus followers. Her message of living downwardly mobile as Christians is counter to the pursuit of excellence and ministry **accomplishment that is prevalent in many churches today. She reminds us** that success is measured differently in the upside-down kingdom of God when we make loving people the point, rather than ministering to people. This book will rattle your missional bones and might even break a few." - **Pam Hogeweide, Blogger at www.godmessedmeup.blogspot.com**

"No other author, from her powerful blog to now this incredible book, has **had more of an impact on my life than Kathy. In the gentlest way possible,**

Down We Go challenges previously held notions of what it means to be a
follower of Jesus. Sometimes it is easy to wonder about the real life of an
author, and if their words are reflected in their actual practice. Rest assured;
there could not be a more solid lover of people, who is open to share the
depth of her wisdom in this book. My hope is that as you read through
these pages, Kathy's compassionate voice will resonate how possible
the journey of downward mobility truly can be." - **Stacy Schaffer, M.A.,**
Therapist and Co-Pastor of The Refuge

"If you wonder where the 'letters' to today's church are, wonder no more!
Kathy Escobar calls us to hear what a living God has to say about how we
can currently live out what Jesus taught in the Sermon on the Mount. It's
incendiary, having changed the way The Refuge approached church and
guides how we operate at The Bridge as well. This call to reflect God's heart
isn't for the faint of heart, but Kathy makes it approachable and doable." -
Donna Van Horn, Co-Pastor of The Bridge, Portland

Acknowledgements

It's almost a joke that in the midst of one of the most weird, wild years of my life I ended up writing this book. In 2010, my oldest son left for college, my husband was activated for the military reserves, and I ended up having back surgery the week before Thanksgiving. That's on top of having four other kids at home and pastoring our crazy little faith community, The Refuge. Somehow Jonathan Brink from Civitas Press convinced me that it was time to bring this material to life and that the perfect time was while my back was healing. If he had actually seen what it looked like to make it happen, I'm pretty sure he would have changed his mind. I am thankful he pushed me to pull this project together and create something cohesive. He has been an amazing cheerleader, editor and friend on the journey; the truth is that I needed **someone to believe in this for me.**

Finishing Down We Go **would also be impossible without the faithful support,** editing help and loving challenge from Sage Harmos, Megan Harris, Stacy Schaffer, Mike Herzog and Phyllis Mathis. In different ways, they cheered me on, challenged me to consider things that needed considering, fixed a lot of mistakes and saw the manuscript from its roughest draft to this final product. **I am so grateful for the ways they handled it with care and love.**

Without The Refuge community, my dreams would still be dreams. There are no other people I'd rather be on this downward journey with; they are my "Jesus in the flesh," my advocates, my brothers and sisters, mothers and fathers, daughters and sons. They help me believe.

Also, my husband Jose rocks. Picture me working on my computer, trying to focus, with kid chaos swirling all around me, and him swooping in and rescuing me over and over again. He is the best teammate and partner; it's a pain in the butt to be married to me and he does it with style and grace.

Lastly, I need to extend deep gratitude to all my blog readers and the online friends I have made along the way. Your emails, comments, phone calls, support, encouragement and love deeply inspire me to keep walking this path, despite its hazards. Thank you for being part of this wild and beautiful journey.

Introduction

For many years in my Christian experience I was taught that life was about "ascending toward God" through a life of prayer, Bible study, worship and hanging around other Christians. Having not been raised in an overtly Christian home, it took me a while to figure out what Christian life was supposed to look like. I learned by observing. It didn't take me long to learn the rules, follow directions and forge a fairly insulated faith life where I said and did the right things and seemed to fit in fairly well. It wasn't all bad. I learned a lot **during those years and in many ways, I thrived.**

The part that I struggled with, though, was the life of ascent that was being taught—a ladder-like living where each day was a step closer to God and away from pain and struggle. My own life didn't seem to be so linear, so simple, and the life of many of my friends—when they had a chance to be honest—didn't seem that way, either. Slowly, I began to see that Jesus doesn't call us to a life **of ascent where we move further and further away from the things of this world. Rather, I believe he calls us to a life of descent, of downward mobility, where we move down into the trenches of real life, real pain, real hope in our own lives and in the lives of others.**

This is in deep contrast to the life of upward mobility that the world—and sometimes the church—beckons us toward. A life of comfort, predictability, and self-protection was never the idea. *Jesus embodied downward mobility and calls us to the same.*

To me, downward mobility is a matter of the heart, not financial resources. It is losing our lives instead of protecting them. Giving away our hearts instead of insulating them. Intersecting with pain instead of numbing it out. Entering into relationship with people different from us instead of staying comfortably separated. Learning instead of teaching. Practicing instead of theorizing.

This book is a reflection of the downward journey I've been on for the past **17 years. Faith is art, not science. Because of this, there are no formulas to** follow or checklists to cross off when it comes to living out the wild ways **of Jesus. We each intersect with God and people in our own unique ways.** Some of you have been on the journey downward much longer than me and have many wild stories to tell; others are only recently feeling the presence of something different; still others aren't sure where to land but just know that it's time to put their toes into some new water and see what it feels like. Regardless of where you are on your faith journey, this material is designed to challenge not only your thinking but also your actions.

In the first few chapters of *Down We Go*, I'll be setting the stage for what I think are cornerstones of downward living. Everything points towards people above programs, relationships above power, and risk over comfort. We must break down the walls that separate people, which create an "us vs. them" mentality, and actively resist the upward pull toward comfort and away from pain. Life down here is active, not passive, and is rooted in the practice of love, not perfection. The practice of love permeates every aspect of downward **living and is weaved throughout this material.** *Section One* **focuses on the core principles of downward living, while** *Section Two* fleshes out the central practices. These Kingdom practices are inspired by the Beatitudes and include **extending love, mercy and compassion, welcoming pain, honoring doubt,** diffusing power, practicing equality, pursuing justice, cultivating creativity and celebrating freedom. My hope is that each of these practices will become integrated into our daily lives in practical, tangible ways. *Section Three*, **the** last section, focuses on ways to sustain life down here, despite the upward tug. This requires cultivating resiliency, redefining success and nurturing supportive relationships with others who are passionate about living out **these ways, as well.**

Each chapter in *Down We Go* includes personal journaling questions to explore, along with group discussion starters so you can talk about these **challenges with other people, too. When ideas are shared, they blossom far more than when they stay in the quiet of our individual hearts. Also included** are practical ways to live these values out. Some suggestions may be familiar to you while others may be challenging or even scary. Their intent is to help you step beyond your current comfort zone.

Down We Go **is for people who are hungry to see the Kingdom of God now,** in the least likely of places, just below the surface of everyday life. It is for people who are tired of ascent and all the ways it seems contrary to the ways of Jesus. For friends who are tired of talking about God in theory and now just want to *do* something. For pot-stirrers who know it's time to shake up the status quo and live out something far more dangerous than they've ever tried before. For lovers-of-people who want real relationships instead of superficial ones. For those secretly bored of going to church every week, listening to the **same message and leaving feeling lonely and disconnected from the power** of the Gospel. For activists dedicated to creating new systems and structures that diffuse power and free the marginalized. For dreamers who dream of what could be and are ready to strap in for the bumpy, scary, beautiful ride **down and then help lead others there as well.**

This material is meant to stir the pot, make you feel uncomfortable, and address real life on the descent. The path we take looks radically different for each of us. Many of my stories are focused on journeying with friends who are healing from deep wounds, abuse, addiction, and mental illness. This doesn't mean that to live life in the downward direction you have to find a way to work at shelter for abused women or start an addiction group. Everyone's story, passions, and experiences are uniquely beautiful. As you intersect with **this material, I invite you to wonder,** *"What does descent look like in my own context?"* Build bridges and use your imagination wherever you can. My hope is that each of us finds inspiration and courage to continually leave our emotional, spiritual, and practical "high places"—whatever they each may be—and move toward living out a more downwardly-focused faith in tangible **ways.**

The world is not desperate for new knowledge; there's plenty of that to last many lifetimes. The world is aching for authentic people willing to be Jesus' hands, feet, eyes, and heart and boldly go where he goes—to those on the **margins of life and faith.**

Thank you for coming with me on this journey down.

We really need each other down here.

SECTION ONE
DOWNWARD MOBILITY

I was talking to a friend the other day about life in the trenches. A church planter and pastor for years, she now teaches leadership at a seminary. We always share stories and tend to end up in the same place in our conversations—downward mobility is not popular, but it's the best thing that ever happened to us. Every day we see God alive and at work in our lives and in the lives of our friends.

The world, and sometimes the church, tells us that life is about comfort, ease and getting what we want. Jesus set the stage for a completely different kind of living—a life of humility, sacrifice and love.

The journey down starts with the inspirational text of the Beatitudes in Matthew 5:3-12, the beginning of Jesus' most table-turning sermon. It's here that he rocks the establishment and challenges us with the core values of a Kingdom-infused life. The first beatitude, "Blessed are the poor in spirit" (Matthew 5:3), sets the stage for every aspect of downward mobility.

Everything down here begins with humility.

Humility stems from a theology of brokenness, an honest acceptance of pain in our own lives and in the lives of others. We begin to see what we didn't see before. When we acknowledge brokenness instead of ignoring it, a door is opened so that we are able to have more honest, authentic relationships with people, in which we can practice love. Embracing a theology of brokenness also breaks down the divide between "us and them" and ways we remain protected from other people, thinking we are better or worse because we are different. In Kingdom living, there is no "us or them." There's only *us*.

This core value of humility is one of the most critical elements of life on the downward path. If we set out on this journey to think we will "help poor people and do good," we will strip not only others' dignity, but also our own. Rather, life down here is being in the thick of it together and learning how to come alongside each other in transformational "with" relationships, instead of only giving or serving the kind of relationships in which we give "to" or do "for" others, thereby missing out on healing in our own lives.

The Kingdom of God isn't going to drop out of the sky; we will have to be active, intentional participants in revealing it. This begins with expanding our view of God beyond our limited experiences and seeing the Spirit at work in unlikely places. When we put relationship with people above everything, we will cultivate authentic transformational community—little pockets of love—instead of spending our energy, building ministries or lifestyles that don't reflect the humble spirit of the Beatitudes. These pockets of love help teach us interdependence, a critical characteristic of Kingdom living.

Another critical element we can't forget as we engage a life of downward mobility is dreaming. Big or small, dreams are part of Kingdom living. They inspire us to try scary things, meet new people, jump into the deep end, or put our toes in the water. Without dreams we can't make "what could be," a reality. At the same time, I continue to learn that dreams are often much prettier when they are just dreams. Life down here doesn't always turn out the way we think it should be, that's for sure.

But that's the beauty of downward mobility. "Pretty" and "easy" aren't the goals. Transformation is.

And one thing is clear: *Down here, there's a lot of room for transformation.*

Chapter 1

It Stinks Down Here but I Really Love the Smell

"So the last will be first and the first will be last."
- Matthew 20:16

I always had it in my mind I was going to be successful. Raised by a single mom who struggled and scraped by to make ends meet, I was determined to go to college, get my degree, make loads of money and do whatever I could to build security for myself. I did pretty well for a few years. I secured a good scholarship to a prestigious college, started rubbing elbows with movers and shakers, juggled a budding career with graduate school and bought my first brand-new car. I was obsessed with "making it" and seemed to be on my way. I started dating my husband during this season and he, too, was excited about our earning potential and bright, shiny future.

Then someone put a wrench in my plans — Jesus. When I first started following Jesus I kept him at a fairly safe distance, going through the motions of faith but staying focused on my controlled life. Over time he started digging up all kinds of things from my past that were hidden and negatively affecting my relationship with God, others and myself. The feelings terrified me at first but I began to recognize the crazy ways I was trying to build a protected, comfortable life for myself after growing up feeling unsafe most of the time.

Pain is Everywhere

As I started to get in touch with my pain, something wild and unexpected began to happen that turned my confined suburban world upside down. *God began introducing me to other people in pain, too.* Christians, non-Christians, **rich, poor, married, unmarried, white, brown, educated or uneducated. I** started recognizing that pain crosses every kind of barrier.

My husband was a little freaked out at first, hearing me express deep pain that I had never shared with him. He was shocked, and also somewhat relieved. In that season, he finally started to really know me—all of me. I felt liberated. He and I became more deeply connected. Initially, neither of us felt comfortable with this level of honesty, but we kept practicing it as best we could.

As I jumped off the career fast track to nurse babies and change diapers full-time, it also became clear that as I was more honest and vulnerable, others around me started to become more transparent, too. Thankfully, during this season, I met some other moms at church who weren't just talking about the latest brand of baby formula. They were sharing how hard it was for them to feel loved, how abandoned they sometimes felt by God, and how much pain they were actually experiencing. They were so brave! The next thing I knew, I was talking about those things as well. It was freeing to be that honest, but also terrifying. It was foreign and definitely not something I had been previously taught "in church."

Then something even weirder happened. The churches I was part of started to get mad at me for talking about pain so much. They wanted to talk about The Word of God, serving, leading and growing—not brokenness, desperation, **healing and fear. But it was too late. By then I had seen too much of the** terrible dissonance between what things looked like on the outside and what was actually happening on the inside. I discovered I wasn't the only one feeling the tension. I started hearing others' stories of shame, guilt, and fear. **I began to listen to tales of deep sadness, grief and loneliness and saw the** painful reality that many people didn't feel loved or fully accepted by God. I began to notice pain everywhere I looked.

Pain was the catalyst for engaging what I call my downward descent; I began entering more deeply into the low places of other people's lives and experiencing Jesus in a way that was completely counter-cultural to what I had learned. For years, I had been fed a theology of ascent. Upward meant victory and success. I had been taught that, with enough prayer, scripture and Christian fellowship, I wouldn't struggle. This ascent theology definitely catalyzed my secular longings to "rise above" and "make it to that place where I wouldn't have to struggle anymore." However, I discovered I couldn't reconcile this idea with the realities of my own story and the stories of so many others. As I reflected on the Gospels of Jesus, I deeply resonated with the reality that he came for the sick, not the healthy, that he was born from below and that he knew pain. Jesus met people in their darkest moments instead of standing on high watching them suffer and waiting for them to get their acts together. He somehow always managed to get tangled up with the riff-raff, the marginalized, the forgotten and the ones crying out in pain.

The tug to follow him into the places Jesus tended to go slowly became stronger over time. I didn't wake up one day and declare, "This is how I'm going to live my life, starting now." Rather, I kept gradually being drawn toward the hurting, the desperate and people on the fringe. I would be at a typical women's Bible study and somehow the person next to me would share that her life was falling apart and I'd stop worrying about doing my homework and start spending time with her instead. Eventually I got kicked out of the Bible study for not doing my homework!

The Cost of Descent

My trek down has not been an easy one. Embedded in my human DNA is a desire for clean, neat, tidy, and "successful," whatever that is supposed to mean. Over the past 10 years I have kicked, screamed, and resisted the downward momentum in more ways than I can describe; most of my resistance is because I have been scared. Scared by what it means to go "down" in a world that praises "up." Scared to follow the calling deep inside my heart that tells me that what the world (and often "the church") says is valuable, is of no value at all in the Kingdom of God. Scared to engage not only with my own spiritual poverty, but also the poverty of others. Scared to stand up against the power structures, on behalf of those being crushed by its weight. Scared to leave the safe confines of church as I knew it.

Without a doubt, descent has cost me a lot. Over the years I've lost money, friendships, status, power, and a whole bunch of pride. Many friends and family don't understand why we've chosen this path. They wonder why we spend so much time and energy on pain and poverty when we used to be satisfied with just going to church. At the same time, traveling down has been the most gorgeous and amazing experience that could have ever happened to me. It rescued my heart, saved my faith and awakened a sense of justice and **passion inside me that had been buried underneath religion and a desire for comfort and safety.**

The Beauty of Authentic Relationships

There's nothing more beautiful to me than seeing hurting people find authentic, healing community. Seven years ago I was on a mega-church staff as a Care Pastor, co-leading a growing recovery ministry and counseling hurting people. When people in pain or trouble intersected with another church leader, they'd send them my way. One day I got a phone call from the **person who ran the Clothing Closet for the local pregnancy care center. She** told me about "this couple with a baby who came in for diapers, but seemed like they needed really serious help."

When I first met Jesse and Elizabeth I discovered they had met as patients in a mental hospital. They fell in love, got pregnant and were quickly married by a justice of the peace. On disability for their mental health issues, they didn't have money, safe friends, or practical support for their family.

They began showing up at the recovery ministry on Friday nights; Jesse usually sat in the corner and didn't talk to anyone, a blank uncomfortable stare etched on his face, while Elizabeth was happy to be out of the house and chatted away with anyone who would listen. Slowly, I began introducing Jesse to a few other safe men who looked him in the eye and asked him how he was doing. I called and checked in once a week. It took almost a full year before Jesse's tough outer shell began to crack. Once it did, there emerged a beautiful, kind, smart, hurting person who had never before experienced God's love, or love from other people in his life.

Our relationship superseded the recovery ministry and when I left to begin a new faith community, The Refuge, they joined the adventure with us. The Refuge was born out of a desire for friends like Jesse and Elizabeth to be a full **and integral part of church instead of being sidelined to the recovery ministry** or stuck as the recipients of charity. The Refuge became a space where there is no divide between the "healthy" and the "sick." We are all in the thick of it together—poor and rich, uneducated and educated, unchurched and churched. Over and over, Jesse and Elizabeth's presence and lives inspire me to continue on this journey down.

Not everything is rosy. Their mental and physical disabilities still exist, and despite the hope and healing that spills out now and then, Jesse continues to battle the past damage of extreme neglect and abuse, and Elizabeth is occasionally hospitalized. Life is still hard. Jesse often wants to die and is sick and tired of being sick and tired. Here's what's so lovely—he's no longer alone in the low and dark places of his experience. He has friends who care and a community that loves him. In my former ascent-driven life, sitting in the next new and exciting Bible study with a bunch of people who looked and thought just like me, I would have never met Jesse and Elizabeth. They would have fit into the category of "those poor people who use the system and never change." Now they're my friends and my family. They share our Thanksgiving table, check on me when I'm sick and love me in a deep way that has changed **my life forever.**

On the outside, appearances would suggest Jesse, Elizabeth and I have nothing in common. Yet, on the inside, we are the same. All three of us want to be known, loved, and valued. We sometimes feel afraid and lonely. We wonder **if God really cares about us and if the people in our lives are going to ditch us tomorrow. We wish we could somehow rise above all our problems and have** piles of money so that we could feel more secure. The more our relationship deepens, the more my eyes and heart open to the beauty of incarnational relationships on the downward journey. Even though ingrained systems of marginalization and ongoing mental health issues make Jesse and Elizabeth's day-to-day life hard, there's so much hope and healing that can happen when our experiences intersect. For all kinds of reasons, Jesse and Elizabeth are probably never going "up."

That means I must go down.

Down Means Up

Descent goes against my basic nature of wanting a controlled, predictable, upwardly mobile kind of life, not only for me, but also for my family. I know from experience that it is far more comforting to be part of a culture where everyone is focused on building security and safety. The magnetic pull "up" is strong. However, I continue to learn how most of Jesus' teachings have a wild, **paradoxical twist: in the Kingdom of God, somehow, down means up**. Much of my previous Christian experience was focused on rising up to be closer to God; now, I'm learning that downward mobility is what draws me nearer to God. When I am with my friends in the darkness and pain, I am acutely aware of God's presence more than in my comfortable places.

I am not alone on this path; there are many others who somewhere along the way realized that "going up" was never the idea, even though we bought into it for a long time. In God's economy, almost everything the world, and often church, told me I should shoot for, achieve or do, now means very little. God's economy is about tangibly expressing love. Now, I am surrounded by a lot of people who do that well.

A few years ago, some friends invited me to lunch to learn more about the work they were doing in India on behalf of the poorest of the poor. They showed a video of precious women and children ravaged by AIDS and living in the slums, sold into prostitution and sifting through garbage to find something to eat. The video was powerful, but what struck me most in the moment was how these smart, talented and educated people sacrificed their careers, money, status and power to care for "the least of these." I was both awed and deeply encouraged to continually resist my human nature, which clamors for the comfortable, and continue on this journey down.

I hope my story will inspire you to keep walking this direction, too.

The Beatitudes

Downward mobility is about discovering and revealing what it means to live into the Kingdom of God as a Christ-follower. The guiding text for a life of descent is the Beatitudes in Matthew 5:3-12. These passages inspire us toward a better way. Jesus' words of blessing to the poor, marginalized and the downwardly mobile were not a threat or a coercion technique to force us into a miserable life. His call to go downward is a methodology for the abundant life. It is the easier yoke. If we crave God's peace and presence, then I guess we have to trust his methods too. It's easy to think more money, power or status will give us security and a stronger sense of self, yet Jesus says it will be exactly the opposite: *to find our lives we need to lose them* (Matthew 10:39).

In fact, the more we read the Gospels, allowing the Beatitudes to sink into our bones and be sewn into our skin, the more we realize that there's really nowhere else to go but down.

Down into the mess of real life.

Down into the ugly places of the human experience.

Down into the places where real people in need of God's hope live.

Here's a reminder of what Jesus said:

> *Blessed are the poor in spirit, for theirs is the kingdom of heaven.*
>
> *Blessed are those who mourn, for they will be comforted.*
>
> *Blessed are the meek, for they will inherit the earth.*
>
> *Blessed are those who hunger and thirst for righteousness, for they will be filled.*
>
> *Blessed are the merciful, for they will be shown mercy.*
>
> *Blessed are the pure in heart, for they will see God.*
>
> *Blessed are the peacemakers, for they will be called children of God.*
>
> *Blessed are those who are persecuted because of righteousness, for theirs is the kingdom of heaven.* - Matthew 5:3-10

To be perfectly honest, almost everything I was taught in much of my initial church experience was completely contrary to this. I was taught to:

"Pull myself up by my bootstraps, believe more, and figure out a way to be strong."

"Not feel too much because pain is somehow bad."

"Find ways to rise to the top."

"Run with the pack and do not question what they tell me to believe."

"Believe that God helps those who help themselves."

"Pray harder, memorize more scripture, and keep asking for forgiveness 'just in case' there was something still offensive in my heart."

"Separate myself from the real world and surround myself with other people like me so that I would be protected from harm."

Of course, no one said these things overtly; they were subtle undertones **of strength and put-togetheredness that permeates much of contemporary** Christian culture. In the spirit of this conversation, I think it is critically important to acknowledge just how prevalent, powerful—and damaging— these completely-contrary-to-the-Beatitudes messages really are. I have a funny feeling I'm not the only one who had some of these messages infused **into my spirituality.**

It's what Jesus was always working against.

It's what we'll always be working against.

Over and over in the gospels, Jesus embodies an upside-down way of living and challenges the status quo—especially the *religious* **status quo. Born to a** young unwed mother in a dirty stall, telling all kinds of crazy stories, eating with prostitutes and tax-collectors, washing his followers' feet, and ultimately hanging on a cross, Jesus was always mixing it up. What should make sense doesn't, and what doesn't make sense actually does.

I always say that I love the Beatitudes. And I hate the Beatitudes. They are **powerful words from a radical man who messed with my life.**

And I have a feeling they're messing with yours. Otherwise, you probably wouldn't be reading this book.

In contemporary culture, these haunting words of Jesus don't make sense. **Success, war, vengeance, power and strength are the guiding principles of** our day. Humility, gentleness, desperation, spiritual poverty, advocating for justice and being persecuted for standing on the side of the oppressed are sure to make us inconvenienced, challenged and humbled.

But who said this journey was about being prepared, secure and sure? The faith I see in the Bible is far riskier, scarier and less certain than what's been modeled to me in many past church experiences. The New Testament is filled **with people giving up all sorts of things that protected them in order to live** out the crazy ways of Jesus after he left this earth.

I chose this downward path because this is the kind of person that I want to **be.**

I want to be a person of humility, willing to give up my safety and comfort for the sake of others. I want to be a person who risks, engaging in the dangerous work of living the Bible instead of only learning about it. I want to be a person of hope, sacrificing my current circumstances to participate in building a better future. I want to be a person of courage, boldly practicing love.

The 12 Steps

I have a lot of friends who are addicts. Even though I don't drink or do drugs anymore, I am painfully aware of how addicted I am to work, approval, caretaking and a host of other things that are extremely hard to stop doing. Seven years ago I finally started working the 12 Steps of Alcoholics Anonymous in an intentional way. As I looked into the history of the 12 Steps I learned they are based on the Beatitudes. When contrasted with the independent, **success-oriented world where most of us live, they are as counter-cultural as** Jesus' teachings.

Much like the Beatitudes, I found that I love the 12 Steps. And I hate the 12 **Steps.**

They, too, are about downward mobility instead of the upward kind. They **are about choosing humility instead of power, honesty rather than pride,** vulnerability in place of self-protection, mercy over "right" behavior.

Here's what the 12 Steps of Alcoholics Anonymous say:

1. We admitted we were powerless over our alcohol-- that our lives had **become unmanageable.**

2. **Came to believe that a Power greater than ourselves could restore us to sanity.**

3. Made a decision to turn our will and our lives over to the care of God as we understood Him.

4. Made a searching and fearless moral inventory of ourselves.

5. Admitted to God, to ourselves, and to another human being the exact **nature of our wrongs.**

6. Were entirely ready to have God remove all these defects of character.

7. Humbly asked Him to remove our shortcomings.

8. Made a list of all persons we had harmed, and became willing to make amends to them all.

9. Made direct amends to such people wherever possible, except when to do so would injure them or others.

10. Continued to take personal inventory and when we were wrong promptly admitted it.

11. Sought through prayer and meditation to improve our conscious contact with God as we understood Him, praying only for knowledge of His will for us and the power to carry that out.

12. Having had a spiritual awakening as the result of these steps, we tried to carry this message to others, and to practice these principles in all our affairs.[1]

I found that the word "alcohol" in the first step could be replaced with any addiction or compulsive behavior. We become powerless over drugs, eating, pornography, controlling, working, people pleasing, and a host of other unhealthy behaviors that destroy connection with ourselves, people, and God. As I progressed through the 12 steps, I couldn't help but recognize their remarkable likeness to the words of Jesus. Like the Beatitudes, the 12 Steps **are a movement away from self-centeredness, pride, control, and feeling good** at all costs to a life of sacrifice, humility and serving others. I think the Beatitudes and the 12 Steps are helpful toward becoming healthier and more kind, compassionate, giving, receiving, accepting, and loving people. I have no doubt that the world could be different if entire faith communities—not just individuals—tried to follow some of these Jesus-centered principles in tangible, practical ways.

It is amazing what can happen when we create a place in the church to practice honesty for the sake of restoration. I have experienced this in my **own life and have seen it in many others through various healing groups over** the years. But it was during my time working through the 12 Steps with other codependents, alcoholics, porn addicts, adulterers, drug users, abuse victims and real people who struggled with shame, guilt, hope and longing, just like me, that something shifted inside in a deep and lasting way. I got to taste the Kingdom of God like I never tasted it before.

I saw what spiritual poverty looked like, up close and personal. Even though we may come from different backgrounds and experiences, most people are really searching for the same things—*to be loved and to love.* Collectively, I **experienced the power of what could only happen** when a group of people ventured out on a similar path together, living these principles in practice, not just in theory. It was prettier—and uglier—than I ever expected.

To be honest, often life down here feels overwhelming. It's hard to live in the dark places of people's experiences. It's sometimes brutal to be tangled up in real life, fear, shame and debilitating struggle. But the truth is that I wouldn't trade it for anything. I've learned more about God and myself than through all the years I'd spent going to church and seminary, attending small groups and **Bible studies and trying to learn** *about* being a Christ-follower. The journey down has forced me away from just talking about loving others to actually practicing love with others.

The Upside-Down Kingdom

As I engage the downward path, I discover that the power systems of the world are inherently inconsistent with ways of the Kingdom, the upside-down kind of living Jesus espouses. Descent is the harder but more meaningful journey. We are battling not only our own fears and inadequacies, but also deeply grooved systems of inequality and power in a culture that thrives on success and strength.

Jesus told us his ways were harder. He said that to follow him meant we were going to have to give up everything familiar, that people would think we were crazy, that we'd be poor, persecuted and rejected, and that we'd lose our security and so many other things we held dear. At the same time, he told us we'd also find life.

We've always opened up our house on Thanksgiving dinner for friends that don't have family in town or another fun place to go. Over the years, the demographic of our gathering has radically shifted, from suburban families who all looked like us, to the oddest group of misfits you could ever imagine. Now, as I look around the circle as we share our thanks, my eyes well up with gratitude. I see the depth, breadth, and diversity of our relationships that now cross over socioeconomics, education,

"In the kingdom of God, somehow down means up."

theology, politics and almost every other thing that normally separates us. Down here, our lives are much richer. It reminds me of the movie *Titanic*. The experience on the upper deck looked so much better, but the lower deck was where the party was happening.

In Matthew 16, Jesus says, *"If anyone would come after me, he must deny himself and take up his cross and follow me."* There are many different ways this verse has been interpreted, but to me it means that to really follow him we will have to give up security and comfort and go where he goes. This means we better strap in, because to follow him, we're going down.

And I do mean down.

I do not believe that what I will share here is the end-all or be-all for life Jesus' way. No one has the market cornered on exactly what living out the

Bible really means. What I share is the experience I've gained, the strength I've discovered, and the hope that stems from what I am learning along the way. Every day I am reminded how tricky this life of faith really is. Some days I want to throw in the towel and run for the hills; on other days I am inspired, **challenged, and awed by the beauty I see in the midst of so much ugliness.**

Yes, sometimes it definitely stinks down here.

But I've learned to really love the smell.

I have a feeling you will, too.

* * * * *

Personal Reflection:

1. What does "downward mobility" mean to you?

2. Where are you seeing pain right now? Is it in your own life? The lives of others?

3. Read the Beatitudes several times. What verses pop out? Consider re-writing them in your own language as a way to connect with some of their power.

4. Reflect on the 12 Steps. How are they similar to the Beatitudes?

5. When you hear the call of Jesus to come and follow him, what does that mean to you?

Group Discussion:

1. Share with the group what "downward mobility" means to you.

2. Where are you experiencing pain right now in your own life? Where are you seeing pain in the lives of others around you? How does pain intersect with a life of downward mobility?

3. Read the Beatitudes out loud together, slowly, several times. Sit with them for a few minutes and then process together how they might inspire and challenge you.

4. Read the 12 Steps out loud. If you are familiar with the 12 Steps, share with the group how they've been helpful to you. If you aren't familiar with them, consider what resonates with you about them.

5. When Jesus said, "Come, follow me," what do you think he meant by this? Have each person in the group share, if possible, a short sentence or two that describes what "following Jesus" means.

Chapter 2

Dreams are Much Prettier When They Are Just Dreams

An eclectic faith community, all equal, love Jesus, pretty
messed up, lead, follow, laugh, cry, serve, Co-Pastors, stories
of brokenness and healing, smoker friendly, The Refuge
- from The Refuge website

The Kingdom of God can easily seem like a dream. It's this idea that feeds our imagination with visions of a world filled with justice and peace. It also feeds my desires for a better world, encouraging me to remain overly optimistic, **a hopeful dreamer. If we buy into the words of Jesus, life is meant to be** something better—something more whole.

For years I worked in church systems and ministries encouraging leaders to look toward the margins and break the divide between the "sick" and the "healthy." I have stood on tables (almost literally) advocating for change. Sometimes the things I have said and done embarrass me, but looking back I think it was worth it because dreams don't become reality by staying quiet.

Dr. Martin Luther King, Jr. once said, *"Almost always, the creative dedicated minority has made the world better."*[2] **For some reason I have always found** myself attracted to the creative minority in the church. I feel connected to the dreamers and pot-stirrers who have ideas of toppling unhealthy power structures, practicing equality as a natural rhythm of life together, honoring doubt and questions, pursuing justice and mercy on behalf of others, and destroying the great divide between "us and them."

As broken human beings, the downward path does not come naturally. We typically don't have many real-life models for what it means to give away power. On the whole, almost every system and structure we live in perpetuates power, strength and policy over relationship. Look at most organizations, systems, or churches and we will usually find charismatic leaders on top, who then find other leaders, who look and think like them, to be a part of their team. Humans tend to replicate themselves, but dreamers believe **this lopsided system can be changed, that the status quo can and should be** rocked.

The only problem is that dreams are much prettier when they are just dreams.

Over five years ago I left an attractive pastoral job at a very large church to plant The Refuge. I didn't really want to leave my old role—I really loved the people—but it became apparent during a dramatic leadership shift that I was no longer a good fit. There was incredible tension over the new direction the church would go after the lead pastor stepped down. I was part of a small pocket of pastors who were advocating for shared leadership and a willingness to shrink in size in order to diffuse power and become more focused on reaching out and deeply caring for the lost and hurting. There was another cluster of influencers who wanted to find a stable, visionary **leader who would aggressively lead and grow the church into a new building.** This experience, although painful, helped solidify my strong beliefs against business models for church and focus wholeheartedly on nurturing a different way.

Armed with a pile of dreams and broken hearts, I, along with one of my pastoral teammates and a group of other dreamers, started our wild little community, The Refuge. We were determined to focus on the values of **community, healing, generosity and equality, despite the cost to our egos and** bank accounts.

The Refuge has been the most authentic, challenging community I have experienced in my Christian journey. It is messy, chaotic, raw, uncomfortable **and unpredictable.** An eclectic group (in a suburban setting), we have an extremely wide range of diversity across socioeconomics, age, education, theology, politics and life experience. The one thing everyone has in common **is a desire to learn to love and be loved by Jesus, others and ourselves.**

The trickiest—and most beautiful—part of The Refuge is its diversity. People are finding a way across the divide and discovering relationship with those who are not like them. Sometimes I sit back and observe the oddest combinations of friends. People who make $600 a month on mental health disability and **never graduated from high school are hanging out with friends who have** master's degrees and make $6,000 a month. Suburban moms are building relationships with addicts. People from fundamentalist Christian backgrounds are engaging those with pagan backgrounds. Right wing Republican voters are actually conversing with liberal lefties and loving each other as brothers. Orphans, outcasts, lepers, prostitutes, pastors, single moms and dads, church **burn-outs, and everything in between are all muddled up together in what I** call "part church-part social service agency-part family."

It's wild. And it's annoying.

Diversity usually sounds best in theory. Most of us profess that groups are stronger and better when they include a wide range of people and experiences. However, humans have a natural propensity toward homogeneity and structures that keep us safely contained with other people mostly like us. A herd mentality permeates much of our current culture—including the church. We tend to stick with other people who look like us, think like us, act like us and believe like us. It makes life much easier. People who aren't like us usually bug us. Our differences can create a wedge between us because we don't know how to hold a space for disagreement. It's why doctrinal statements are important for many churches and ministries. They create a clear, discernible line that keeps those inside comforted, knowing the person next to them **generally buys into the same things they believe.**

At The Refuge, these lines are intentionally blurred. We choose to live in **the tension of coming from completely divergent life experiences. We believe** radically different things about God and life while still finding a way to love one another. Because we always have a culture of an open floor and a lot of dialogue, friends sometimes blurt out things that we might completely disagree with theologically and practically. I can't tell you the amount of times I cringe inside at the raw and pure sharing at our gatherings, because I know how uncomfortable it sometimes makes me and others feel. Some may have **an urge to swoop in and set them straight, but our culture is one that trusts** God is at work in mysterious ways and so we don't need to control others to make ourselves feel better.

We allow these conversations because they intentionally disrupt the status quo. As tough as they are, they inevitably lead to conversations of healing and restoration. They allow people to discover the Kingdom of God is much bigger than they could possibly imagine. They help people think outside of the box in a way that is restorative.

As much as we wish these conversations immediately led to fast healing, they don't. Healing usually comes at an incredibly slow pace. In fact, it often seems like people are getting worse and not better. Our natural desire for quick results urges us to lose patience with friends who seem to be barely making any progress. Add in social awkwardness, anger at God, deep insecurity and **visible pain, and the result is a wide range of possible ways to be annoyed.**

Most people don't go to church to get annoyed.

Many of us thought that going to "church" was about being inspired. Yes, it's **important to be inspired by God. But it is also possible to go only for the feeling** of inspiration. My friend Karl calls it "inspiration addiction." It is the powerful pull toward being entertained and inspired while sitting in our seats. I was definitely an inspiration addict. I remember leaving many a church service energized and filled up, thinking how amazing it was to listen to a powerful song, watch a moving film clip or hear a stirring sermon that made me laugh or cry. The problem is that very few of those inspirational moments translated into change in my real life. It became about getting a fix once a week.

Often, though, our addiction to inspiration shows up far beyond a weekly church service. We expect that the relationships we're in, the groups we go to, or the people and places we spend our time will somehow make us feel good, inspired, happy and encouraged. When they don't—when we somehow don't get the high or hope we are looking for—we move on to try and find it **elsewhere.**

When I read Jesus' interactions with the crowds and even his followers, I don't see Jesus immediately going after inspiration. Jesus disrupted people's world as much as inspired them. I see conversations full of dissonance, tension and confusion, and people leaving certain situations with Jesus scratching their heads. Others felt outraged. Yet those who stayed in the tension wept with gratitude. One thing feels fairly clear to me—his message, his delivery and the end result of his time here on earth wasn't consistently inspiring or feel-good in the ways we usually seek. Rather, over and over again, Jesus pointed **toward the upside-down and counter-cultural ways of the Kingdom of God:** *A life of sacrificial, tangible love regardless of the cost.*

For Jesus, the ways of love, sacrifice, justice and mercy do not come cheap or easy. The downward path into the Kingdom of God requires transcending our differences to discover something truly inspirational. At first, these relationships often don't leave us feeling inspired and infused with hopeful energy like a powerful sermon and worship service seems to. Sometimes they leave us feeling inadequate, angry, frustrated, confused, or a little empty and tired. But if we learn to stay in the tension, we end up discovering the **depths of something that an inspiring message can only hope to achieve:** *real relationship.*

Learning the ways of love through incarnational relationships with others **is messy.** Jesus understood this. He consistently stepped into and through the mess as opposed to away from it. He taught, healed, prayed, and gave everything—even his life—to show us the way through the mess, so we could discover how to live in love and hope. He knew we needed to get past the **things** we *thought* were inspirational to uncover the things that actually *are* inspirational.

Entering into messy places is a core characteristic of downward living. We need a diverse mix of intentional relationships in which to tangibly practice love. Also, consistent with the first Beatitude and an attitude of spiritual poverty, to live down here we must consider a theology of brokenness that embraces humility as the starting place. It also means we must develop eyes to see what others do not see and to begin to make visible what is often **invisible to the upwardly mobile.**

Jesus School

My downward journey has picked up speed from being part of The Refuge community. I call it my Jesus School: a place to learn to love Jesus, others and myself, and a place to be loved by Jesus, others and myself. This school is a tough one! Through being part of this community I am learning more than ever that love initially hurts. *Receiving and giving love among broken, real people is brutally hard in the beginning, but yet, not impossible.*

Relationships will be the most difficult and spiritually transforming experiences we will ever participate in, but they require a cost—a cost that when we're really honest, we may not actually want to pay. Deep down, most of us have learned to avoid pain. We long for the very connection and closeness we actively resist. It's part of the human condition God is working to restore. I am as guilty of it as the next person. I'd much rather connect with easy people who don't require anything of me and constantly tell me I can do no wrong. But in reality, I have always learned the most, grown the most and been challenged the most in the dissonance of intimate relationship.

Sacrificial love—a giving of myself—requires more of me than sometimes I want to give. I wonder if that's a small piece of what Jesus was saying about love—*there's no greater love than laying down our life for our friends* (John 15:13). When I give a piece of my heart and my life to another person, I am sacrificing myself. This kind of sacrifice is foreign and goes against many messages the world tells us about independence, self-reliance and doing-whatever-it-takes-to-feel-good. But it is only when we give away ourselves that we discover the meaning of love. In giving it away we become love. We become the incarnation of Jesus.

Living into this love requires comparing what we're doing to what Jesus did.

So what does this look like practically?

My friend, Jake, was a Christian leader for years. He led many students to Christ through a popular campus ministry and loved engaging with kids on a deep, heart level. About six years ago Jake began asking some really hard questions about his own practice of ministry. He started saying things that made leaders above him uncomfortable. He kept looking around at the "pretty people" who were chosen as leaders to replicate the ministry and wondered about those on the margins who weren't given the same love and attention. He started thinking about a painful reality after over 20 years as a Christian: *"I don't know any poor people."* As a result his faith began to melt down.

If the Gospel is true, then the place that we should be looking to live out our faith is not only to the pretty and popular, but also towards the margins— the poor, unloved, lonely, rejected, outcast, marginalized, and oppressed. The problem is that when we've lived insulated in systems that don't include those people, the only way to cross the divide is to extend a hand from up above and make ourselves available to serve at a soup kitchen or do some kind of charity volunteer work.

For Jake, he couldn't reconcile his current model of ministry with Jesus'. Staying protected and keeping his hands clean was no longer an option. He knew that his faith in practice wasn't aligning with what was stirring in his heart. When he started processing that out loud, people started getting anxious. They told him it was just a phase, a mid-life crisis, and that he'd be "back" soon.

When we began exploring his questions together, he told me that he didn't know any poor people in Denver. I knew plenty and invited him to come with me for a field trip or two. As we ventured out, he began seeing poverty, mental illness, addictions and deeply engrained systems of oppression up close and personal. Now he's ruined, so tangled up in the mess and mire of incarnational relationships that sometimes he wants to run for the hills just like me.

Here's what's so important to know about his story, though. He listened to the stirring deep in his heart and began to say out loud, "Something's wrong here. There's got to be more to faith than what I've been doing." He became part of the "creative minority" dedicated to revealing the Kingdom of God, and it wouldn't have happened if he continued to go along for the ride on the upward ascent. Here's what he says now about life in the low places:

> *"It kicks my ass most days. I see how easy I've had it and how hard it is to live without resource day in and day out. Sometimes, it grates on me because there don't seem to be any fast solutions. I like to solve problems and get things done.*

It doesn't work that way when we're talking about issues of poverty, mental illness, and injustice. Mostly, I'm learning how much I really don't know, how incompetent I can feel. But Jesus' words always ring in my ear—'For I was hungry and you gave me something to eat, I was thirsty and you gave me something to drink, I was a stranger and you invited me in, I needed clothes and you clothed me, I was sick and you looked after me, I was in prison and you came to visit me.' Jesus didn't say I needed to feel good about or understand it or have anything nailed down. He just said to do it."

Jake simply took the risk to discover why Jesus called us to descent.

This incarnational life in the trenches of real relationships taxes us, stretches us, moves us, and transforms us. And when I follow Jesus into the messy places, I am learning extremely important truths about downward mobility and life in the Kingdom. I am learning that I have to give as much as I get. In real relationship I can't sit passively, be inspired, and write a check for the offering plate; that just won't work. Incarnational living requires my blood, guts, time and energy. Most of us aren't great at the long haul and are even worse at conflict. We have a hard time living in the tension of not getting all of our needs met all of the time (think how many leave churches and groups because they don't have the right kinds of programs, speakers, meeting times, and a host of other reasons). I can remember my husband Jose and I complaining about our desire for "more of this, or more of that" and migrating to a new group or church to start over, hoping to meet our need to have it "work" for us.

Part of life in Jesus School is actually experiencing a sense of "need." There are many Christ-followers who are excited to serve, give and "be needed." However, the other side of the coin—to need—sometimes gets overlooked. With the recent infusion of missional language in the wider church conversations, this distinction shouldn't be missed.

I hate needing and love being needed. In authentic missional living, both must exist.

Jesus modeled this for us at the Last Supper in John 13, washing the disciples' feet. Jesus made a significant point in this moment: to be a disciple you must not only give but also receive. Receiving is intimate and sometimes foreign to those of us who like to stay in the giving seat. In Jesus School, part of our **learning is to humbly learn how to receive love, care, encouragement and support from others.**

Like most schools, this kind of Jesus School is not always fun and games but a lot of hard work and challenge. Jesus' ministry to the broken, the lost and the poor provides a guiding framework that is definitely bumpy. There are definitely times I want to drop out, but I know down deep the things I'm learning here go far beyond the confines of The Refuge. It is strengthening my relationship with God, myself and with others in ways I hadn't previously experienced. I may not get the inspirational fix I sometimes long for, and might often be irritated, bugged and frustrated, but I do get to participate in the beauty and hope of real people practicing the ways of Love.

A Theology of Brokenness

In a consumer-oriented world, a theology of brokenness is not popular. The kind of authenticity and rawness present in most of the in-the-trenches communities or ministries I know of is scary for a lot of people. I completely **understand that fear. I prefer answers, healing and clear-cut movements that are tangible and measurable. I want results, to see people change fast in a** way that seems apparent. I like a finish line.

A theology of brokenness embraces our spiritual poverty, questions, doubts, and desire for love, hope and redemption, and reminds us that the stink and the beauty are wrapped into one. We can't just focus on the group of people who will confirm that our ministry is a success. Instead, we must include people who will challenge our definitions of success and stretch our imaginations about what the Kingdom of God looks like. It turns things upside-down. It includes people we wouldn't. This is the message of the Gospel of **Jesus Christ.**

I also recognize the tug toward successful ministry is strong. People look for powerful, smart, charismatic leaders with clear-cut answers and the ability to motivate. This is an age-old problem, reflected when Jesus first entered the world as a newborn baby. Instead of a powerful king who was going to kick butt and take names, the promised messiah ended up being a humble servant **who saved the day by dying.**

Still, even though we know the story, we continue to look for powerful kings instead of humble servants. In Mark 2:17 Jesus said, "It is not the healthy who need a doctor, but the sick. I have not come to call the righteous, but sinners." Yet over and over many of us reject our sickness—and the sickness in others—and do whatever we can to appear healthy and hang around others who look healthy, too.

A theology of brokenness is a way of seeing the world that is contrary to much of what we've been taught. Instead of a "rise-above" mentality, a theology of brokenness ascribes to a "go lower and deeper" one. It doesn't mean that we wallow in our own brokenness or the brokenness of others, but instead, we acknowledge that success is not defined by everything looking neat and tidy. Jesus promised there would be pain and suffering in this world but that joy, hope and peace were available in the midst of it. Rejecting brokenness usually leads to a false faith where we are pretending instead of living authentically.

Years ago I was confronted with this tension in a very real way. I was involved in a women's group that required me to be honest with my brokenness. I remember being extremely angry about having to admit I didn't have it all together. I didn't want to admit out loud that I actually was hurting and struggling because it meant somehow my faith wasn't strong enough and I was somehow failing as a Christian. When I kept these fears and doubts to **myself, they caused a lot of collateral damage, but once I started sharing the truth out loud, I discovered that most of my friends wrestled with similar** feelings. When I began accepting my brokenness instead of resisting it, a wide **expanse of freedom opened up that not only drew me closer to others, but** also brought me closer to God in a more authentic, honest way.

Thankfully, a theology of brokenness does not mean the absence of hope; the beauty is that there is hope in the brokenness and healing in the midst of **pain. It is good to remember that hope and promise are threaded throughout** the Beatitudes: in our mourning, we will find comfort; in our spiritual poverty and persecution, we will experience the Kingdom of God; in our hunger, we will be filled.

Jesus didn't expect people to figure it all out. In fact most people didn't have a clue about what he was doing, including his own disciples. But maybe that's the point. Acknowledging we don't have it all together requires us to face our brokenness. An "I've got it all figured out" attitude leaves no room for God or others.

A theology of brokenness also directly confronts our desire for comparison. Embedded in much of our thinking is that change is linear, fast and clear. We subtly or directly expect ourselves (and others) to make the ascent up the ladder, one rung at a time. Once we're up the next one, we are not supposed to look back. Each rung is a stage of "getting better" and we keep pushing ourselves to take the next step up and escape from whatever was on the rung below.

A theology of brokenness begins with the reality that life is messy and complicated. Think how frustrated we get at ourselves or other people when we can't seem to get over a past hurt or struggle. Success, and the lack of it, has a way of breeding contempt. Many have a "but we're/they're supposed to be better by now" ideal that is unrealistic when we're talking about deep issues of abandonment, insecurity, fear or abuse that so many people have in their life history. A theology of brokenness smashes the "up the ladder to perfection" idea because humanness and life is far from linear. We are up, down, and all over the place. Most of the people I know have life journeys that look far more like roller coasters than ladders.

The most radical shift in my faith came when I embraced my own brokenness in a deep and central way. I had resisted it for a long time, constantly angry with myself for not climbing the ladder fast enough. When I finally settled into the idea that maybe, just maybe, Jesus would love me even in the midst of darkness and failure, something deeply shifted in how I viewed myself and others.

I recently shared with some friends that "maybe wholeness begins with accepting our brokenness." Instead of resisting and rejecting brokenness, we can accept and acknowledge it. It doesn't mean that we stay there or encourage others to stay there either. Acknowledging the brokenness means transcending it by discovering it doesn't define us. It opens us up to a new way of seeing the world that is much more honest, real and grace-filled.

We see this played out in Luke 7. A sinful woman burst into Simon the Pharisee's house and wiped Jesus' feet with her tears. From the outside, it would appear that all of the "appropriate" people would get the kudos and her ugly, disruptive, uncomfortable entrance would be chastised by Jesus. Instead, he rebuked them and honored her heart and her devotion by **telling everyone that she loved much because she was forgiven much. In this** moment he was reminding us all that a theology of brokenness was better than a theology of put-togetheredness. A theology of brokenness requires developing eyes to see life, the world and ourselves, through Christ's eyes.

Making the Invisible Visible

I often tell people that from the outside, The Refuge experience can look ugly **and confusing. A weird hodgepodge of outcasts thrown into a room together** with socially awkward moments and uncomfortable silence, there's nothing neat, tidy, or exciting about it. However, there's much more going on than meets the eye. You see, when my friend, Jack, is outside smoking a cigarette and chatting with some friends, it is one of the only times all week someone safe and loving asks how he is doing. When my friend, Janice, pulls up two hours early to help set up for our gathering, it might be the first time all week she's been out of her house. When my friend Samantha speaks up and shares during our gathering, many people don't know that when I first met her she wouldn't even look me in the eye when she talked, because she was so filled with shame and guilt. It's almost impossible to see the beauty on the surface, unless you listen to the wonderful back-story of change and hope that informs **their lives.** *Understanding requires looking beyond appearances and seeing what Jesus might see.*

Appearances are also very deceiving the other way. People can look like everything's "fine," when inside their hearts are breaking, their marriages are crumbling and they are in the pit of depression, all while trying to keep it all together. Hurt, struggle and invisibility crosses economics, social classes and faith experiences. Seeing what Jesus sees requires looking deeper than what meets the eye in whatever circles we are in. It is noticing the person across the room who is alone and uncomfortable, sensing when someone just needs to talk and engaging with our neighbor and listening to their story instead of rushing to close our garage as fast as we can. It looks different for each of us, but the essence is the same—there's always a lot more going on for people **than meets the eye.**

One of my dearest friends is a single mom who struggles with mental illness and self-injury. Lydia is the worst cutter I've ever seen. Feeling God's presence **and hope is hard for her. Feeling included, loved, and protected is even harder.** Shame, guilt and self-hatred come instinctively for her. I've known her for five **years and if someone was measuring her progress against a linear theology** of "if you do this, then that happens," she—and we as her support system— would be utter failures. Nothing looks better on the outside than it did five years ago; she's still on services, needs a lot of counseling and support and battles wanting to die.

However, over the past few years I have seen Lydia learn to try to trust men for the first time; before, she had only been used and abused by them. Now, she is able to call a few men from our community when she is in trouble and ask for help; they sometimes take her to doctor appointments and take care of her son when she needs a break. We recently celebrated six months sobriety from cutting, the longest she's ever gone in her life. Should she relapse, she'll have a strong network of people who will love her still and help minimize her shame. She is one of the most caring, loving people I know. Slowly, she is starting to believe that too. To most of the world she'd be in the pile of **invisibles, those that are never seen or valued by others.**

New eyes mean that we see with our hearts into the real and sacred stories of each other's lives. *We make what is invisible, visible.* **I believe wholeheartedly** that Christ-followers could change the world, a city and their communities if we humbly and actively participated in *making the invisible, visible*—**if we** **were part of calling out the dignity, beauty and worth of every human being** regardless of race, age, gender, socioeconomics, religion, brokenness, weird- **life-circumstances and social status.**

One of the biggest problems in every community, including most churches, is that so many people actually feel invisible, worthless and purposeless. They are not sure they really matter to anyone. Stuck in shame, hiding, and feeling self-contempt, they go through the motions of their day. Some live on the streets. Some live in apartments. Some live in nice houses. Some squeak by on social security disability income, while others collect big bonuses at their high tech company. Some use their money to buy drugs. Some use their money to buy stuff they don't need to numb their pain. Some go to church every week. Others worship other gods in different ways. Some believe in nothing, while others wonder if God has forsaken them.

The problem of invisibility has nothing to do with money or religion. Invisibility has to do with our disconnectedness from the heart and soul of another human being, which then disconnects us from the reality of God. It has to do with our weird prejudices that lead us to believe that certain people are acceptable, and other people aren't. It has to do with our busyness, self-centeredness and tendency to hoard and self-protect. It has to do with generations upon generations of invisibility in families, with no end in sight. It has to do with our fear of truly engaging in the messiest parts of other's lives, that cause us to pretend we don't see, don't know or don't have time. It has to do with being known and seen in the midst of our own mess and our tendency to want to stay invisible, too.

Invisibility means we're no longer there, nobody can see us and our capacity to relate to one another is virtually extinguished.

My friend, Janice, felt invisible. In her fifties and never married, she struggles with a wide range of debilitating health issues. She has five years of sobriety after a 30-year cocaine addiction. She can articulate so clearly what others may think or feel but never say. She says that sometimes she feels like she lives in "God's Ghetto." Here's what that means to her:

> "I know I'm his, but it sometimes feels like maybe I'm a second-class citizen. A first-class citizen gets all his miracles and he does awesome stuff in their lives. They get relationships. They have something to do with their time. They don't seem as lonely as me. They get money, at least more than me, it seems. They can move around, do things, instead of feeling stuck in their house. They didn't get abused. I kind of feel like I get a glimpse of good things, the leftovers, but not as much as other people. If God has anything left to give at the end of the day, I wonder if maybe I can at least get that. The times the Ghetto feeling gets the worst is when I go 2-3 days

without human contact. That is when the doubts really set in and I wonder why God doesn't let me have a better life."

Unfortunately, God's Ghetto is populated with more people than we think. Many feel they don't matter to God because if they did, they certainly wouldn't be stuck with some of what they're stuck with. They feel invisible to God, **and invisible to others, too.**

Jesus consistently made the invisible, visible.

He called out the image of God in people—all kinds of people, from all walks of life. The outcasts. The shamed. The lonely. The confused. The broken.The sick. He heard their cry. He stopped. He listened. He touched. He offered **healing.**

We will never know the other ways he engaged with people; many of the **incidents recorded in the Gospels leave** much to our imagination, but we do **have these examples blaring at us.** Jesus never talks about right beliefs, doctrinal statements, or church services. He simply said, *"Come, follow me."* That means we are called to realize our need for God, restore dignity, sacrificially love, willingly share, and notice the least likely. We are challenged to enter God's Ghetto and make the invisible visible, too.

God, give us new eyes to see and help us make the invisible visible.

To be able to walk the path toward making the invisible visible, to tangibly love and serve others with Jesus' love and hope, we first have to be touched **by it ourselves.** *We can't pass on what we don't know ourselves.* This means we have to continually confront our brokenness, shame, and need for healing, **our own feelings of being invisible.**

Healing doesn't mean, "Once I get healed, then I can pass it on." It's a continual life-long spiritual transformation process. As we are transformed, **we get new eyes to see more clearly, new hearts to feel deeply, and new ears** to listen more intently. We then begin to notice what we didn't see before, **next door to us, in the next cubicle to us, in the next chair to us, in the next** neighborhood over from us, across the city from us. We become compelled to care.

Jesus School is about engaging incarnational relationships in the muck and mire of real life, but it isn't very inspiring in ways we typically think. Embracing a theology of brokenness and learning to see the world through new eyes isn't initially pretty, either. Entering into God's ghetto requires making the invisible, visible. However, the promise given by Jesus in the blessing of the Beatitudes is true. When we engage the practice of love, the reality of the Kingdom of God comes shining through.

Down here, we see beauty in the least likely of places, hope seeping out of the darkness, and love and mercy expressed in ways beyond words. Even though dreams are always prettier when they are just dreams, I wouldn't trade this path of descent for anything. It's where we intersect with real lives, real healing, and real hope.

Personal Reflection:

1. What scares you about raw, messy, incarnational relationships?

2. How addicted to inspiration are you? What draws you to it?

3. **What is your Jesus School right now? What are you learning right** now about yourself, God and others at this season in your journey?

4. When you look around, what are you seeing now that you used to **not see?**

5. Have you ever felt like you were in God's Ghetto? How?

Group Discussion:

1. **Share with the group your honest feelings about engaging in raw,** messy, authentic relationships. Are they easy or hard for you? Why?

2. Connect together on the idea of "inspiration addiction." How has it influenced you? How has it potentially kept you from following **Jesus?**

3. **What is your Jesus School, the place where you are learning the most** **right now about the ways of Jesus? What are you learning there?**

4. How has the theology of put-togetheredness damaged your relationship with God, yourself and others? How can the theology of brokenness heal those relationships?

5. Engage with the idea of God's Ghetto. Have you ever felt some of **these feelings?**

6. When you look around you, what are you seeing now that you used to not see? What is becoming more visible?

Chapter 3

There is No "Them or Us"…Only Us

"I call you my friends" - Jesus (John 15:15)

For many of us, a lot of God-inspired dreams reside under our skin. We know we want to live differently, with more passion and freedom, and we are ready to get our hands dirty and our hearts broken. We are geared up to experience God's Kingdom in action, but before we jump in, important distinctions need to be made between typical "missional ministry" and living the ways of Jesus, in action, on the path of downward mobility.

Missional ministry often begins with an us/them mindset that is build upon a foundation of, "We're going to be good Christians and go help those poor people who are not like us." I believe this heart to serve comes from a sincere place, but it perpetuates a dangerous divide. Jesus levels the playing field, modeling an incarnational way of living that requires far more of us than we typically expect. He calls us to a sacrificial life of love, not sporadic acts of service that keep everything on our own terms, with our hearts and lives at a **protected distance.**

To live the path of downward mobility with others we have to break down the **barriers that separate them and us.**

It starts with getting in touch with our own spiritual poverty and examining our ministry motives. When we're honest, we are broken just like "them." And when we see this, we discover there is no dividing line. We're all part of the Kingdom of God. Some just can't see it yet. Barriers crumble when we relinquish our need for quick fixes and learn to live in the tension of life in paradox—where God's love exists, even when we can't see it. Black or white, in or out, and good or bad thinking won't work in the low places of the human experience; we need to become comfortable with a single, new category of just "us."

My friend, Ken Loyd, has journeyed with people who live outside in downtown Portland for many years. (He does not use the word "homeless"). Wise in so many ways, one of his favorite things is to remind people that, "there's no us and them; there's only us." There's no question that from the outside it's hard to see what someone who is educated, married with kids in the suburbs, and gainfully employed has in common with someone who lives on the streets and never graduated from high school. But on the inside, we are more similar than different. We feel insecure and afraid at the same time we long to be loved and known. We feel invisible at the same time we long to be connected to God and other human beings. We're all more alike than we often think.

Breaking Down Barriers

Deeply rooted in our culture are divisions that separate people. We make sense of the self by connecting with people "like us." We make friends and build relationships with people who have similar backgrounds, educations, passions and theologies. Individuals and groups with resources and power very rarely mix with people without them, and we see this perpetuated in class systems, racial divides, and the deep chasms between groups we see in many neighborhoods.

A first step to breaking down "us and them" is to get in touch with our own spiritual poverty. This goes back to the Beatitudes. At the root of this divide is the need for love and validation. We long for God to love us. And instead of embracing the love of God, we engage in pride, which is our own attempt at validation. We attempt to earn God's love instead of accepting what we already have. But if we think we are better than others, the divide will always exist. An honest realization of our own need for God is embodied in a humble spirit that says: *"We realize we can't do it, a program can't do it, nor can our skills and abilities do it."* This is in contrast to our natural propensity to control and manage.

The barriers exist because we're afraid to acknowledge our pain. Pain usually intersects with spiritual poverty. I know plenty of people who show **no outward appearance of struggling, but inwardly they are experiencing** tremendous pain and suffering. I used to be one of those people. It doesn't matter how successfully suburban or even wildly upper class people are— everyone experiences pain. When it comes to finding hope in the midst of pain, those who look like they are at the bottom have remarkable gifts they can offer to those who look like they are on top. Jesus gave himself for all, **and we can learn to give ourselves to one another, as well.**

As we acknowledge our own pain, we cultivate the ability to feel, comfort **and enter into the pain of others, too. Before I started embracing my own painful story, I was unable to have true compassion for others. Sure, I could** offer simple, trite advice or offer to pray, but I didn't connect on a deep, heart-level because I wasn't in touch with my own heart. The Apostle Paul's wise **words resonate with my experience:**

> *"Praise be to the God and Father of our Lord Jesus Christ,*
> *the Father of compassion and the God of all comfort, who*
> *comforts us in all our troubles, so that we can comfort those*
> *in any trouble with the comfort we ourselves receive from*
> *God." (2 Corinthians 1:3-4)*

Acknowledging pain helps us tear down the barriers that keep us from relationship and our own humanity. When we give up self-protection we **allow ourselves to feel and care. We begin to weep with others and weep for ourselves. We become acutely aware of the human struggle not only in** others' lives but also our own. We let go of quick fixes and simple solutions and embrace the long, hard journey of relationship with other people where we cry together, celebrate together, and feel each other's pain. It frees us to offer each other the comfort and hope we've received from God.

This also means that we actually have to be in relationship with others beyond the surface. We can't cry over a story we don't know. Likewise, we can't know a story without really getting to know another person.

Breaking down the barriers also requires examining our wider motives. Is it just about proclaiming our faith and making sure people know we are

Christians, or helping people quietly and naturally intersect with Christ's love, freedom and hope, through relationship? Breaking down "us and them" means we become active networkers and bridge builders within our local communities, fostering peace, partnership, and open-handed generosity with **a diverse range of people. Why? Because inside each person is the image of** God just waiting to be discovered. We unveil that image through the gift of loving relationship.

We can't ignore that Jesus invited us into something active and tangible. Jesus was all about restoring people and bringing sight to the blind. He was intentional about setting things straight and reconciling the world. Unfortunately, what often happens is that the latest buzzwords and models in **ministry distract us, and we miss that these things actually build barriers that** keep us separated.

Love is the New Buzzword

To break down the barriers between "us and them" we must begin with love and examine our motivation behind relationships. Is our driving force to feel **good about ourselves and be able to say at the end of the year,** *"See how cool we are because we did all of these great things for other people?"* Or is it about being so in tune with Christ's heart for people that we are compelled **to love, naturally?**

Early in the life of The Refuge, a few church leaders shared with me how they were becoming "missional" and asked if we were going to be missional, too, as if it was the latest and greatest thing that no one had ever heard of before; surely we would want to jump on the bandwagon. Nothing triggers all my church craziness more than buzzwords and the latest trends.

As I was sitting across the table with leaders who had been in paid ministry, making decisions for churches for years, I angrily thought, *"You don't even really know a poor person, do you? You have never ever been in close relationship with a single mom who just got beat up by her ex and is trying to raise her babies on $1,000 a month, have you? You have never held someone's hand when they've relapsed, have you? Because if you had, you wouldn't be asking me that question!"* My thoughts are not always nice, but I try and come back around, remembering how broken our man-made systems of **ministry have become.**

The allure of the latest buzzword is to jump into the latest trend of what might work. But the buzzword only lasts until we discover it doesn't. The Kingdom of God and the downward path require getting our own hands dirty and understanding that none of us are exempt because of our position, class or time constraints.

Jesus was never about words without actions, being hip and cool, strategic visions, or the latest trends. He was always about real love. If the missional movement is doing anything, it is getting people out of their seats and into their communities. But that's only the beginning. Missional ministry requires the practice of love. The reason I shy away from the word "Missional" is **that it gets adopted by church leaders as,** *"See, look at us, we actually do care about the poor!"* when so many of the other systems and practices remain **inwardly-focused and upwardly mobile.**

Jesus-mission-oriented life is much more than periodic, exciting service projects and occasional short-term mission trips, while everything else remains structurally and programmatically the same. This often means **being focused on serving the people in the pews (or in the newest and** most comfortable chairs) and making sure they are happy (so the offering plate is happy), and bringing people "to us" instead of having to engage in sacrificial living in meaningful, authentic ways that get under our skin, make **us feel uncomfortable, and change our hearts forever.**

I think Jesus' methods are actually quite simple when we look at how he lived out his ministry in the Gospels. There were no bells, whistles, programs, or gimmicks. Over and over, we see him model direct interaction with people, primarily those on the fringes. He worked with a select group of people and invited them to practice love, which meant engaging those on the fringes. We have complicated many of his simple ways. To me, missional living—individually and corporately—is a stripped down, simple approach to practicing the ways **of Jesus without the trappings of worldly models and measures.**

Missional shouldn't be a buzzword or a program. Rather, *missional is a way of living.*

It is a way of the heart, and is something that is better left unsaid in words and promotional materials, but rather practiced in humble, simple, natural actions that don't get any press. It is similar to the way Jesus taught us to pray in the Sermon on the Mount—just do it and don't make a show of it.

Missional is *the upside-down, inside out, and beautifully uncomfortable ways of the Kingdom* that are counter-intuitive to the worldly principles of business school and success that have infiltrated our church culture.

Missional is *messy, chaotic, situational, and in many ways utterly unmeasurable.* It doesn't fit in a box and can't be packaged or programmed. It must be lived.

Missional means *embracing the values of the Beatitudes in Matthew 5, not only in action but also in our core DNA.* This includes spiritual poverty, the ability to mourn and feel, humility and gentleness, advocacy and social justice, mercy and compassion, and sacrifice at great costs. Jesus uses the guiding words from the Sermon on the Mount to powerfully demonstrate that his ways will be hard, sacrificial, and intensely counter-cultural.

When it comes to being in the darkest parts of our cities, our neighborhoods, or people's hearts, one thing feels clear: we're not one formula, book, or leadership skill away from being able to do anything. If missional really means anything it's that we're radically humble, painfully aware of how complex real life is, and in desperate need of God's spirit really showing up.

I don't think the world, our cities, our neighborhoods, or our hurting friends care about the word "missional" or any of the other buzzwords we toss around. What they're wondering is: *"Who will bring some love and hope into this darkness?"* **Jesus started his public ministry with the words of the** Beatitudes and ended it with this reminder, on his last night with his disciples: *"Love each other in the same way I have loved you. There is no greater love than to lay down one's life for one's friends"* **(John 15:12-13).**

With friends, there is no, "us and them." There's only "us."

And "us" begins with love.

Why Prepositions Matter

To engage love in practical ways we have to begin changing our prepositions. My friends at the Center for Transforming Mission in Tacoma, Washington do amazing work equipping leaders who are journeying with people in hard places around the world. They espouse a theology "from below," a principle of ministry that centers on Jesus' people bringing the Good News into dark places. Their work is built upon the premise that authentic transformational relationships can not be built upon power or inequality. This idea is contrary to much of what we've been taught or unknowingly bought into when it comes to advocacy and helping relationships.

In most Christian and typical mission-oriented circles, the most prevalent preposition has become the word "to." The style of the preposition "to" is paternal. This idea is built on principles like:

"I have something I need to give **to** you."

"I have wisdom I need to impart **to** you."

"Here's the advice, biblical truth, or kernel of supposed life-changing knowledge I have to give **to** you."

The problem with the preposition "to" is that it begins with an "I'm up and you're down" perspective of power that is patronizing and disempowering. Someone has more resources, knowledge, and put-togetheredness than the other. This posture often ends up making the one on the receiving end feel like a project or a loser.

The preposition "for" is another easy reflex for most of us. The style of the preposition "for" is maternal. It's when we want to do things *for* a hurting **person.**

"Let me makes these calls **for** you."

"I don't want you to hurt, so let me fix this part **for** you."

"Your anxiety is giving me anxiety, so let me do what I can to take care of this **anxiety for** you."

"Let me get what you need right now **for** you."

The problem with this kind of approach to others is that it creates codependence. Helpers get sucked into helping and also end in a one-up role where they are the ones who need to take care of the person, make things happen for them, or remain in a role where they always "serving" people; it stays on those terms. Again, it's a one-way relationship, only a little nicer and with better perks for the hurting person.

Our human default is to "serve the poor **because we have something to give to them or do for** them." This keeps everyone involved in typical one-up, one-down kinds of relationships. Many aren't interested in being in relationship beyond a helping **moment.**

TO is paternal and can create oppression.

The preposition "with" changes everything. **It means:**

"I am **with you in this moment, will stand** alongside you, and am not walking ahead of you but alongside you."

FOR is maternal and can create codependence.

"I am in the same boat; I struggle, too, but my struggle may just look different."

"I want to share life **with** you, not just take care of you or tell you what to do."

WITH is incarnational and creates transformation.

"You have some things I need to learn from you, too. Let's learn from each other."

"I will let you into my life...I want to be **friends with** you."

"With" removes imbalanced power from the relationship. It recognizes the fundamental dignity of the person and says, "I am here with you." It begins with listening for the deeper story that informs the suffering. It waits patiently for the person to ask for help, if needed, because sometimes people aren't ready for help. Sometimes people just need people to sit with as they work it out on their own.

There is no question—"with" is scarier. It means I let others know me instead of hiding behind doing good works at a protective distance. I make myself vulnerable and let others into my life, experience, and heart, instead of just taking care of them to feel good about myself. Within the professional, clinical culture, as it is customarily taught, these kinds of "with" relationships may look like bad boundaries. "With" relationships are messy, **unpredictable, hard, confusing, and sure to tap into our pain, history, fears,** and annoyed, frustrated places. I understand how easy it is to stick with "to" and "for" modes of relationship. They protect us because they keep us in a place of power. They keep the focus off of us and on the other person. In the end, we don't need "them;" they just need "us." Even though that's easier, I believe that "*with* each other" relationships create true transformation.

Living in relationship "with" people is much more enriching. I experience it up close in the life of our community. My friend Jamie struggles with mental illness. She is a brilliant advocate and can smell out people who want to make her their project, or who try to put themselves in a "to" or "for" relationship from the start. She articulates what it feels like to be in "with" relationships so well. **She says:**

> *"I hate it when people try to help me but don't really want to be friends with me. They see me as a project, as someone that needs to be fixed, but not as an equal human being. To be honest, it is really demoralizing. At the same time, I can do that to others, too, trying to control people or situations that are not exactly what I had envisioned them to be. But every time I experience real 'with' relationships, I'm more convinced there's nothing more beautiful, freeing and healing."*

I wholeheartedly agree with Jamie. "With" relationships are incredibly beautiful. They break down power differentials that strip dignity and keep people stuck. "With" is actually more protective because it keeps us from becoming someone's mother or father, rather than a friend. When there is a mutuality of relationship it opens up room for transformation and cultivates hope on both sides. The divide between us crumbles, allowing for God's image to be reflected in simple but powerful ways.

Learning to Live in Paradox

We don't like living with the tension of paradox. It's chaotic and physically disrupting. It's two opposing ideas that often appear to have equal value. Father Richard Rohr, a Franciscan friar and author, said this about paradox,

> "A paradox is something that appears to be a contradiction, but from another perspective is not a contradiction at all. You and I are living paradoxes, and therefore must be prepared to see ourselves in all our reality. If you can hold and forgive the contradictions within yourself, you can normally do it everywhere else, too."[3]

I was talking to a friend on the phone the other day who is in a season of deep healing in his life. In sharing with me the story of a recent interaction that went sour, he asked me if he was a perpetual screw up, doomed to mess up all his relationships. In that moment, that was what felt real to him. He could only see his darkness and completely forgot about his light. I responded with **the most honest answer I could:** *"Yes, you often screw things up, but that doesn't discount the reality that you are also loving, kind, compassionate and wise. They both exist in you at the same time, and one doesn't discount the other."* He, like me, has a hard time living in paradox.

Living in the gray or in the tension of two contradicting things, existing at the same time, is difficult for many of us; for those who come from a very conservative, evangelical, or fundamentalist tradition, it's even more difficult. Some of us have been taught that things are either black or white, right or wrong, good or bad and dark or light.

I know this well in my own life. In the past, any doubt at all meant a complete lack of faith because, in my mind, doubt and faith couldn't co-exist together. That has radically changed over the years and holding the tension now—although still difficult at times—is much easier. I also used to refuse to accept I could be good and bad at the same time. I'd either have to be "all good" or "all bad," but there wasn't anything in between. That looked like doing all kinds of things to be a "Super Christian" or swinging completely the other way and defining myself as a "miserable, unworthy, shameful wretch."

Most human beings I know, when they are being honest, are a mixture of good and bad, light and dark, ugly and beautiful, strong and weak, confident and fearful. There are a wide variety of paradoxes within us. It's what makes us human. The problem that many of us have encountered in our spiritual walk, though, is that very little of what we've been taught helps us embrace these. Reckoning with this tension is no easy task, but is necessary on the downward path. If we cannot accept these paradoxes in ourselves, we won't be able to accept them in other people either. In the trenches of messy, incarnational relationship, there are an awful lot of paradoxes.

Jesus himself was full of paradoxes. He was a king and a humble servant. A saver of lives who lost his own life. An incredible teacher and one of the most challenging-to-understand communicators of all time. He often taught in seemingly opposite directions to reveal the living heart of the Kingdom of God. A gift we can give to ourselves and to our relationships is learning to embrace life, ourselves, and others in paradox. The more I get in touch with my own story and travel with other people along the way, the more convinced I am that this extremely difficult work of the heart must happen to love God, ourselves, and others well.

It's easy for many people to articulate: "Of course I know I'm good and I'm bad at the same time." But on a gut level, when we dig a little deeper, it becomes more apparent how much work is being done underneath the surface personally, relationally and spiritually to resolve the conflicts, and the negative emotions as quickly as possible. If we can't accept the paradoxes in ourselves, it is impossible to accept them in others. This means we won't be able to live in free and generous "with" relationships because we will constantly be consciously or unconsciously working to squeeze the paradox out, instead of learning to live in its tension with others.

My friend, Claire, recently intersected with this idea of paradox, and it has deeply affected her. She sees how hard it is to live in the tension of two contradicting things existing at the same time. As she's actively involved in journeying with people in hard places, she knows that part of her growth and learning involves embracing paradox. Here's what she says about it:

> *"Instead of dividing myself into either ducks-in-a row Claire or messy, struggling Claire, I am practicing a new season of integrating both aspects. It is hard for me to embrace*

that both of these can actually exist at the same time. My Christian experience told me that I had to work as hard as I could to get the struggle completely out so I could be free. The truth is that I never could, so I just buried it and put on my game face. Now, in a safe community, I am finding it difficult to admit that I have present issues that aren't relegated to some distant part of the past. The beauty is that the more I share, the closer people feel to me, which is completely opposite of what I would expect."

I relate with Claire's struggle and have found that the more I embrace both sides of me—my good and bad—and share that honestly, not only do I feel **more connected to others, but others have said they also feel more connected to me.**

Radical shifts can happen in our own lives and in the lives of those we engage with if we can learn to embrace paradox. Instead of rejecting the ugly, real, human being stuff, we can learn to accept all parts of ourselves. We can stop **being mad at God (and ourselves) for not changing us fast enough. As our capacity to give grace to ourselves increases, we also develop more grace** for others. Embracing paradox also cultivates resiliency because we begin to see more joy in suffering, peace in tribulations, and wholeness and healing in brokenness. Lastly, it widens our ability to interact and relate with people very different from us.

These are necessary ingredients for breaking down the divide between "us" and "them." It is much easier to talk about this in an intellectual sense than it is to integrate it into the deep places of our hearts and lives. However, it is a critical piece of living in the low places of our own and others' experiences. **Real people live in paradox.**

The Way of Interdependence

Jesus' call of love is an invitation to learn the ways of interdependence. True **interdependence means we rely on one another in a way that is healthy and** creates an effective balance of power. Interdependence includes not just **vulnerability and a willingness to be transparent with how we are doing and** feeling, but also willingness to let others' love, mercy, wisdom, and help seep into our lives. It is a freedom to be ourselves—with our unique abilities, strengths and weaknesses—and love others without being compelled to change, reject, or avoid them. Interdependent hearts are open to feel others' pain without letting it suck the life and hope out of them. It is a life of spirit-infused sacrifice connected to other people instead of a life of narcissism.

People do not want to feel like projects. Independence and codependence, like "to" and "for" relationships, create an imbalance. Interdependence requires healthy balance. It is the kind of connection the Apostle Paul spoke **of in 1 Corinthians 12:12-27, where the parts of the body are intertwined together, doing what they are meant to do, forming a wholeness they could never form alone.**

Our basis for interdependence is the undeniable dignity that each human **possesses. When we begin with the dignity of each human being, we can** begin to transcend the judgments that typically tear us apart. It gives us the courage to be whole in the midst of brokenness.

My friend Renee is gay. When she came out of the closet, her dad put a Bible on the table and said, *"This is how I feel about it. This book says it is wrong, and I don't want to have anything to do with you anymore."* **When she was** first invited to hang out at The Refuge she said that there was no way in hell she was setting foot in a church. For multiple weeks, she drove around the parking lot and left without ever getting out of her car, before finally getting the courage to walk through the doors.

As she slowly began to ease into community life here, she began to make friends. Even though I heard her story, I knew that she'd never experience the full measure of love if she stayed in hiding. One evening she decided to tell her story. I'll always remember that moment because I saw one of the most conservative guys in the room start to cry. Later, he told me that he was so sorry that he had been a stone-thrower and that knowing Renee as a person **changed everything.**

Over time, their friendship blossomed in many wild and wonderful ways. He entered into her life, and she entered into his, not in a "to" or "for" way, or in an unhealthy codependent or detached independent way. They became interdependent friends and even ended up working together. She became part of our family, too. We needed her as much as she needed us. Her voice, her heart and her presence made all the difference, and when she moved away, we all felt the gap.

Renee shared her experience with me:

> "I have felt myself grow over the past year. It's so nice to have consistency in my life, to know that no matter what, I can come vent, laugh, and feel safe. When I shared my story, I wanted everyone to know the real, exposed, not perfect, raw and in-person side of me. I feel like I know myself better and have finally been able to let others into my life, too. I think the one thing that has helped me is how diverse our group is. We have people from all walks of life who have been through and experienced so many things. If one person hasn't felt something or done something there is almost always someone who has. I feel safer knowing that they are all as messed up in their lives as I am and that they are not going to judge me for the things that I have been through and done. It's a great feeling to know that you are not alone in your struggle."

When we began to hold Renee's dignity, it opened up the space for her to be honest, vulnerable, and present, which cultivated interdependence. If Renee had been a ministry project, we could have kept her at arms' length and made our relationship all about her. Instead, she received the gifts of others' stories in the same way we received the gift of hers.

Vulnerability begins with transparency. It is learning to be honest with each **other about our story, but it goes a step further when we learn to let others** in, too. It shifts from a one-way relationship to a two-way relationship, where both are giving, and both are receiving. This creates interdependence. Renee wasn't the only one who took a risk; we all did. This kind of interdependence is counterintuitive to much of what we have been taught. "To" and "for" relationships, codependence and independence, are ways to control, run from pain, and avoid failure. They protect us from living the real, uninhibited, tangled up ways of the Kingdom in interdependent relationship with people

and God.

Jean Vanier, the founder of L'Arche Communities and Henri Nouwen's inspiration, reminds us how difficult it is to live this way. He says:

> *"There is always a warfare in our hearts; there is always the struggle between pride and humility, hatred and love, forgiveness and the refusal to forgive, truth and the concealment of truth, openness and closedness. Each of us is walking in that passage toward liberation, growing on the journey toward wholeness and healing."*[4]

The alluring alternatives to interdependence, which include independence and codependence, are far easier to embrace. But they don't produce life. We need healthy relationship to survive.

Although many use the word "codependence" in recovery circles, codependence is a human condition that crosses a wide range of experiences. It includes an unhealthy pattern of control, care-taking, enabling, people-pleasing, and suppressing our own desires for the sake of keeping the peace in relationship with others. Even those who appear confident often have strong codependent characteristics underneath. Codependence is far easier for me than interdependence! Those of us who struggle with codependency tend to **give but never receive, remain out of touch with what we want or need, stay** stuck in roles of martyrs, peacemakers, victims, or care-takers, and act out of **fear instead of freedom.**

Western culture values independence and an "I don't really need anyone else" mentality. It's a way of being that either overtly or covertly says that we don't need to be close to people in our lives, and that we can handle things solo and make our own destiny. Independence isn't inherently bad; it is healthy to be free and strong apart from other people. The problem is independence often means we aren't engaged in the relational stuff of life. The shadow underneath a lot of independence is fear. Independents tend to rarely connect on an emotional level with other people. They reject input, think their way is right, and try not to need God much since they have their own bases covered. They can be friendly and kind, but the message underneath is still a clear "I don't really need you."

To live these downward ways of Jesus, the great divide between "us and them" will need to be smashed down. Pain is the great equalizer, the ingredient that diffuses the split between the healthy and the sick and reminds us we are **all human beings in need of love and hope. As we strip away our reliance** on buzzwords or ministry gimmicks we can lean more firmly into the simple **ways of Jesus that are centered solely on loving people. An integral part of** love is accepting the paradoxes that exist in others, as well as ourselves, and learning to live in their tension. With time and practice we can engage in transformational, interdependent "with" relationships alongside each other, **and learn at a far deeper level what it means to love and be loved, to need and be needed, to give and to receive.**

* * * * *

Personal Reflection:

1. When you think of "to," "for," or "with" relationships, which type comes more natural to you?

2. What scares you about "with" relationships? What inspires you about them?

3. Think of some paradoxes in your own life. Write them in your journal. "I am _____ and _____." How easy or hard are these to accept?

4. Do you have more of a tendency to be codependent, independent, or interdependent? Write which one best describes you and why.

Group Discussion:

1. Have you ever been the recipient of a "to" or "for" relationship? What was it like for you?

2. Can you see ways that you might have engaged in "to" or "for" relationships with others? What did that feel like for you? How do you think it felt for the person you were in relationship with?

3. Consider the idea of paradox. If you feel comfortable, share with the group some of your own paradoxes. Describe two contrasting things that live in tension within you.

4. How easy or hard is it for you to live in the tension of your own paradoxes? How about in the paradoxes of others?

5. Do you consider yourself more of a codependent, independent, or interdependent person? If you are in a group or organization, which of these might define your group? How do these patterns play out?

Chapter 4

"The Kingdom Isn't Just Going to Drop Out of the Sky"

"Your kingdom come, your will be done, on earth as it is in heaven." - Matthew 6:10

I was at a conference a few years ago and one of the speakers, Alexie Torres-Fleming, who is an advocate in New York for the marginalized, reminded everyone that contrary to popular belief, *"The Kingdom of God isn't going to just drop out of the sky."[5]* We have to be active participants in creating it, willing to sacrifice our pride, time, money, and a lot of other comforts in order to make it happen.

Alexie had abandoned an extremely successful career to live as an advocate in the housing project where she was raised. She traded a life of upward mobility for a downward one. As I listened to her share this passion for action, something deep inside resonated. Her heart for justice, mercy and love superseded her desire for a comfortable and cushy life. I resisted the urge to make a fool out of myself, but I wanted to stand up and shout, *"Yes, yes, yes! This is it!"* Her message embodied the gospel and Jesus' call to us to tangibly act on his behalf and bring his hope and healing to a world in desperate need of love.

As followers of Jesus, we don't do good deeds simply out of a sense of duty. We love our neighbor tangibly because this is the fullest reality of the Kingdom of God. Loving our neighbor reveals how deeply God loves them. We become

God's physical hands, feet, heart, eyes, ears and mouth. We incarnate the **presence of Jesus.**

A spiritual thought does not bring the Kingdom of God to earth, but a spiritual action does. The sum total of many hands, feet, hearts, eyes, ears and mouths changes the world. Our part isn't changing the world so that others believe what we believe. Instead, it's so Christ's spirit of humility, gentleness, peace, love, mercy and compassion can be infused into a dark and broken world, bringing redemption, reconciliation and healing. Many forces are working **against us.**

First, if we have God in a tiny box, limited by small definitions of who God is and how God works, we will not be open to creative imagination or allow our lives be fueled by a more expansive view of what's possible. We'll also have to reckon with humanity's gravitational pull toward comfort and the vast difference between "building a ministry" and "cultivating community." These new ways are way harder, requiring us to go against the flow and resist our tendency to default toward what is easy, defined, contained, or successful in the world's eyes. None of these new ways of living out our life and faith are **possible without a wider view of God.** *Without taking God out of the box, we'll never be able to make what could be, a reality.*

Expanding God

I was walking down the hallway at my son's junior high school a few years ago, when I saw the following words of wisdom from Mark Twain on the wall:

> *"Twenty years from now you will be more disappointed by the things that you didn't do than by the ones you did do. So throw off the bowlines. Sail away from the safe harbor. Catch the trade winds in your sails. Explore. Dream. Discover."[6]*

Every time I see a sappy inspirational quote like that my heart is always stirred. This one reminded me that the world was not changed by people who stayed in their safe, protected houses or within the confines of what was socially acceptable. Change always happens when people take risks.

The Bible is packed with stories about people who didn't want to be risk takers but were pushed, challenged and strengthened by God to risk anyway. Risk takers need fuel, something that propels them to keep going, even when there's no clear road map to follow. That fuel is a sense of the deeply developed story about the Kingdom of God. The problem is that story can only be developed after we risk. The longer we take the path of descent, the more we find ourselves seeing the value of following Jesus.

A story gives us the fuel to follow our dreams even when people think we're nuts, and to be so compelled to live out our passion that the traditional benefits don't matter. The best fuel is the kind of stirring that comes from God at work inside of us, prompting us to take steps we're scared to take and trust in ways we don't really want to trust. It requires an openness to the wildness of God that is not easily grasped, especially in a world often guided by an "if/then" framework that teaches a + b + c will equal d.

God must not have read the "if/then" memo because things never seem to work that way for almost anyone I know. Rarely have my "if/thens" come to fruition. I'm not surprised. They were usually about money, building a strong and stable foundation, and other things that had nothing to do with loving **people.**

Kingdom cultivators will need to be more open to the mystery of God.

Prior to beginning the path of descent, much of my spiritual learning had centered on the ability to know and define God based solely on accurate scripture interpretation. I was taught that if we studied the Bible enough, we could essentially figure out God and be sure of what he meant. This confines **God to the limits of our human understanding, instead of embracing the** mystery of what we don't fully know. This only works well within the confines of homogeneous Christian circles. A downwardly mobile life requires letting go of our preconceived notions about God and remaining open to God's vastness beyond language or our own experience. As we make room for unknowns, doubt, mystery, unique expressions, and others who see things differently than we do, we continually widen our view of God.

To live in the trenches with a variety of people, we will have to quit trying to manage and pre-define their experience with God. Individuals are all over the place with God—hopeful, disconnected, joyous, disappointed, confused, wondrous, and everything in between. Many Christians have been inundated with the idea that intimate relationship with God is always happy, close, personal and fulfilling. When we're not feeling that way, we can think something must be "wrong" with us. *When we let go of corralling people's experiences with God into a tame, manageable place, something significant shifts and freedom opens up to a fuller range of emotions and experiences with God.*

We also have to let discomfort teach us. When I was in seminary, one of my spiritual formation group facilitators challenged us to explore the feminine side of God through a guided reflection. I'll never forget the class members' interesting responses—arms crossed, hearts closed off and all kinds of negative, angry reactions. I remember feeling uncomfortable, too, but an openness to be challenged and remaining hardened are two different things. **Living in the tension and wrestling with discomfort helps us grow. Jesus** was the consummate question-asker, tension-creator and comfort-remover. Learning Kingdom ways is unsettling. Our beliefs are important, as they are a part of our faith, but the word "belief" has come to mean our reasoning **about God and the dimensions of the box that we put God into.**

What would it look like in a community of faith if we recognized belief as important, and honored it, but do not have it serve as a gatekeeper for being together? What would it look like if we allowed the larger community to continually shape and reveal our understanding of who God is? I have seen God grow bigger, and more real in people's lives because they are experiencing **an unadulterated version of their own, rather than my version.**

A few months ago a new woman started coming to Refuge gatherings. She had no previous church experience, would not call herself a Christian, and came only looking for community after a long season of loneliness. She **shared with our group that she had no idea what God was supposed to be** like. She just knew that when she was with the friend who had invited her to The Refuge, she felt loved and cared for in a way she had never experienced.

She said, *"If that's God, great. If that's not God, that's fine, too. The only thing I know is that it makes me feel better."* Years ago I would have felt the incredible urge to put her big idea into a little box and make sure she knew **this or that about God in the moment. But over the years I have seen what**

can happen when we listen instead of talk, and learn instead of teach. To me, **that simple moment was a holy encounter, a reminder that God is wild, big,** and at work in people's hearts.

As a spiritual mentor journeying with a wide range of friends, letting go of controlling people's experiences with Jesus and leaving room for a wide range of expressions does cost something. It's chaotic and a bit unsettling. My controlling tendencies can leave me thinking, "I should do something to bring that person over to the land of right-thinking" (or at least to use words that will make me feel more comfortable). I am learning to hold that at bay and take my grip off others' spiritual steering wheels and let God do the driving. The **point is not to avoid understanding who** God is; the point is to keep our means of **understanding open.**

God, expand us and help us expand our understanding of you.

As we expand our "God borders" personally and corporately, we'll provide room for people to explore what it means to know and follow Jesus without feeling judged, squeezed down, or forced to conform in order to be in relationship. As we learn to let go, we stop being know-it-alls and start being humbler, kinder people open to God's spirit at work in our own lives and in the lives of others.

Reckoning with the Gravitational Pull Toward Comfort

A while back I was having a conversation with a good friend, who is a therapist **and life coach and was in church leadership for decades. When she was part** of a growing church several years ago they taught their leadership to identify three types of people when they walked through the door—"Green Zone" people were folks you really wanted to stay because they had stable jobs, previous church experience or charisma, and knew how to give practically and financially. "Red Zone" people were all of the above but also had leadership potential, too. The more Red and Green Zone people you could assimilate, the better.

"Blue Zone" people, however, were another story. Blue Zones were a little on the messy side, maybe those who were recently divorced, single parents, or maybe didn't possess the greatest social skills. They were drains on the resources and needed to be kept at a minimum.

The big idea in terms of building their church was to nurture and develop as many Red and Green Zone people as possible, remembering that they had certain expectations that needed to be met—they tended to want good worship, teaching, a solid kids' program, and to be with other people who were similar to them. Since they are the ones who pay the bills, they keep the ministry wheels spinning round. Blue Zones weren't bad, but they just weren't valued. No one would think about building a church around Blue Zones. That would be crazy!

As she was telling the story I started to laugh at the absurdity. Yet, I know from experience it is no laughing matter. It's real. Harsh as it seems, emphasis continually gets placed on those with resources because they are the ones who provide important foundational elements—money and people—for ministries to be successful.

Over the past few years I have become painfully aware of how much easier life is when you have resources. Doors open. People return phone calls. Practical parts of life are easier. Churches and ministries want you.

I call this force "the gravitational pull toward comfort." The pull is the underlying attraction we have toward those who have more than enough money and whose lives seem put together. By comfort, I mean resources and experiences that make us feel more stable and secure. It is good that people do well, but we need to understand how the attraction to them can detract us from moving toward the marginalized and those who are struggling.

I know this in my own life. Raised by a single mom, scraping by on my own through college, I have an innate drive to build the most secure and comfortable life I possibly can. I wanted to do anything I could to not have to worry constantly about money. I went straight from college to graduate school to add extra assurance that I could make a good living. Then I got married to an educated man with a stable career. We focused on building a secure life for ourselves and for our children because that makes "sense."

The contemporary churches we were part of seemed to have a lot of people like us—educated couples with good jobs and stable families who knew how to give, serve, and participate in church activities. On the whole, we were all Red and Green Zone people. I liked the comfort and predictability of not only having enough resources to keep our lives working well but also being surrounded by other people who were essentially in the same boat. It worked for a long time. I was insulated from people who struggled with a lack of resources. In fact, looking back, not one person we were close to was without resources. **We all had houses, cars, medical insurance, and the ability to put** food in our refrigerators and gas in our cars, without thinking twice about it.

Oh how things have changed for us! Now we are part of a community where the majority of friends live on the margins when it comes to resources. Many do not own homes or have insurance, and often aren't able to easily fill their refrigerators with food or their cars with gas. These friends are single moms, divorced dads, struggling couples, disabled men and women—beautiful people who often fall into the category of the marginalized. The prettiest part is that we are all mixed together—those with resource, those without it—side by side in the trenches of life with one another. There are no Green Zone, Blue Zone, or Red Zone people and decisions aren't made based on who gives and who doesn't. I think it's lovely, but it's definitely not comfortable.

In our community, we do our best to resist the gravitational pull toward comfort and stability and do what we can to look toward the margins. **Regardless of whether we have resources or not, all people share the same thing in common**: *A desire to love and be loved, a desire to be heard, and a desire to be known. We long to be connected to something bigger than us and to taste freedom, hope, joy and purpose in the midst of real life.* These are our **common denominators, the things that we all share.**

In many organizational systems, intentionally or unintentionally, the pull toward resources and comfort influences decisions at deep levels. It also perpetuates a cycle of oppression and separation between people. Those with resources and power tend to make the rules and influence most systems. At the same time, we need to respect that resources, in and of themselves, are not bad. Yet, many Christ-followers have adopted ministry philosophies that create comfort and predictability instead of shaping them around Jesus' creative and unpredictable deference toward the hurting, marginalized, and **underrepresented.**

Having resources, power, voice and influence are gifts that can be used to create a nurturing and thriving community instead of a mechanism to keep **people separated and protected. Unfortunately, the pull toward those with** resources is so engrained in our ways of living that we often don't even notice. It's always interesting to me that on the whole, there are usually a **lot of people who have resources grouped together and a lot of people who** don't have resources grouped together. Very rarely are they intertwined and interconnected with one another in loving equal community—the kind that **Jesus calls us to.**

When we segregate instead of integrate, we perpetuate the divide. A true reflection of the Kingdom of God is when those with no resources and those **with a lot of resource live together in brotherly and sisterly love. When love** is present, economics, education, mental health, gender, and a host of other things don't get in the way

I often get glimpses of this in The Refuge community, the weird combination **of people who are learning the ways of love together even though it appears** **we may have nothing in common. I have a great deal of respect for my friends** who could do fine in an average church, but have said in their hearts, *"I have* *something to learn here that I can't learn when I keep hanging around people* *who look, think, believe, and are just like me."*

When I consider the gospels and the wild life of Jesus I see how the Kingdom he proclaimed looked radically different from the ways of the world. In his economy the first were last and the last were first. He had a gravitational pull toward the marginalized, the outsiders and those on the fringes of life and faith. To be like him, we will need to fight against our human pull toward **insiders, comfort and resources.**

This looks like inviting and involving those with the least amount of voice and power instead of the most. And let's be clear, this often contradicts the traditional leadership structures in many churches and ministries, who defer **to those with power and a voice because that is who pays the bills and carries** the most clout. It is indeed easier to build a stable foundation when you find big financial givers. The part that is rarely talked about is what then needs to happen to keep those supporters happy. When we continually defer to those **with resources and comfort, the least and the last will not be heard beyond the occasional sound bite.**

True change will come in our systems when we refuse to defer only to resource and **open up space, power, and voice for those without it.**

At The Refuge, we have tried to never defer to comfort. That's why we're poor. But it allows us to intentionally create a space for those who have never had a place to use their voice, share their hearts and gifts, or have their dignity restored. They would be crowded out by those who are prettier, seem more talented, more capable, or able to write the biggest checks. This is not to say that gifted and talented people don't have a place, but they're not the **only ones who do.**

Downward living requires refusing to be controlled by money. Jesus called out the reality that we can't serve both God and money (Matthew 6:24).

My friend, Sabio, has been part of our community since the very beginning. He's a single dad with a job at a nonprofit that barely pays his bills. He has a huge heart for community and understands this gravitational pull toward resources and comfort in a practical way. You see, he lives on the margins **and has watched the strong and powerful move ahead in many systems while** those with less visible resources are ignored. Here's what he says about living in a community that is fighting against the gravitational pull toward comfort:

> *"I'd say that those of us that stick around The Refuge have this in common—we admit to being spiritually poor. That doesn't equate to everyone being financially poor. Some folks here have resources and still understand that they are poor in spirit and know that they need God and each other. It hasn't always been this way, I'm pretty sure that we started out with a lot more folks who could seriously provide for a new church financially.*
>
> *Our identity was much more attractive in the beginning, though we didn't know exactly what we were doing. From the beginning we always walked the talk as well as we could that*

everyone would be honored and loved for who they were, not for the checks they wrote.

A funny thing happened as everyone's voice was persistently honored with equity instead of deferring to the big donors and we continually admitted our spiritual poverty—many people with margin just started gradually leaving. I miss them, because I came to know some of them. I discovered that unintentionally I drove one of these people away when I spoke strongly in defense of doing things "with" people, instead of the usual "to" and "for" ways of doing things. I was strident in defending that as a core principle in our relationships. I didn't hold back and assumed that this well-intentioned person would hang in there and at least wrestle with the idea. Instead, they just left.

I am sure it is much easier to do things "for those people" (if you are not one of those people) and it must be rewarding to do something good by writing a check. I wouldn't know. I'm just guessing. I don't know what the big answer is to having enough moolah and mojo to do the beautiful and hazardous work we do together for Jesus, other than to keep your overhead low and your friends close at hand."

I am thankful for Sabio. He helps me remember to *keep our overhead low and our friends close at hand.* In actively choosing to live with people in the uncomfortable spaces, he is creating the type of community I really need. He is leading the way for others to see the reality of the Kingdom of God. Sabio's presence forces me to continually wrestle with what it means to live with those who are not like me.

As I reflect on Scripture, it seems Jesus was pretty clear on this one. Over and over again, he told us what Kingdom living looked like, and it always pulled in a different direction than where most people seemed to be going. It usually looked a little funky, odd, and off-kilter to the norm. It shook up the status quo. It tilted toward the marginalized, spiritually poor, hungry and desperate, and shook the foundations of the systems that default to religion, power, **resources and comfort.**

Cultivating Kingdom living requires reckoning with our gravitational pull toward comfort. If we keep justifying it and letting ourselves continually be pulled that direction because everyone else is doing it, we will end up with even more structures and relationships that perpetuate power and keep those on the margins silenced and disempowered. In the same way the Kingdom isn't going to drop out of the sky, issues of power and resources won't dissipate until we stop deferring to it.

Little Pockets of Love

Another way we can actively participate in cultivating the Kingdom of God now is by nurturing what I call "little pockets of love." Imagine the shift that would happen if people actually viewed Christians as cultivators of little pockets of love. To me, church has nothing to do with a building, sermons, worship songs, kids program, places to sit, or a pastor to look up to. Instead, it is about creating a space of love for one another. Eye-to-eye, face-to-face, heart-to-heart, and life-to-life. People knit together on the journey, somehow committed to living, growing, learning, eating, trying and loving together.

My working definition of church is: "People gathered together in some way, shape, or form to learn and practice the ways of Jesus and pass on love, hope, mercy, justice, and healing in a broken, weird world."

I believe people are the church and we can live out our faith in diverse ways. Two people can be the church, 2,000 people can be the church, and anything in between can be the church. It supersedes language and isn't limited by our definitions nor by the type of gathering or experience. When I am with another person cultivating little pockets of love, it is "church."

Throughout the years I have been transformed through little pockets of love. Very little happened for me in the big venue or the places where everyone was just like me or where I could easily hide. The places where people called out what was deep within me, stuck with me even when I wanted to run away, pointed me toward God's real heart for me, and challenged me to pass it on—those are the places where I seem to learn the most.

There are many different expressions of pockets of love beyond the ones I've been part of at The Refuge or in other small, intimate and challenging groups.

They are in houses, pubs, the streets, AA meetings, homeless shelters, prisons, schools, traditional churches, workplaces, social clubs, neighborhood gatherings, and a score of other places. Pockets of love are places where the gospel can be lived out through hearts in action. Where Christ's light can shine into the darkest of places, truth can be spoken, hope can be borrowed, and food can be shared—the kind that fills our stomachs and our spirits.

We often say The Refuge is a place to "learn to love Jesus and others, and to learn to receive love from Jesus and others." How often do we allow **our focus to include receiving love from God and others? In many churches** and ministries, little emphasis is put on loving ourselves even though Jesus inextricably ties these two together, telling us to love our neighbor as **ourselves. If we are going to be able to love our neighbor, we must at the** same time learn to love ourselves, to let God's love touch our hearts. **Self-hatred, self-doubt, insecurity, depression, disconnectedness, and loneliness** plague so many yet we often haven't created spaces that help shift these damaging patterns.

In the Oscar-winning movie *Precious*, a hurting, abused, unvalued girl finally **discovers someone who believes in her, who sees beyond the surface and calls** out her beauty and strength. It's a powerful story of redemption for victims of poverty and severe sexual, emotional, and physical abuse. Her alternative **school teacher is the catalyst and invites the main character, Precious, into** *"a little pocket of love"*— a place where she can receive love and begin to find **hope and purpose despite terrible circumstances. It was a glorious picture** of "the church" and what can happen when containers are created for God's healing and hope to enter through relationship with people.

At the heart of God's mission is the restoration of people. But unless we **actually create a space where people can emerge from their wounds, doubts,** fears, and failures, it is doubtful they will ever discover that love.

Finding a new story takes time and hard work, but it is possible. After many of years of living in an emotionally abusive relationship, my friend, Rachel, left her husband, taking her two kids to try to rebuild their life. The path for her was bumpy; she had issues with court, custody, mounting bills, and the ongoing demands of being a single mom. In these moments, there's a desperate need for ongoing support, for a little pocket of love.

She says:

> *"My loving sisters and brothers have a supernatural way of balancing giving, receiving, and loving in an extremely safe environment that has allowed me to walk through this very tough journey. They allow my questions, my anger. They love me unconditionally, so there is no fear of being too 'difficult.' They have filled in the gaps (and there are many). Whether it's helping out with paying the bills, lending a hand to help me move, or babysitting, they have shown me love in a very tangible way.   It's truly been a matter of life and death for me."*

Our role in her life wasn't to save the day and make her life easier; we couldn't do that anyway. It was to create a space for her to find her voice, get her feet on the ground, and learn to love herself after years of being beaten down.

If we look at the life of Jesus, it's hard to imagine the church would be anything other than a diverse scattering of little pockets of love—places **where the beauty, strength, and goodness that is within each person has a chance to come out. Where God and man somehow intersect in mysterious, supernatural ways. Where Jesus-in-the-flesh is alive and well, calling out hope, forgiveness, purpose, passion and love.**

Still, as Alexie reminds us, it doesn't happen magically. It requires much *intention, grace and endurance* to nurture little pockets of love.

I do not think there is a great need in this world for the building of more churches; however, I think our families, neighborhoods, cities, and the world can be radically changed if more intentional communities—little pockets of love—are cultivated.

The Difference Between Building Ministries and Cultivating Communities

The book *Community and Growth* by Jean Vanier has impacted me more than almost any book I've read. Written in the 1980's, it's a solid—and challenging—

primer for a life of descent. He says:

> *"Christian communities continue the work of Jesus. They are sent to be a presence to people who are living in darkness and despair. The people who come into these communities also respond to the call and the cry of the weak and the oppressed. They enter into the covenant with Jesus and the poor. They meet Jesus in them."*[7]

I think it can be fairly easy to build what we typically and historically think of as "church" or a "ministry." There are fairly good business models for it, which usually include a clear vision, a financial foundation, and strong leaders to carry it out. It's trickier to find ways to knit hearts together and gather **around a common purpose while allowing for a wide range of diversity and** perspectives. Nurturing a spirit of justice and action, sharing meals and resources, and creating a safe and challenging container to learn to love and be loved by Jesus, ourselves, and others requires a whole different way of thinking.

When we started The Refuge, we tried to mix the *attractional* **model (come to us) with the** *missional* model (go to others). **We wanted people to come** to our wider gathering so we figured out a way to make sure that we included **music, teaching and a fairly good vibe. We decided early on that there would** be no "membership." At the same time, we were certain that we wanted to make sure that no one ever said, *"I* **go to** *The Refuge because I love the teaching, music, or kids program."* We always wanted people to say, *"I am* **part of The Refuge** *because of the people."* We intentionally didn't ramp up **music or teaching and get people addicted to something that we believe is a** "want," rather than a "need."

Most of our life together didn't happen at that main gathering. Instead, it happened in eye-to-eye and heart-to-heart encounters throughout the week. People got confused. They kept waiting for us to find our stride and ramp up our programs, and after about a year of muddling around trying to find ourselves, it became clear that we were mixing models that can't be mixed.

Slowly, we began to let go of the need to make people happy and lean into what was deep within our hearts. We had a deep desire to cultivate a diverse, experiential, advocacy-infused and transformational healing community without walls. We also found that it was not as attractive to churchgoers as we hoped. Many people simply weren't interested in downward mobility, even though this is what Jesus invites us into. People were looking for inspiring teaching, good music and something amazing for their kids once a week. It just wasn't who we wanted to be. Slowly, we learned to be comfortable in our own skin and lean into what was already within us.

Over time, The Refuge has become more clear about who we are and who we're not. I have also become more aware of who I am and who I'm not. Each of us is different and wired with unique passions for ministry. The beauty of the Kingdom of God is that is allows and invites this diversity. My hope for each person, each community, dedicated to the downward journey is that we **individually and corporately learn how to become comfortable in our own** skin instead of trying to be something we're not.

Fortunately, many people are longing for a something deeper that "going to church" won't fill. The on-going exodus out of church (and sometimes Christianity) by our younger population continues, with hoards of people giving up on the system and finding ways to live out their faith apart from the traditional containers. Many are tired of seeing new wine continually poured into old wineskins. Since we need to be active participants in cultivating the Kingdom now, we have to create new wine skins—radically different models of living in community together in a wide variety of contexts. We'll have to turn our attention and energy toward realizing the distinct differences between cultivating communities and building ministries.

First and foremost, cultivating a community requires an extremely high level of relationship that most of us haven't really learned to do well. Many have spent a lot of time focused on learning what the Bible says to believe, but haven't learned to practice what it says to do. Christianity has largely become a system of belief, as opposed to the practice of love. Even though we know it doesn't work that way, we keep thinking that "teaching about Jesus" will **somehow eventually equal love.**

The way to learn how to become like Jesus is to love. The only way we can learn how to love is to practice it in close relationship, and have our lives rub up against each other, including doing so with people who are different from us. Loving people just like us is not that difficult.   Loving people who never change, who bug the hell out of us, who aren't kind or thankful, who don't pass on grace even though they've received heaps of it—that requires much more work. In other words, love is best practiced in the spaces that require it. Isn't that exactly what Jesus challenges us to—to live into the spaces that **only come through a path of descent?**

Cultivating community requires embracing that the long view isn't very sexy. **Because life change rarely happens in a snap, slogging it out over the long** haul with people is brutal and tries our patience. In messy, incarnational relationships, the fruit is sometimes hard to see and often imperceptible to the naked eye. The "results" our human nature tends to look for are sometimes elusive.

My friend and teammate, Karl, has been around the ministry block for many years. He has been part of little communities, mega-churches, start-ups and well-established para-church ministries. One thing he and I talk about is how challenging it is to cultivate community, as opposed to building something using old models that perpetuate power differentials and keeps hearts—and leaders—at a protected distance.

He says:

> *"A community is not designed, period. You do not get to sit around and dream about what you want to build or even the people you want to reach; you only get to be with the people that are around you. You don't get to show off the superstars and hide the weirdos in the back someplace. In a community, there is an assumption of equality, of mutual interdependence, and that means everyone must be heard."*

As followers of Jesus, cultivating community requires a level of relationship many haven't been taught, especially in seminary. Karl adds:

> *"On a personal level, it is hard to not be in charge, to predetermine an outcome. I understand the carefully crafted 90-minute experience where I know how to get people to emotionally connect and bond with me. It is far more difficult to live a less edited life, to show up for people who will never*

pay me back or help the church get bigger. Seminary taught me how to be aloof to lead, but I did not take one course on how to be a friend. It is so clear now that the only skill I need, but do not have, to build a community, is the ability to be a good friend."

Through The Refuge community, Karl is learning how to be a friend. So am I. Learning to be good friends who sit in the midst of pain and suffering without easy answers, is not at the top of most leaders' lists, but it is an essential ingredient of downward living. When I talk to individuals who are daily in the trenches with hurting people, we seem to share many of the same stories. We never have enough money or support, we have volumes of hard and beautiful stories, and we are constantly asking God, "Are you sure this is what you had in mind, because it's way harder than we thought?!" Yet we can't abandon living this way because we're seeing God in the here and now.

Downward living requires letting go of old ways and leaning into new philosophies and practices.

The old way says, "If you give people what they really want, they'll come and take part." The new way says, "Our responsibility is to give people what they really need: an opportunity to be known, loved and valued in intimate, interdependent relationships with others." This is what scares people off the fastest and is also the kind of living that is a marker of authentic community.

The old way says, "We need to give people opportunity to serve 'the poor' or 'other' people so they can get out of themselves, and help address their self-centeredness." The new way says, "We will do more than reach down and offer a hand, which helps us recognize our own need for humility. We **will go down and experience how much we actually have in common and** how desperate we all are. We have more to learn than we have to give."

The old way says, "Figure out how to be self-sufficient as quickly as possible, maybe even before you start. Do what it takes to build an infrastructure that will support itself and feed into it to keep it humming along." The new way says, "Abandon the infrastructure if it means sacrificing people and relationships for the sake of a structure that always needs to be maintained. **Feed your people and community with love, care, respect and beauty (and** understand this will probably never pay the bills the way you had hoped)."

The old way says, "Go find people that can fulfill specific roles, individuals who can get the jobs done that you need to get done to strengthen your infrastructure." The new way says, "Who is already here and how can their gifts and passions be best expressed even if there are gaping holes in the things we think should happen?"

The old way says, "We measure success by numbers, financial viability, and a solid list of programs." The new way says, "We can't really measure success. We just know it when we see it. It looks like places where people have experienced Christ's touch and love, even though their circumstances may remain the same. It's where feeling loved and accepted changed everything underneath, where a person's dignity got restored, where an artist felt the freedom to express, where someone came and went but took with them a taste of a different way, or where some never set foot into a weekly gathering **but read something online that gave them hope and made them feel less** alone."

Honestly, I sometimes like the old ways better for one simple reason: It was so much easier to pull off. This new way is harder. But once you've tasted, felt and experienced the Kingdom of God in messy places, you're ruined. In a Jesus-inspired way, the downward descent seems to be the only option.

Spiritual leader and social change advocate Mahatma Gandhi said, *"Be the change you want to see."*[8] We can't live these "in-the-trenches" ways without God's wind and expansive spirit blowing through us. We can't make these changes without continually acknowledging our spiritual poverty that breaks down the barriers between "us and them." We can't live this out without a willingness to become interdependent and reject the gravitational pull toward comfort. Dr. Martin Luther King, Jr. adds, *"Change does not roll in on the wheels of inevitability, but comes through continuous struggle. And so we must straighten our backs and work for our freedom. A man can't ride you unless your back is bent."*[9]

Changing powerful, deeply-rooted ways of doing things in the world and the church won't come cheap or easy. But one person at a time, one community at a time, change can indeed happen. It starts with us. With God's spirit fueling us, we can make what could be, be.

Making What Could Be, Be.

As a dreamer, I like to imagine what could be.

Despite some of my cynicism about church systems, I am still an idealist. Change is possible; otherwise I would have given up a long time ago. I am still foolish enough to think that our wild "God dreams" are possible. I think when **Jesus said** *"Your Kingdom come, your will be done on earth as it is in heaven"* (Matthew 6:10), he meant that the Kingdom was possible now. I also know it's possible because I see it every day in small and beautiful ways. I see the marginalized, forgotten, neglected and abused finding love and hope through **healing community.**

For a lot of us, it's hard to dream. Almost every time I challenge people to dream it stirs up fear and trouble. We've hoped before and had many of our dreams dashed, mocked and called unrealistic or impractical. I know that many have tried to make their dreams a reality in systems that rejected them, and they've lost a lot of hope. The thought of opening hearts back up again is too scary. Others are in the midst of living out dreams and are finding how hard they can sometimes be. Often can think of all the reasons these dreams won't work, so why even try?

But here's why I think we should try. These Kingdom ways aren't supposed to be a pipe dream, or an elusive, unrealistic and unobtainable idea that we know will never happen. Jesus' ways of upside down living require imagination and hope. They require crazy people willing to live out what's embedded deep inside their hearts, regardless of the cost. They require courageous women and men who risk their money, time and pride to go against the flow of the powerful status quo and create little pockets of love that reflect Jesus, rather than the world. They require humble disciples, followers of Christ, who try as best they can to heal the sick, feed the hungry, care for the poor, love the unlovely, and pass on hope in places where there is none. Most of all, these **Kingdom ways require people with eyes to see more beauty and hope in the** often ugly, messy, downward journey than on the predictable, comfortable **upwardly mobile path.**

The other night I was with some Refuge friends at our house talking about dreaming. **Even though I want people to dream big, I also want people to** dream small. To value little and simple ways we can move toward more of Christ's love, life and hope in this world. I shared with my friends how many years ago I dreamed of the kind of community I am now a part of—one that was inclusive, authentic and healing, and valued generosity, equality and the practice of love, above all. I shared how, in my dreams, it looked completely different. Trust me, it was a lot prettier, easier, bigger and brighter. Yet, even though my original picture was different, the real flesh and bones of what I had hoped for has come true. I'm experiencing it in real life. I am grateful but also not afraid to keep dreaming for more. I want others to have a chance to **taste and see, too.**

So I keep dreaming, trying to play my small part in the bigger story. I'm **reminding myself, and others, that this downward path is worth it. Despite** being messy and unpredictable, it's also filled with unbelievable beauty and **hope.**

When I stop and allow myself to really imagine, I dream that we'd be people who took Jesus' words seriously. We can't just talk about it, but we actually have to be forgiving, loving, sacrificing and humble. I hope we become people willing to give away our stuff, care for the widows and orphans, die to ourselves, hug lepers, love our neighbors, lay down power and make peace **with our enemies.**

I dream that all people would feel valued, regardless of our differences. I **hope we become people who refuse to let color, socioeconomics, gender,** theologies, shapes, sizes, or social abilities get in the way of seeing the image of God and respecting each other's worth, value and contribution to this world. I hope we will continue to find ways for women, men, white, brown, poor and rich to work equally and fully alongside one other as brothers, **sisters, leaders and friends.**

I dream that the divide between "us and them" will continue to crumble.

I dream that Christ-followers will form into an underground army of advocates, that we will stand with the marginalized, oppressed, poor and unlovely, and will risk our pride, position and power so that someone with none could get a little.

I dream that damage from the past and present will not paralyze us from living out who God made us to be; instead, we'd use our story to help another **person.**

I dream a whole bunch of us will find ways to create little pockets of love in places that desperately need them so that we will be known by the world as "those crazy people who never give up on the hurting, the lost, the oppressed and the outcasts."

Never be afraid to dream.

Personal Reflection:

1. Consider how your view of God has been expanding during this season of your faith journey. What are you learning about God, yourself and others?

2. Have you ever deferred to those with resources? What was that like?

3. Have you ever been marginalized, and experienced others' neglect? What was that like?

4. Which ideas about cultivating community are you drawn to? Which ones scare you?

5. Which of the "old ways" are difficult for you to let go of? Why?

6. Respond to Gandhi's idea of being "the change you want to see." What is God stirring up in you to try and change?

7. Dreaming is sometimes hard; it opens us up to hope in a way that can terrify us. We sometimes see these kinds of inspiring words and let them prick our hearts, but actually risking ourselves to really engage with what they could mean in our real lives is a whole different story. What are some of your dreams? What is God stirring up in you?

Group Discussion:

1. How has your view of God been expanding? What has that looked and felt like for you?

2. Process together some examples of "the gravitational pull toward comfort"—where you've seen it happen and how you've intersected with it.

3. From your collective experiences, what are some differences between "building a ministry" and "cultivating a community?"

Which comes easiest to you? Why?

4. When you look at the contrast between the "old ways" and "new ways," which of the old ways are hardest to give up? Which of the new ways **inspire you the most?**

5. When you consider Gandhi's thought, "Be the change you want to see," where is an area you are called to be a change agent? What are some of your dreams? What is God stirring up in you?

SECTION TWO
CREATING LIFE DOWN HERE

The dreams of making what could be a reality are embedded in many of our hearts. **Some of you are already seeing these dreams lived out in reality and** need to know you are not alone. Others are considering stepping into new ways of living out your faith and need a reminder you're not crazy (well, you are, but at least you're not alone). And yet others of you have a stirring inside and aren't quite sure what to do about it.

The downward descent requires embracing and fostering a culture of healing. Such a culture has very specific attributes that must be practiced to actually develop. Each of these practices includes a central and guiding ingredient from the first beatitude--*humility*. "Blessed are the poor in spirit, for theirs is the kingdom of heaven" (Matthew 5:3) becomes our guiding text and the foundation for living out the wild ways of Jesus. Each of these practices begin **with humility:**

- **Extending love, mercy, and compassion**
- **Welcoming pain**
- Honoring doubt,
- Diffusing power
- Practicing equality
- Pursuing justice
- Cultivating creativity

- Celebrating freedom

These kingdom principles are counter-cultural; living them out will mean that others around us might get mad at us, worry about our well-being, or think that we aren't being very good Christians anymore.   Rocking the boat and refusing to toe the line of the status quo usually will result in some kind of tension or conflict in relationships, either personally or corporately. As you **move through the upcoming chapters, my hope is that each of you will listen** to the stirring in your heart, *whatever that looks like*, **and consider ways to** continually transform some of these ideas into practice.

It's also easy to nod our head and say, "Of course, these are no-brainers. These are elements that should be in place for those that follow Jesus." The assumption that they must be true does not make them true in reality. *We must actively work to create them.* **Consistent with almost everything Jesus** challenges us to do, it is far more difficult to live out these principles personally and corporately than at first glance, especially with countless strong forces **against us.**

There are also a few things to remember as we explore these Kingdom practices on the downward road of making what could be a reality. If we can't practice these ourselves, we can't pass them on to others.   We can't take people where we ourselves aren't willing to go.

This downward journey looks different for everyone.   Like everything else in the Kingdom, there's a wide variety of creativity available, many diverse possibilities for living out these ideas. The key is to embrace where you are at in your culture, context, and experience and apply them there. There's no perfect formula or right way; these are broad strokes designed to stir up creativity, imagination and action.

Within each of the following chapters are also a few practical ideas to consider. The way to integrate some of these values into our lives and our experiences is to practice them not once, not twice, but continually.   This kind of faith **learning is not science and will require a high degree of stumbling, bumbling** and falling down. Failure is an equal part in the experience, but affords us the opportunity to get back up and try again.

Keep remembering: *There are many forces against this kind of living.* **I feel**

the tug almost every day, and it's a resistance that can be discouraging and tiring. Jesus knew it was going to be hard, but he left us with his power and example to continually strengthen us on the journey down to the low places **where he and many others live.**

Chapter 5

Extending Love, Mercy and Compassion

*"Christ has no body on earth but yours, no hands but yours,
no feet but yours. Yours are the eyes through which he is
to look out, Christ's compassion to the world. Yours are the
feet with which he is to go about doing good. Yours are the
hands with which he is to bless now." - Teresa of Avila*

When you think of Jesus, what comes to mind? If you think of a Christian, is it the same picture? When average people think of Jesus, their responses usually land in this area: *loving, kind, merciful, compassionate*. **Unfortunately, when** people are asked, "What are some characteristics of Christians?" research consistently shows the words on the tip of many people's tongues are **probably more along the lines of:** *judgmental, critical, homophobic, mean*.

Sadly, a lot of the work Christ-followers have done throughout history to care for the poor and marginalized around the world often hasn't translated into the overall perception of Christians. We can blame all kinds of people and circumstances for our bad press, but I don't think we can escape that Christians have gained a bad reputation. We tend to be known for our politics instead of our love, mercy and compassion. Why? Because many **have become entangled in contemporary culture that tends to focus on the** self, independence, survival of the fittest, and a "let's not get our hands too dirty" attitude.

The needs of the world can sometimes so overwhelm us that we don't even know where to start. We think the small part we play won't make a difference. Mother Teresa nips this doubt in the bud, saying, *"If you can't feed 100 people, just feed one."*[10] When we're stuck in a cycle of thinking that in order to be worthy, our practices have to be big and affect a large amount of people, we become paralyzed and miss out on what's right before us. **In denying our capacity to feed 100, we never feed one. Small, simple** acts go further than we think, especially in a harsh and cruel world. Let us never underestimate what a kind word might mean for someone, or what a cup of cold water might mean for another. One is always better than none. Something is always better than nothing.

Everything begins with love. Jesus makes the command to love one of his most defining statements. He summarizes the entire law with it: *"Love the Lord your God with all your heart, with all your mind, with all your soul and all your strength, and love your neighbor as yourself" (Mark 12:30).* We **can** talk about love, preach sermons about love, read books about love, quote scriptures about love and long to love. However, the bottom line is: *The only way to actually learn the ways of love is to extend it, try it, do it, risk it, live it—to enter into another person's life and let someone into ours.*

Mercy and compassion are essential components of love. Emulating Jesus, Mother Teresa is known for this kind of love; it flowed from her tangible care for the sick, the dying, the neglected and the forgotten. She extended mercy and compassion to people, not in words, but in actions. Many think of Mother Teresa's example as out of reach for average people, but in our own unique ways, we are all called to incarnate Jesus. The essence of downward **living is embodied in a life of extending love, mercy and compassion to others.**

Jesus shows us the way by continually reminding us it's the people who matter; doctrine, rules and the outsides of our cups mean little in the light of love. He calls us to focus on people and on hearts. He tells us to sacrifice ourselves, stop and help, shore up wounds, offer healing touches, and look the outcasts in the eyes and remind them of their worth. This is what we as **individuals, as a wider body, should be about.** *If we are really living out the Gospels the way that Jesus modeled for us, then we should be known as the weirdest, craziest risk takers and lovers of people in town.*

Extending love, mercy, and compassion requires us to first receive it ourselves.

It will also mean leaving the predictable confines of our own churches, homes and neighborhoods to actively seek the lost, hurting, forgotten, and marginalized instead of expecting others to come to us. This core value of inclusion rocks the foundation of much of what we've been taught about church and Christian life. As we break down the obstacles that keep us separated from others, we must tangibly engage in the essence of Jesus' downward ways—restoring human dignity.

If we are really living out the Gospels the way that Jesus modeled for us, then we should be known as the weirdest, craziest, risk-takers and lovers of people in town.

We Can't Give What We Haven't Received

"I know there's grace for everyone else," says my friend, Shawna, *"but I don't think there's any for me. I am too far gone."* Shawna expresses the same sentiment of so many others I know—often including myself: **We have trouble receiving love and grace for ourselves. Shawna has a long story of neglect and abuse. Always struggling to get by, she never felt truly accepted or loved. Despite her generous** and kind heart, it is extremely difficult for her to believe she's lovable. Over a lot of time in healing community and after many conversations reminding her of her value and worth, it is starting to sink in that she is, indeed, loved. It didn't happen **overnight or in a sudden epiphany. Rather, it has been through the slow, gentle pace** and practice of life together in community.

Over and over, she resisted love, but we wouldn't relent. Slowly, she started to let go of self-hatred and lean in to God's love, our love. As she practices **receiving love, mercy and compassion from others, it is increasing her ability** to love and connect with others. Now, when I see her in a conversation with someone else, looking them in the eye instead of at the floor, offering kind words and care, I am filled with gratitude for the wild and beautiful ways God **can heal and restore through loving community.**

The potential danger of missional mindsets being focused on hand-out "to" and charity-like "for" relationships that are more focused on us feeling better, than actually getting into the muck and grime of real poverty and pain. "With" relationships usually come from people who are in touch with pain, hurt and **struggle, and have tasted grace, mercy and compassion.**

When I consider the story of the Good Samaritan in Luke 10, I can't help but think that the Samaritan man was someone who understood what it felt like to be on the outside, on the margins. Maybe that is what motivated him to stop and help. I do not think the only way to extend love is if we have a painful story, because thankfully everyone hasn't endured the same level of hardship. However, without a heart connection to God's redemption, grace and mercy in a practical and sincere sense, it is challenging to pass these gifts **on to others.**

In my early years of learning what it meant to be a Christian, I lived with a lot of shame, guilt and self-hatred. Deep down, I often felt I wasn't forgiven by God and remained stuck in a cycle of feeling unworthy of love and grace. I was extremely harsh and critical toward others who didn't look, think or believe like me. I'm embarrassed now by some of the ways I treated others, but I honestly think it was propelled by the anger and shame I felt inside. As I grew in experiencing God's grace, I became better able to pass it on to others **more freely.**

It's interesting how common Shawna's story is—harshness toward ourselves that can't seem to be shaken. We fail to see the importance of loving the self. We miss the second part of Jesus' command. He says to love our neighbor *as we love ourselves.* Self-love is not taught in many Christian circles because it gets associated with self-centeredness. What's most ironic, though, is that self-hatred is completely narcissistic and self-centered.

When I was unable to share the pain of my past and what I was struggling with in my heart and head, I had a block to connecting with people. I could go through the motions of connection, but deep down I knew something was missing. That missing ingredient was my inability to accept, honor and embrace my own story. I wasn't bringing my true self to my relationships, so I could never be fully loved for who I really was—with all my good and all my **bad mixed together. As I began to embrace my whole story, and share more** openly in safe relationships, I found that my capacity for love, mercy, and compassion greatly increased. When we reject our own stories, we somehow reject others, too. When we accept our own stories, we can authentically **accept the stories of others.**

I call this integration. Integration is a wholeness that comes from acceptance of our strengths and weaknesses instead of a constant resistance and rejection of anything negative. Integrated people are safer because they aren't in hiding; they aren't trying to pretend to be someone they're not or keep others at arm's length for fear of being found out. They are centered, **solid and safe.**

Safe does not mean tame; the ways of Jesus are far from tame. Safe is the ability to hold a sacred space for people to share their real life. It is kind, loving presence without judgment or control. The safer we are, the more likely those who are in desperate need of love, mercy and compassion will be willing to engage in true relationship with us. Jesus was a safe person; people were wildly drawn to him, seeking his love, mercy, and compassion. Safe people embody the same quality; hurting people gravitate toward people **who naturally and freely extend love, mercy and compassion.**

My friend, Carrie, is a single mom who left an abusive marriage and has been navigating life alone for many years now. A sexual abuse survivor, she struggles with feeling loved, protected and safe in this world. Through redemptive community she is healing and learning how to live in freedom. A **champion for safety, she says,**

> *"Having safe people in my life that didn't run away when I was hurting has been one of the most healing parts of my journey. At first it was incredibly hard to tell people my story. Knowing other people in the same boat as me and struggling with the same things in their relationship with God, with themselves, with other people helped me feel much less alone."*

Safety comes from embracing our own story and pain and realizing it doesn't define us; once we can do this, it's far easier to pass it on to others. Carrie now provides a safe haven for other single moms finding courage to leave abusive relationships and rebuild their lives. The number one ingredient that she brings to these relationships is safety. She is in touch with her own story and God's love, mercy and compassion, so she can pass it on to others.

Leaving the Ninety-nine for the One

Once we engage in our own story of pain and suffering, we can begin to see that others share many of the same feelings. This awareness provides us with deeper understanding behind what it means to "go out" and answer the call to love others. The gospels are filled with stories that center on "going," extending love, mercy and compassion to people and places in desperate need of it.

> *"Blessed are the merciful, for they will be shown mercy."*
>
> *Matthew 5:7*

Last year my family went to Kenya for a mission adventure. A Kenyan friend invited us for a week of teaching, playing with kids, and intersecting with their ministry. He asked me to speak to the pastors and leaders at their Bible college about life in the trenches with people. He told me, "Kenya doesn't need more evangelists. It needs more pastors." Immediately, the Parable of the Lost Sheep passage came to mind. Jesus says:

> *"If a man has a hundred sheep and one of them wanders away, what will he do? Won't he leave the ninety-nine others on the hills and go out to search for the one that is lost? And if he finds it, I tell you the truth, he will rejoice over it more than over the ninety-nine that didn't wander away! In the same way, it is not my heavenly Father's will that even one of these little ones should perish." (Matthew 18:12-14)*

It's easy to read the Bible for *personal* application and completely miss the *community* application. We must consider both. My friend, Karl, always reminds me that Paul's letters weren't written to individuals but were written to bodies of people, to the church as a whole. When we read the Bible from a "we" perspective instead of an "only for me" perspective, things shift. Actually, they get much harder. Personal holiness doesn't require the connection and sacrifice that real community does. I don't know exactly what direction Jesus was going with this parable, but maybe he was talking about **the hundred sheep being the whole community of believers, or the church.**

There is a strong allure to tend to the "Church of the Ninety-nine," **the ones** who already fill the pews. This group tends to be louder and stronger. Jesus, **in this parable, tells of the shepherd who is willing to leave the Ninety-nine to** find the One (to me, the One is the outcast, marginalized, oppressed, doubtful misfit, who somehow doesn't cut it with the Ninety-nine). That One is worth it. That One is his. The One is valuable enough to drop everything and go find it.

The Ninety-nine are the ones who pay the bills for many churches and ministries and help make things go. They are the ones whose voices are loudest, who have the most power and the most influence. It leaves many **shepherds saying,** *"If we can just keep the Ninety-nine happy, maybe we can somehow figure out how to help the One."* I understand the dilemma. The church of the Ninety-nine is powerful; its culture is deeply embedded into our models, practices and almost everything related to contemporary church.

It's easier to tend to the needs of the Ninety-nine, and let the Ones fend for themselves. Toward the end of my time on a mega-church staff we were told we needed to stop using the words "desperate," "messy," and "broken" because they were making some "big givers" uncomfortable. They wanted to hear more about the Bible and were becoming tired of hearing stories from "those recovery people" every week. In that same season I was also told that it was time to focus on "key leaders who don't drain our resources," instead of "hurting people that take too much of our time."

This parable paints a stark reality that flies in the face of our desire to protect the Ninety-nine. The shepherd actually leaves the Ninety-nine to find the One. What if Jesus realized that wholeness was not possible without the One?

I don't think you can have a church of the Ninety-nine and a church of the One. If we focus on the needs of the Ninety-nine, we miss that a central part of the community's wholeness is in finding the One.

I never want to dismiss that God does amazing work in the Church of the Ninety-nine. God is alive and well, changing lives in all kinds of ways. Yet, I often can't help but think that we've missed the whole point. We've built structures and systems in Jesus' name that were precisely what he was **challenging.**

My friends, Ken Loyd and Jessica Stewart, work with people who live on the streets in Portland. I have seen their work up close and personal and here's **what always challenges me.**

They focus all of their energy on seeking out and finding the Ones.

They go where no one else is willing to go. They hold people's hands when they are going through withdrawals during detox. They lift people out of the bathroom after almost overdosing, needles still in their arms. They look in the eyes of people who are treated like trash and tell them they are beautiful. The Ninety-nine do not help them in the work they do; sure, they get a few checks now and then, but on the whole, the people who support their work the most are fellow rag-tags who believe that the Ones are worth it, that the only way these people will ever feel Jesus' love is if someone brings it to them.

Ken and Jessica are masters at inclusion; they make those who have always felt excluded, left out and less-than, feel respected, part of and included. They believe, as I do, that Christ's love, mercy, and compassion are inclusive **and radical. Instead of trying to change people, they love them as they are.**

Removing the Obstacles that Keep People from Coming and Going

Regardless of how easy it is to nod our heads and agree with the importance of intentional inclusion, how often are the rituals we've established actually designed to keep the One out? Last year I went to a Catholic mass for a Quinceañera for one of my daughter's friends. I appreciate these kinds of celebratory, sacred moments to honor life's passages. The priest was brilliant, sharing a beautiful homily about Jesus, the master teacher of love. It was very stirring.

I appreciated the beauty of the moment until it came time for communion. I knew it was coming before I walked in, but I got sucked into the priest's lovely message about Jesus' heart for people and forgot about the very strict guidelines around the Eucharist. He clarified that communion was only for **Catholics, and even then you had to have gone to confession at least once in** the past year. I respect traditions; they are highly valued across a vast variety of denominations and churches. Each are entitled to their strong beliefs and practices about the way things should be, but I don't agree with them. The church has created a barrier to participating with God in one of the most sacred events in the Kingdom. It has created a rule to shut people out. The **more we exclude, the less love, mercy and compassion is extended.**

As I sat there listening I noticed how ugly and sad it felt. I remembered a time when I was a kid and went to church with a friend of mine. No one in my family regularly attended church, but I was very interested in God. When **communion was being served in that Protestant church, I stood up to get in line when her mom stopped me, coldly saying,** *"You can't take it unless you've been baptized,"* which I hadn't. They went and took Christ's body and blood, and I sat there by myself, feeling stupid, ashamed and confused. Over thirty years later I can still remember what it felt like to be excluded.

Many of my friends feel excluded from communities or relationships for a wide variety of reasons; sexual orientation, economics, shameful life experiences and lack of belief seem to be the most common reasons people are excluded. **Jesus was the master at inclusion, reminding us that people always supersede beliefs, and that restoring dignity was far more important than ensuring that** someone was following social rules or norms. He embodied the practice of **love by modeling a radical inclusion that brought those from the fringes into the fold of his love, hope and healing.**

To become people who extend God's love, mercy and compassion, we will need to model Jesus' actions and become masters at inclusion. Mixing with people who make us feel uncomfortable is where we learn the most; these kinds of inclusive relationships are an excellent training ground to engage with our prejudices or barriers to love. My friends who minister on the streets around the United States never expect people to come to them; instead, they go to where the pain is—where love, mercy and compassion are greatly needed. It would indeed be easier if they could set up shop and provide a service that would bring hurting people in the door so they could care for others on their terms, but that ministry model is utterly flawed. Jesus didn't expect people to meet him on his turf. Instead, he went out, extending a web of love and healing, bringing love and hope to places of pain.

A few friends connected to The Refuge live in government sponsored housing; they call it the "ghetto." It's very unassuming and looks like a typical apartment complex in the suburbs of Denver, yet, underneath the veneer is a subculture of poverty, drugs, child neglect and pain. I try to drop by every week to hang out with friends and bring a sliver of love and light into what often feels like darkness. Every time I am there I remember how forgotten this segment of society feels.

Caring for those who fall in the category of "suburban poor," is not quite as popular as caring for those that live on the streets or in urban slums. These friends are not going to easily enter into any structured church program. They don't have gas, can barely make ends meet and have little desire to be part of typical church systems. But the common thread is a desire for love, for someone to care about them, and for connection.

My friend, Jeremiah, likes to say, *"When someone comes to see us, we feel loved, respected, not so forgotten. It's the highlight of our day."* It is disrespectful to not be willing to go where hurting people are and only expect them to come to us. Every time I visit I feel even more clear about this: church has absolutely nothing to do with a gathering. Instead, it has everything to do with bringing Christ's body to a dark, hurting world through incarnational relationships and actively participating in restoring the dignity of others.

Dignity Restorers

To extend love, mercy and compassion in a broken world we must learn how to restore dignity where it has been lost. Dignity is the inherent value established by God that resides deeply within every human being. At the heart of the practice of love is the recognition of someone's dignity. To love is to see that intrinsic value in each other. Mercy and compassion flows from this deep and core belief in the value of others. When we love the way God loves, we're calling out the inherent value in people that was established in the beginning of creation and reiterated at the cross. Human interaction is at the basis of restoring each other's dignity.

Not everyone can see his or her own dignity. Not everyone knows he or she is worth more. To love is to engage in the practice of restoring our capacity to see the inherent value of every individual.

Marginalized people usually find themselves on the outside, for various reasons. They are the Ones to the Ninety-nine. This feeling of exclusion can strip people of their capacity to see their own dignity. They become accustomed to being beaten down, used and subjected to abuse, prejudice and disrespect.   My friend, Lynette, puts it this way: *"I have never in my life known anyone who cared about what I thought or felt. The only thing I've ever been good for is to be used. I have no idea what I'm supposed to do with people being kind and caring toward me. I only know how to respond to abuse and being ignored."* Slowly, she's trying to learn to take in the good and allow some of her dignity to be restored.

Many churches have somehow forgotten one of the most important things that Jesus did, that he modeled for us so beautifully–*he restored dignity to people who had lost it.* The sick, lame, broken, desperate, outcast, marginalized, the least and the last. Over and over, he healed them, lifted their heads, and touched them with hope—hope that the Kingdom of God was available now, and it wasn't only for the learned, put-together, well and powerful. It was available for all who were humble enough to admit their spiritual poverty and need for God.

I believe strongly that the world needs more dignity restorers:

- People who are willing to call out God's image in those that don't know it's there.

- People who are willing to sacrifice their own jobs, time, heart and money to change systems that keep others oppressed.

- People who use their own power and privilege to make room for those without it.

- People who are willing to give a rip about that one person who everyone else has given up on.

- People who see beyond gender, politics, religion, socioeconomics and anything that divides and segregates us, so they can engage in deep and meaningful relationships.

- People willing to go the long haul and offer compassion and love to the hurting, instead of trite advice and easy spiritual answers.

- People who will stand between the stone throwers and the one about to be stoned and advocate on their behalf.

- People who touch the untouchable.

- People who see the best in others, instead of the worst.

God, help us be brave vessels of your love, mercy, and compassion wherever we are, wherever we go.

A start to being dignity restorers is to restore our own dignity first. We must get in touch with who we really are, who we were meant to be and not what we thought we had to become to feel better about ourselves as Christians. We need Jesus' healing as much as those we are trying to reach. We need the humility to reach out and touch his garment, seek his ways, surrender to love, and receive God's mercy and compassion, so we can then pass it on to others.

My dream is that we would individually and collectively put our resources, hands, hearts, buildings, power, influence, hopes and prayers into restoring dignity in person after person, in natural and beautiful ways. As we do, I believe that the image of God, uncovered in his people, shining brighter and brighter, will diminish the darkness of this world like never before.

My hope is that we will be people and communities deeply dedicated to freely offering love, mercy and compassion to others. That we will somehow be known as "those weird people who love others unconditionally, tangibly and in all kinds of crazy, unexplainable ways." The world needs more people willing to restore dignity where it's been lost, people who go to hurting people, instead of expecting them to come to us. People who touch people who need touching and include people who need including. People who look into the eyes of people who are used to looking down in shame. People who **are unafraid to welcome pain.**

* * * * *

Personal Reflection:

1. What is it like for you to receive love, mercy and compassion from God? From others? How does this affect your ability to extend it?

2. What parts of your own story do you need to consider embracing more fully?

3. In considering the parable of the Ninety-nine and the One, what are some of the ways you have seen this lived out in the churches or communities you've been a part of?

4. What would "going" look like for you, in your context? What would you have to leave?

5. Think of ways you have felt excluded from or uninvited to the table. What was that like for you? What did you learn through that experience?

6. Why is respecting and valuing human dignity so central to extending love, mercy and compassion?

Group Discussion:

1. What parts of your story are you learning to embrace more fully so you can share love, mercy and compassion more freely with others?

2. Share together your responses to the idea of leaving the Ninety-nine for the One. Why is it so hard to leave? What are the pulls toward staying with the Ninety-nine?

3. What is God stirring up in you in the areas of "going?" What would "going" look like for you in your context?

4. Share ways you have felt excluded from or uninvited to the table. What was that like for you? What did you learn through that experience that shapes your current practices?

5. Process together why dignity is so central to extending love, mercy and compassion. What happens when it's not present?

Ways to Extend Love, Mercy, and Compassion

1. Start telling your own story more freely, more honestly, in a safe circle of friends.

2. In the beginning of this chapter, self-hatred, self-doubt, insecurity, depression, disconnectedness and loneliness were mentioned as feelings that interfere with the ability to be compassionate towards ourselves, as well as others. Are there one or more of these feelings that you are bumping up against? Are you aware of the origin? Make an effort to speak out about these messages with a close friend this week, and try not to edit or hold back.

3. Ask God to show you who around you is neglected, abandoned, forgotten or lonely. Check in with them, go hang out for a while, bring food or flowers, and just "be" with them without offering advice or trying too hard. Are there single moms or dads who could use a day or night off, who may be pleasantly surprised about the offer? Can you think of someone in your life experiencing a divorce, death, or loss of some kind? Do something special for them this week, to remind them that they are not alone.

4. Intentionally seek connection in your community or neighborhood with people not like you. If that scares you or feels too overwhelming at first, find out what agencies or ministries serve people in need and how you might be able to be part.

5. Consider Mother Teresa's admonition: "If you can't feed 100 people, just feed one." Find the one. If you need some specific direction, look up your closest local food pantry location. Connect with the staff, and ask what you might be able to do to support their efforts. Think about Matthew 25:35: "When I was hungry, you gave me something to eat."

Chapter 6

Welcoming Pain

"We must embrace pain and use it as fuel for our journey" -
Kenji Miyazawa[11]

A while back one of my youngest sons fell through the coffee table and badly cut his leg open. I noticed something during the whole crazy experience that really struck me. In the midst of the drama I didn't try to make him stop crying. I allowed Jonas to express anything he needed to express. He was in and out of pain, amazingly articulate about what he was feeling and experiencing, but **when the doctor whipped out the needle in the emergency room to prepare** for stitches, it got ugly. My oldest two kids and a few friends were in the room with me, and we'll never forget his yelps.

During that moment, my daughter Julia and I leaned over him, stroked his face, and whispered that we were with him; we let him scream as loudly as he needed to. Inside I was terrified and overwhelmed while doing everything I **could to be strong for him. Seeing my baby in that much pain felt so unnerving.** When it was over, we stepped back and took a deep breath, knowing he had **made it through the worst.**

I hate pain. For many years, I was the consummate pain avoider, the one who tried to sweep it under the rug, pretend like everything was just "fine" and put on my happy face. It also wasn't something I learned in church. I had **been hiding pain long before I ever set foot into a church or dedicated my life** to following Jesus. Once I did become a Christian, though, and entered the world of discipleship, I did pick up on an unspoken but obvious cue: *"Actually, we don't talk about pain here, either."*

I will be honest—I was so relieved. I had an incredible amount of pain stuffed down that stemmed from my shameful past and deep insecurities. In my first few experiences in churches, I discovered that I actually didn't need to worry about the pain; I just needed to worry about the promise—the promise of new life, wholeness, strength, peace, and power. The only bummer was that the pain was still there; however, it sometimes came out in wonderfully helpful ways like performance addiction and perfectionism. Most of us know **these two behaviors can help people get far in ministry circles.**

Pain is a natural part of life at one time or another, and most people carry some of it all of the time. It will always be expressed; in some way, shape, or form, it always comes out. The questions that need to be asked, especially for **those who are trying to follow the ways of Christ individually and corporately, are:** *How can we learn to welcome the pain instead of run from it? How can we be people and places that aren't afraid of pain, and who acknowledge its presence, purpose, and power?*

Occasionally I facilitate a support group for women who are healing from sexual abuse. We sometimes talk about inviting pain as a guest to the dinner table. How do we treat guests that come to our house? We treat them kindly and engage with them. We don't ignore them and pretend they aren't **there. We welcome them into our presence instead of slamming the door in their faces.**

The majority of my experience within Christian circles has been an avoidance of pain. There is a subtle and sometimes direct aversion to welcoming pain into our lives and communities. I understand why. There is the implied but unspoken hope that turning to Jesus will make you happy all of the time, and **your problems will end. But Jesus does not remove us from reality. Instead, Jesus redeems reality.**

It is hard to be in the messy, bloody, unpredictable places of people's real lives—in the addictions, job losses, shame, insecurities, abuses, divorces, **wayward children, deaths, doubts, loneliness and depression. Gaping wounds** are not pretty. To protect ourselves from pain, we sometimes send a subtle message that says, "*Please put a band-aid on that. Do something to make me feel more comfortable, and then I can be in relationship with you.*" We don't want it in our face, so we send people off to "*get healing.*" We recommend counseling and certain books to read, and hope our friends will figure it out—fast.

All these possibilities separate "healthy" people from "hurting" people. A **mixed-up message is heard: that pain can be separated from our regular** experience, instead of embracing the reality that most people are pretty desperate and suffering in some way. Pain is just a different story for each of us.

Jesus was fairly clear that he came for the sick, not the healthy. I think we're all sick, but it's a matter of recognizing, embracing and welcoming it so that God can enter into it and bring continued healing. And until we create a loving space for pain to be acknowledged, it won't go away.

My friend, Conrad, followed Christ for 30 years, attending church and Bible studies every single week. He was involved in Sunday school, lay leadership, and almost any other ministry activity available. During all these years he was also battling a severe, debilitating sexual addiction that no one knew about—**not even his wife. Filled with intense guilt and shame, he acted out daily for** almost 40 years. Never once did he consider saying anything out loud. The **systems he was in felt far too scary and unsafe.**

> "*I know it seems stupid, but I used to believe that I was the only person in my church that struggled with sexual addiction, that I was the only person who had not been freed from my addiction when I was 'saved,' that maybe I hadn't really been saved because I still struggled with sin.*"

Conrad finally found a safe, intentional community that welcomed pain, and he found the courage to say out loud for the first time, "This is what I struggle with." It opened up the doors to his healing in ways that changed not only his **own life, but also the lives of many others. Now, he is part of helping others** welcome their pain as well, providing love, guidance and support to take the **brave steps towards honesty.**

I often say Alcoholics Anonymous is one of the most powerful, thriving underground churches in the world. They have hit upon a Kingdom principle that is missing in so many churches – *create a safe place to express pain and admit the unmanageability of our life apart from God.* This opens up the road to healing that exponentially changes lives, hearts, and relationships.

AA has managed to pull this off without overtly using the word 'Jesus', either. That's *living the ways of Jesus instead of talking about the ways of Jesus.* AA has a culture that embraces a mentality of "*Yes, we're all desperate, and we know it. We know it enough to walk in the door, put our butt in the chair, and admit we have a problem.*"

If we examine the stories of Jesus, this is what he did. He stepped into people's pain and created a safe space to address it. He didn't avoid it. He didn't shame people for it. He just went right to it. By speaking into it he empowered people with the capacity to address and transform it.

"Blessed are those who mourn, for they will be comforted."

Matthew 5:4

We can't lead people to places that we ourselves aren't willing to go. In order to create and cultivate a culture that welcomes pain, we will have to become more aware of our pain and learn to say it out loud. We as leaders have to be willing to step into their own pain to show others that it doesn't define us. Once we can talk about it, we can begin to chart a way through.

12 Step programs are safe because no one gets to hide. Everyone attending is aware that by showing up, you are calling out your pain. Pain is a great equalizer and levels the playing field. That's why most recovery meetings have a very successful businessman next to a nearly homeless guy, next to a girl waitressing to put herself through college, next to a stay-at-home mom.

Part of our role as Christ-followers on the downward journey is to stay in touch with our pain, issues, tendencies, and addictions (we all have them), so we can live in reality instead of denial. We can then offer the world and each other our real selves instead of ones we constructed in order look good and avoid pain.

I used to be an incredibly skilled hider and pretender. On the outside, I looked confident and bubbly, but inside I was a mess. Through a bizarre twist of circumstances, I ended up in a small women's group at a very conservative church when my kids were very young. When my friend asked me to join, she said it, "Wasn't really a Bible study, but wasn't really a therapy group. **It was somewhere in between, a place to become more honest about our** relationship with God, ourselves and others." I was tired of being cooped up with my little kids all day, and they had free childcare, so I decided to give it **a try.**

It didn't take long, though, before I realized I wasn't putting my toe into the baby pool. No, this was jumping into the deep end. At first I thought I would sink and tried to weasel my way out of having to participate by pulling the, "You're not reading the Bible enough for me" card. The truth was I was really **scared.**

It took me a long time to finally feel safe enough to share, and over time I was able to express deep pain from my past—an abortion, sexual abuse, and what it felt like growing up in a house filled with alcoholism, drug use and depression. It felt like the floodgates opened and tears that were held back for years finally had a safe place to flow. I began to realize that even though I hadn't been acknowledging my pain, it was coming out in unhealthy ways like overworking, perfectionism, and anger. Even though I wasn't in touch with it at the time, it was seeping out. Pain always does.

When we avoid pain, we also learn to avoid feeling. By cutting off a very real part of our own humanity; we stop being human. Part of the downward journey means becoming people who can feel at deep levels and create safe **spaces for others to feel, too. We do this by mourning, by calling out the very** real sense of pain and suffering that comes from loss, wounds and the real junk of life.

In Matthew 5:4 Jesus reminds us, *"Blessed are those who mourn, for they will be comforted."* It's not hard to recognize that much of Western culture stinks at the art of mourning. We are uncomfortable with pain and sadness. It gives us a level of anxiety we don't like, so we do what is most natural—try

to soothe and smooth it over instead of learning to sit with it.

Over the years I have experienced interesting dynamics when it comes to crying and the expression of pain. In women's groups, when someone is brave enough to cry, before one tear even falls to the floor, tissues get whipped out and comforting words start flowing. In mixed gender groups, men hardly ever cry and it becomes even more rare for women to make themselves vulnerable. Regardless of the setting, once the tissues get passed out along with the indirect message "please stop crying," the hurting person is blowing their nose and we're moving on to the next person. We need to learn to hold the space, back off from our trite words of wisdom and give people room to let what's inside, out.

At the same time, we need to respect that pain takes time to heal. Again, our culture of "quick fixes" can deeply impact the safety people feel when they finally enter their pain. They need time and grace. **We can never measure** what equals healing. Since we are not God, we can never fully know what is going on in a person's heart, mind, and life. Healing does bring certain fruit. Yet, we must not assume that particular behaviors or outward markers are **sure signs of healing.**

One of the things I appreciate about Alcoholics Anonymous is that while there are specific markers to movement and sobriety, there is also an understanding that relapses are natural parts of the journey, and that meetings and an ongoing need for support will probably forever be part of our lives. They don't offer simple solutions or expectations that life is suddenly going to be different. However, what is present is a possibility for change and healing that comes from hearing about others' experiences, strength, and hope.

Another way to welcome pain is to cultivate continued trust in God. I always tell people who are beginning to embrace their pain that "God can hack it." God is always much bigger than our pain, but we don't discover that until **we expose it. I wonder if one of the reasons we are afraid of pain is that we** are afraid that God won't help with it. We assume that when God doesn't take away the pain it must mean God doesn't care. God's seeming inability to make things easier for hurting people can be frustrating and confusing. In reality, though, God can handle pain and knows how to enter into it like no **other. We see this clearly through the lens of Jesus as he hung on the cross in** pain.   The question for us is, will we give God room to work in us, or rush to make others and ourselves feel better?

A life of descent means learning to be people and communities who invite pain to join us at the table, to welcome it instead of push it down. We can't pretend it's not there or tell it to heal itself before it knocks on the door again. We have to face our fears and enter into the darkest places of each other's hearts and lives. We must cultivate trust that God is always present, moving, healing and restoring in ways that our limited perspective sometimes can't seem to see.

Once we get past the initial fear, creating a space at the table for pain is far more possible. As I began to face my own pain, I recognized the value this space could represent for others, too. I set out to replicate this kind of safe container in the different churches I attended. Every time, by God's grace, I was able to carve out a solid niche of honest, safe people who were longing for healing and deeper connection. What never seemed to happen, though, was a full integration of these groups into the wider church. We were always looked upon as "those

God, help us be people who are willing to welcome pain.

people who needed healing" and subjugated to the margins instead of being embraced as a central piece of the faith community. The Refuge is the first community I have been part of where pain is openly welcomed beyond just words, with men and women together on the journey toward healing.

My friend, Brian, has a long, painful story of deep abuse and addiction. A pastor for years, he found ways to hide his pain through working harder at ministry. He was gifted at leading his congregations but could never share out loud the behaviors and thoughts he struggled with daily. Eventually, his actions caught up with him, he lost his ministry and he ended up trying to take his life.

He met a Refuge friend in the mental hospital; she struggles with depression and ended up needing another hospitalization. A friendship formed, and when he was released he intersected with The Refuge community as a potential haven for healing. He says:

> *"For decades I've struggled with shame and guilt while pretending to have it all together. Sometimes, the road to healing seems impossible, with negative self-talk crowding out all other thoughts, and with remorse, fear, and self-loathing engulfing my mind, body, and spirit. But a little bit more each day I get glimpses of grace. It hurts like crazy, but it's starting to feel more like healing. I have desperately needed a place to be honest, and connect with people who knew pain, too, but were somehow finding new life in the midst."*

Brian only recently opened the door to expressing pain, but he is already experiencing the relief that comes from having a container in which to let his inner processing emerge. The teachings of Jesus tell us clearly that, while we are in this world we will suffer, but because of God, we can have hope in the midst of this suffering and know that we will be blessed when we mourn and receive God's comfort.

Going Through the Wall

A lot of people I know are wrestling with their faith. They're willing to recognize the pain, and want to address it. They may have hit a wall in their spiritual journey and find themselves tossing, turning and churning about what it means to follow God in ways that are unfamiliar and scary. Often, it can feel lonely and disorienting, leaving them to wonder if they're the only person who doubts or questions much of what they once believed. It's even more confusing when others around them are perfectly fine with not moving toward anything new. This can sometimes induce the feelings that something might be wrong with them or that they're the only one in pain. Once we begin **to welcome pain to the table, we can begin to create and foster a culture of** emotional and spiritual healing.

This idea of hitting the wall translates well to the spiritual journey and the value **of pain. In** *The Critical Journey: Stages in the Life of Faith*,[12] Janet Hagberg and Robert Guelich explore the critical stages in our spiritual journey. No matter how much we try and avoid it, the authors suggest we will encounter the inevitable wall.

The authors highlight six primary stages in our spiritual journey:[13]

1. *Recognition of God* – This is the stage we start to believe and turn our lives over to something bigger than ourselves. It's the beginning of our faith journey.

2. *Life of Discipleship* – In this stage we begin to learn more *about* God. We discover the rules, doctrines, and guiding principles of our faith. This season is filled with immersion into Bible studies, Sunday School classes, and other venues that help us learn more about our faith.

3. *The Productive Life* - We become good at serving and doing things *for* God. After we have a firm foundation of knowledge from the Life of Discipleship, we turn our energies toward service and work on God's behalf. This can take a wide variety of forms, but the essence of this stage is "doing."

4. *The Journey Inward* – During this stage, *welcoming pain is necessary*. It is a season where we begin to figure out a new way to do relationship with God, ourselves and others. It is usually filled with pain, doubt, and angst, and is a confusing season for people.

5. *The Journey Outward* – Here, we learn to live, serve and love from a completely different position because we have a deeper sensitivity to pain, suffering, and doubt. This newly acquired understanding allows us to minister out of compassion and love and not be scared to sit with others in their pain as well.

6. *Life of Love* – In this final stage, we are so compelled by love that people may think we've lost our minds and have gone off the deep end. We don't care at all about money, possessions, or what others think of us. The only thing we are compelled by is love.

Hagberg and Guelich point out a few observations that are important to highlight.[14] First, they make clear we can't skip over any stage. The spiritual formation journey is initially a linear process of development. There are no shortcuts or "work-arounds" available that allow us to jump from Stage One directly to Stage Four without first going through Stages Two and Three. But once we have gone through a stage, it is possible to skip or revisit those stages **during new seasons.**

Stages of Faith, adapted from Hagberg and Guelich's *The Critical Journey:*[15]

STAGES OF FAITH	CHARACTERISTICS	HOW WE GET CAGED	HOW WE MOVE TO THE NEXT STAGE
STAGE ONE: Recognition of God "We Believe."	A sense of awe and need for a Savior and greater meaning in life. A sense of innocence and openness.	If we stick to a sense of worthlessness or ignorance and don't believe we are really worth "more".	Become part of a strong group. Take on more significance. Follow a charismatic leader that provides some direction.
STAGE TWO: Life of Discipleship "We are learning about God."	Meaning comes from belonging. Answers found in a leader, cause, or belief system. Sense of rightness and security in our faith.	If we become rigid in righteousness and following the rules, develop a "we against them" attitude, keep switching faith communities.	Recognize our uniqueness. Identify giftedness. Recognize what we can contribute to our group, church, system, etc.
STAGE THREE: The Productive Life "We are about doing things FOR God."	Uniqueness in community, sense of belonging to a community or ministry and being part of the Body, greater responsibility in some areas of our lives (work, home, church).	If we become overly zealous in "our way" or become weary in well-doing. If we are self-centered or view our lives as performance.	Lose sense of certainty (things we thought worked don't anymore). Experience faith or personal crisis. Feel abandoned by God, others. Looking for direction and seek guides.

Second, it is very possible to get stuck in any stage along our journey. Hagberg and Guelich call this getting "caged." The chart below details ways we can get caged at each stage, and suggests ideas to keep moving and avoid staying stuck. Remember that no stage is good, bad, right, wrong, or better than another. Each stage is its own particular chapter in our ongoing relationship with God.

Unfortunately, from my perspective, many Christians live their entire faith journey in Stages One through Three. These first three stages focus primarily on performance. This keeps churches and ministries in business as their fulfillment produces dedicated followers, people who sit in the pews and learn, tithers, and volunteers who pull off the daily demands of the ministry or organization.

Between Stages Three and Four is a critical juncture, or what the authors call, "The Wall." The Wall occurs when things stop functioning for one reason or another. The Wall shocks the person into a state of contemplation. It could come from a life experience like a death, divorce, trauma, job loss, or an addiction or deep pain uncovered. It can also be precipitated by gradual **ambivalence toward things we were once passionate about. Regardless of** how we find ourselves at The Wall, it is a place where we start to say, "This just isn't working anymore."

STAGES OF FAITH	CHARACTERISTICS	HOW WE GET CAGED	HOW WE MOVE TO THE NEXT STAGE
THE WALL "Things just aren't working anymore… There's got to be more."	Confusion, fear, loneliness, ambivalence, resentment.	RESISTANCE AT THE WALL: Strong egos, self-deprecators, guilt/shame-ridden, intellectuals, high achievers, doctrine-focused, people-pleasers.	GOING THROUGH THE WALL INVOLVES: Discomfort, surrender, healing, awareness, forgiveness, risk, acceptance, love, closeness to God, discernment, melting, molding, solitude, and reflection.

STAGES OF FAITH	CHARACTERISTICS	HOW WE GET CAGED	HOW WE MOVE TO THE NEXT STAGE
STAGE FOUR: The Journey Inward "We need to figure out a new way to do this relationship with God & others."	Life or faith crisis, loss of certainties. The things that worked aren't working anymore. Search for direction, not answers. Pursuit of personal integrity in relationship to God. God is released from the box.	If we always question everything and are consumed by self-assessment, become immobilized, don't keep moving.	Let go of self-centeredness. Accept God's purposes for our lives. Seek wholeness through personal healing and pilgrimage. Be willing to commit to whatever it takes.
STAGE FIVE: The Journey Outward "Learning to live out of a totally different place."	Surrendered to God. A renewed sense of God's acceptance. A sense of deepening relationships. A sense of calling, vocation or ministry.	Not really caged at this stage but others can view you as: Seemingly out of touch with practical concerns, careless about "important" things, and not diligent in certain areas.	Not striving, just evolving. Growing deeper Seeing God in all of life. Being God's person. Letting go. Available to others in a new, more present way.
STAGE SIX: The Life of Love "It's all about God."	Living in obedience to God, wisdom gained from life's struggles. Compassionate living for others. Detachment from things and stress, life abandoned.	Not really caged at this stage but others can view you as: Separate from the world, that you neglect yourself and that maybe you're "wasting your life."	

Almost everyone hits The Wall somehow, at some point, whether we walk up to it or slam into it a little more dramatically. Unfortunately, many are taught and trained to ignore The Wall and move back to Stage Three as fast **as possible.**

Far fewer people do the courageous work to break *through* The Wall and discover what lies beyond the initial stages. The latter stages are primarily **about growth as a human being, as opposed to performance. Stage Four or** The Journey Inward can initially seem like a scary place where everything feels up for grabs and all we once knew is gone or doesn't bring life. In Stage Four, we can't hide behind performance. We no longer feel safe, satisfied, or energized in the system that used to get our heart, time and money. The typical ways we used to experience God don't work anymore and we find ourselves with more questions than answers. As we allow ourselves to feel **pain and let God into places we have not wanted to go before, the damage of** our wounds becomes apparent. Sometimes we are bleeding, deeply scarred, and wondering if we'll ever be whole again.

This is the most confusing stage and also the most glorious. As we begin **to let go of comforts that protected us well, we can see that they actually** kept us from growing as human beings. Unbound, we can begin to see God **more clearly. We can begin to discover a deeper, richer, more mysterious** relationship with God.

Likewise, because of its messiness, this stage is where those who have not experienced it will say, "What in the $#*!^!+@ is happening to you?" There is the potential to be seen as crazy, heretical, lost, stupid, or unfaithful. People can view us like the Prodigal Son and hope we'll come back home as soon as possible. Stage Four is where we need nurturing guides, fellow sojourners who will stay with us and remind us this is a critical stage in our faith journey where we must listen deeply and not lose hope when all we once knew feels **stripped away.**

Without experiencing this Journey Inward, I don't believe we will be able to live in the low places of people's painful experiences. This stage is where our own story begins to intersect with the bigger gospel story of pain, suffering, redemption and hope.

The hope is that we will transition into Stage Five where we are serving, loving, and living from a free place that gives life not only to us but also to others. In the Journey Outward we live from a more whole, integrated position in our faith and personal lives. We are more vulnerable not only with God but with other people and are genuinely committed to community. We serve and love others out of profound desire and passion, instead of out of duty, obligation, or attachment to an organization or institution. As this happens, the meaning of suffering and the meaning of love take deeper root. We comfort others with the comfort we've received, and we love others because we've experienced Christ's love like never before.

"Until we allow ourselves to engage with our own pain, we won't be able to welcome it in others."

Movement between The Journey Inward and The Journey Outward is more fluid. We don't wake up one day and say, *"Okay, it's all crystal clear now! Here's my new purpose and there's no turning back."* But we can live in Stage Five with a greater sense of freedom, compassion, depth and a willingness to not know all the answers. Mystery is not something to solve, but a recognition we don't need all the answers to be whole.

Stage Six living may come at later ages in our lives where we have greater freedom to live out all we've learned from the Journey Inward and Outward. My seminary professor used Mother Teresa as an example of Stage Six, where any trappings are completely lifted. This is difficult when we have kids at home, mortgages to pay, and practical things that tie us down. However, it is hopefully a part of each of our journeys, where over time we are humbled, poured out, and dedicated to a life of love and service in a pure, unconfined way.

The Kingdom of God is in dire need of more Stage Four, Five and Six people. It's not that Stages One through Three aren't important, but there's a glut of folks who tend to live there. Brave people are needed to live the wild ways of Jesus in action; once we've gone through The Wall and know pain and suffering in a deeper way, we can travel with others in dark places more freely. It's there that we learn to become safer people who know how to **welcome pain.**

People who have wrestled with their own pain recognize the need for safe space. They become safe people, leaders who can sit in the midst of someone's pain without answers, and allow the pain to speak.

Safe People

I use the word "safe" a lot. For me, safety doesn't mean comfortable or insulated, but rather it's a container for people to be their real selves, in all their joy and in all their pain. Over the years some people have pressed back on the word "safe," thinking that it means, "anything goes" or "people are never challenged or encouraged to move forward." To me, nothing could be **further from the truth.**

Safe people create space for change like none other.

Jesus was safe in ways that created radical change in people's lives. He gave them space to be honest about their pain and suffering, so they could work through it. He walked toward those in pain instead of running the other way, and his presence created a container for healing that stirred hearts and **changed lives.**

In order to live well on the downward descent, we need to practice becoming people who are safe.   We need to cultivate safer communities and spaces for people to grow, change and heal. It takes a lot of practice in relationship with each other where we rub up against our judgmental tendencies, fears, insecurities, selfishness and woundedness. At the same time, because we are **each a living paradox we also get to experience freedom, compassion, love** and hope through these relationships.

Safety doesn't mean anything goes, no matter the cost; instead it is long-haul relationships where we are willing to accept others' flaws and weaknesses **because we are radically aware of our own. We begin with grace and** recognize that spiritual transformation takes time and looks vastly different **for each person. It requires us to learn to be more honest, more willing to** engage in healthy conflict, and to have the ability to stay in, instead of run from, relationships, when the going gets tough.

To be cultivators of safe spaces, it's helpful to better understand what makes a person (or a community) safe, and what makes them unsafe.

Unsafe people (and communities):

- Tend to be extremely judgmental and defensive.

- Are quick to offer advice to others but remain unwilling to receive input or feedback.

- Think they have all the answers and reflect certainty that their opinion or perspective is somehow superior.

- Blame others for their mistakes but refuse to take responsibility for **any of their own.**

- Often demand trust as implicit in the relationship without having to offer any work on their end to earn it.

- **Remain closed to change and are extremely rigid in their beliefs.**

- Offer unsolicited advice, quick fixes, and do not take no for an answer.

- Use their power to make others unequal with them.

- Avoid conflict all together or create disproportionate conflict to somehow gain control in their relationships.

- Project that somehow they "have it all together" and rarely express their own struggles or weaknesses.

Safe people (and communities):

- Offer love and acceptance freely, without strings attached.

- See beyond the surface to the good that's within us.

- Are good listeners, willing to sit with painful stories instead of fixing **or giving unsolicited advice.**

- Help us feel comfortable being ourselves and challenge us to grow, stretch and practice.

- Value relationship over opinions or differences, and nurture a spirit of equality with those different from them.

- Receive help, input, and feedback instead of only giving it, and engage in healthy conflict instead of avoiding it.

- Are honest and kind, willing to say the hard things in love.

- **Remain humbly connected to their stories and pain and are willing to** share their weaknesses and struggles with others.

Safe people and communities continually create spaces for transformation. A truly safe relationship will almost always cultivate movement, and a safe community tends to cultivate spiritual transformation.

The safety I have experienced within groups and friendships over the years never allowed me to remain stuck. In fact, it has always propelled me to move. The container of safe relationship gave me a place to see—up close and personal—my character flaws and pain, which motivated me to *want* to change. These friends pushed and pulled me, but it was never out of a "to" or "for" relationship. Instead, it was in the spirit of "with." The community stood with me as I processed what it meant to engage in transformation. It was **common to hear,** *"I know how you feel, but let's not stay here for too long."*

Almost every single person I am in relationship with (including myself), no matter how messed up, doesn't want to stay stuck. We need people who will **love us where we are but remain willing to engage for the long haul as we learn, grow, and try to experience God in the midst.** *We need incarnational, in-the-trenches relationship that can hack pain.*

Becoming safe people and safe communities doesn't come easily, either. The Christian community is well known for its judgment. People are often waiting for us to leave, tell, yell, critique, use, or "scripturize" (what I compare to throwing out scripture like candy). Only talking about becoming safer won't work.

I don't think safe comes naturally for most of us. Our instinctive bent is toward being judgmental, controlling, selfish and self-centered—the antithesis of safe. Also, a lot of us don't come from relationally healthy families where safety was truly present. To top it off, many Christ-followers have been taught that our mission in life is to "speak the truth in love" to all who aren't living out their faith or lives the way we think is appropriate. That kind of love ends up looking mostly like shame.

The true test will be actions over the long haul: grace, truth in love, the ministry of presence, and tangible unconditional love, extended over time. Safe is not a science, and we are sure to make mistakes and unintentionally damage hurting people no matter how hard we're trying not to. The difference is that safe people and safe communities do what they can to stay in relationship. They make amends quickly and live in a place of grace and forgiveness.

God, help us become people and communities that can welcome pain.

Safe containers help hurting people express pain in ways it needs to be expressed.

Until we allow ourselves to engage with our own pain, we won't be able to welcome it in others. Practically everyone I encounter feels like they are the only one "as messed up as they are." But when they intersect with others who freely share their pain and struggle they quickly realize they're not alone, that others feel intense pain, too.

When I look at Jesus in the gospels, he was a magnet for pain. Countless people came to him pleading for help and healing, asking and begging for relief from their pain. In a variety of ways, he somehow could connect with their pain. He recognized their torment, saw through their eyes to what was within, stopped and was present instead of ignoring their pleas. Clearly, those in pain were drawn to him like a moth to a flame.

If we are emulating Jesus, then the world should be drawn to us, too. This will require us to get in touch with our own pain and journey and practice being safer people over time. It will require a willingness to courageously go through The Wall in our spiritual journey and wrestle with a deeper **understanding of God, ourselves, and the world so we can become more connected to other strugglers, too.**

* * * *

Personal Reflection:

1. What are some areas of pain in your life that you are learning to integrate into your life and your story?

2. Have you gone through The Wall yet? What was the experience like for you? What did you learn about pain through it?

3. Which stage of the faith journey do you feel like you are in now? What does it feel like for you in this stage?

4. Which of the characteristics of safe people do you think you embody? Now, look through the characteristics of unsafe people; which ones do you sometimes emulate? Write about that in your journal.

Group Discussion Questions:

1. How easy or hard is it for you to welcome your own pain? How about others' pain?

2. Which stage do you see yourself in on your faith journey? What are you feeling and experiencing during this stage?

3. Share with the group if you've had a Wall experience. What was it like? What did you learn about pain through it?

4. Read aloud the characteristics of safe and unsafe people. Be honest about which ones you struggle with emulating or leaving behind and why.

5. Brainstorm together a list of harmful or helpful things people have said to you when you have been in pain.

Ways to Welcome Pain to the Table:

1. Begin to embrace your own story: where you came from, what you struggle with, the low places of your experience and what thoughts often rattle around in your head that are hard to say out loud about yourself, God, your relationships with others.

2. Read the book *Changes that Heal* by Henry Cloud and examine patterns that you might have from the past that create barriers to relationship with yourself, others and God.

3. Recognize if there is anything that you use to "numb" out your pain or the pain of others. Do you overwork, eat, drink, spend or over-watch TV? Try to start paying attention to when you choose those vices, and talk to a close friend about what that felt like.

4. Go to a free Codependents Anonymous meeting for a while; it will feel weird and foreign if you've never been to one, but listen in on the stories and consider where they might intersect with yours.

5. The next time someone cries in your presence, resist offering a tissue. Rather, just sit with them in their pain and listen instead of talk.

6. Model vulnerability in the relationships, groups, and settings you are in by sharing your struggles (if the group is safe enough).

7. Think about what it would look like to start your own "not a therapy group and not a Bible study." Are there people you know who would like to be a part? Consider practicing what that would look like.

Chapter 7

Honoring Doubt

"Doubt is uncomfortable, certainty is ridiculous." - Voltaire

Years ago, when I was fairly new to the Christian faith, I remember asking my pastor some really hard questions about the Bible. I was a young believer, zealous in my desire to learn. Our pastor, a young and dedicated biblical scholar, felt extremely certain about particular Bible passages and would begin rattling them off as responses to my questions. Even though my Bible knowledge was minimal at that point, I felt something was a little off in the way he responded. He sounded like he knew 100% what God meant. When I challenged him about his certainty by asking, *"Well, how do you know that's exactly what God means?"* he responded by rattling off a bunch of other Bible verses to defend his answer.

As an infant in my faith journey I left it at that, but wondered if maybe I was just too young to understand these lofty biblical truths at such an early stage in my faith. Now, looking back, I realize I was asking the right questions, but wasn't mature enough yet in my spiritual walk to stand up for the reality of my doubts.

A few years later I finally had a safe enough place to share some of my doubts with other Christian women who were wrestling with their own doubts. We each expressed deep pain at silently feeling guilty for our doubts and our longing for a place to say them out loud. As we did, our faith increased, rather than decreased.

Now, in the trenches with people each day, I see how critically important it is to create more spaces to honor doubt. So many people struggle with God but often feel like something must be wrong with them. Almost every time I share my doubts out loud other people say, *"Really? You feel that, too? I thought I was the only one."*

Part of the downward journey includes growing in our ability to honor doubt— our own doubts and also the doubts of others. Real people doubt, and trite certainty doesn't seem to help hurting people. The pain and brokenness in this world is often confusing, prompting us to sometimes doubt God's power and love. Downward living requires courage to embrace our doubts and trust that faith can hack it. We also need learn how to unhook belief from faith, as well as begin to respect that right thinking doesn't necessarily translate into a deep and active faith.

Real People Doubt

A few years ago my 15-year-old daughter asked me an out of the blue question. "Mommy," she asked, "What was there before God? I know God made the world, but how did he come into existence in the first place and what was 'there' before?" The first thing that crossed my mind was whipping out John 1 or Genesis 1; the only problem is those scriptures don't properly answer her questions.

Instead, I resisted the panic rising in my chest and the fleeting thoughts that because I had no good answer, maybe my faith was a sham, or even that I was actually an atheist. I responded, *"Julia, way to go, asking the world's most profound questions that no honest person can fully answer!"* Right after that, the next question that got fired from the back seat by one of the nine-year-old twins was, *"While you're at it, Mom, how do we know the Bible is true?"* Yeah, just an average day driving home from basketball practice for the Escobar family.

The Webster's definition of doubt is: *"to be uncertain about something; be undecided in opinion or belief."*[16] Some synonyms for "doubt" include: *apprehension, confusion, disbelief, lack of confidence, misgiving, mistrust, quandary, skepticism, suspicion, uncertainty, and reluctance.* Do you recognize any of these in your life right now? The antonyms or opposites include: *belief, certainty, confidence, dependence, faith, reliance, and trust.*

Seeing the contrast between these words makes me cringe because I realize how much has shifted in me over the years. I used to think the sign of being a good Christian was a rock-solid certainty that I could back up with exact scriptures. Now, I believe a critical element of our faith journey is a willingness to wrestle with doubt by honoring it, recognizing that it is part of faith.

There's a biological phenomenon in human nature to, when we are threatened, either fight or flight. When it comes to our faith experiences, some of the same reactions apply. We may respond to critique or questions with violence and anger, whether it's in the quietness of our hearts or in our actions or words. Or we may retreat, hide, run and pretend nothing's wrong or that there's nothing we can do. These two ways—fight or flight—are the two most prevalent responses to conflict or tension.

Jesus' life reveals a third way of responding that I call *an active presence,* a hope for what's possible, a willingness to walk the fine line of remaining in conflict or tension with love and truth. Most of my dreams for living the ways of Jesus embody this "third way." It forces me to reckon with my tendency to **respond with anger and violence toward a system that I disagree with, while** resisting my daily desire to check out, run for the hills, and let everyone else figure it out.

Doubt is embedded in a life of descent, while certainty is often synonymous **with ascent. Even Jesus himself expressed doubt in the Garden of Gethsemane.** As honest sojourners, we will always be living in the tension between doubt and faith. Similar to the practice of welcoming pain, if we can't embrace **doubt in our own lives it is impossible to allow it in others.**

As frustrating as doubt can be it is part of the human experience. We doubt we are lovable. We doubt God is good. We doubt all kinds of things, whether we say them out loud or not. In the quietness of our hearts, in the darkness of night, most people, regardless of their beliefs, education, and socioeconomic **level, wrestle with some form of doubt.**

Honoring doubt is similar to welcoming pain—living in the tension and not feeling the overwhelming need to make it all better and tie it up with a neat and tidy bow. Julia's question can never be fully wrapped up by slapping a scripture on it. The challenge this leaves me to wrestle with is to ask, *"What does that mean for my faith? Can I live with the not-fully-knowing? Can I still believe the big God story while I question some minutia?"*

Everyone I know doubts. Many of us have been taught that certainty comes from right belief about words in the Bible, that if people could just "believe properly and trust Jesus," everything would be okay. That might work for some, but tell that to my friend who's teetering with sobriety during one of the most difficult seasons of the year. Tell that to my friend whose husband just ditched her. Tell that to my friends who got kicked out of their church after dedicating years of their lives to building it. Tell that to my friend who is still single after years of hoping to find a partner. Tell that to my friend who **goes to bed hungry so that her children can eat.**

I always think back to the early disciples—they were there, in the flesh with Jesus, and they still had a lot of trouble believing. Here we are, 2,000 years later, trying to make sense of this great mystery and what it means for us in **the world.**

My friend, Melinda, was raised in a very charismatic family and then married a pastor. They served in an extremely fundamentalist church for years, toeing the line and insulating themselves from the rest of the world. Slowly, things started to shift. She began asking questions; he started to get mad about her questions. An affair ensued and brought them to a crisis not only in their faith but also their relationship. Their former community could not handle the level of honesty, pain, and doubt they were experiencing. It didn't fit into their paradigm. So Melinda's family ended up with the marginalized, with those on the outside of "the church." They had a deep desire for God but no **safe place to wrestle and heal.**

I intersected with Melinda first through a blog post where she said out loud, *"I think I might be an atheist and I have no idea who I can talk to about this."* It turns out that morning she felt like one, but in reality, she was experiencing a normal shift in a maturing faith and only needed to not feel so alone in the process. She had hit The Wall but also recognized she didn't want to give up.

She hung in there with God and continued to nurture a different kind of faith that wasn't about rules, beliefs, or what someone tells her is right. Her faith has become a far deeper experience, a knowing that sometimes can't be defined by language. Her journey became a beautiful reminder that God can handle **our doubt as much as God can handle our pain.**

Life down in the trenches requires us to become people and communities who honor doubt. This includes not only doubt about God, but also doubt about ourselves. We must integrate into our practices many of the same things that **help when welcoming pain such as being more honest, providing safe places** to wrestle, and trusting that God is at work in ways we sometimes can't see.

Like pain, we need to accept doubt as a natural part of our experience instead of resisting it. This can be extremely difficult for those experiencing a deconstruction-reconstruction process when it comes to faith. Often, our questions aren't a detour back to the original familiar destination, but actually a journey into the wild outback beyond a map.

Over the last several years, I have been learning to let God and myself off the hook in different ways, and it has brought a freedom I hadn't before **experienced. I am reconciling in my heart that some doubts will never be fully** answered this side of heaven. This allows me to stop getting mad at myself for not going back to a spiritual place that I don't think exists anymore.

We serve people better when we stop trying to resolve what can't be fully resolved and focus on the very simple essentials instead: love, love, and love. Most people, regardless of their specific faith orientation, tend to agree on **one thing**: *the importance of love.*

It also helps to give others a lot of room for doubt instead of trying to control or manage someone else's experience. My friend Jake described it this way:

> *"I honestly was insulted by how people who I had once shared*
> *a similar faith with started to treat me. They dealt with my*
> *doubt like I had caught a bad cold. They promised to pray for*
> *me and assured me that it would pass. One person attributed*
> *it to a 'mid-life crisis.' I found out how much people depended*
> *on me to continue to believe the same way, the same things,*
> *the same bullsh*t. My doubt actually scared some people."*

To live into descent, we must learn to live in the tension of people's spiritual journeys and give up our impulsive need to bring people over to our way of thinking. We need to have faith that God is big enough to handle doubts. God doesn't go away when we doubt. God simply gives us room to process it so we can approach God more freely.

Also, we must let go of our need to make people understand God's love in a pre-packaged way. The doubt that is hardest for me to accept is when people doubt God's love. I want to jump up and down and try to convince them, *"See, see, see! You are loved! Please, please, please believe it now!"* But of course, I am human, too, and those same beliefs about being loved are hardest for me to grasp for myself no matter how much convincing is in the mix.

> *"We need to accept doubt as a natural part of our experience instead of resisting it."*

In the trenches with people I am learning to let go of the false notion I can convince anyone of anything. *I'm not one sentence away from making someone understand Jesus' love.* Yes, we can love tangibly, stay in for the long haul, and continually point towards God, but we cannot convince anyone of anything; that job is the mysterious work of the Holy Spirit. I am thankful God's Spirit is relentless in pursuit of our restoration.

One of the problems I have experienced is that we can tend to get so frustrated with people's "lack of progress" in this area of love that we get tired of trying to convince, and simply give up. What if we gave up worrying about convincing and just relaxed, recognizing that a natural part of life is sometimes doubting we are loved? The Kingdom of God can stand up to doubt. The question is, can we?

A few years ago my friend Nadia Bolz-Weber, who pastors an inclusive missional faith community in Denver, posted a blog that included a simple cartoon that often comes to my mind. It said, *"Faith needs doubt like children need love."*[17] Without love, children wither. Love poured into kids builds strength in them and allows them to grow and develop. Doubt does the same thing to faith.

My daughter Julia's question makes me think. My lack of a wonderful, spiritually-acceptable answer doesn't make me throw in the towel; actually, it deepens respect for my faith and for the faith of others. Doubt causes me to engage my faith. It helps me see that faith is bigger than me, the walls of a church, the confines of a particular culture, or even the lack of an answer to an obviously profound question.

How One Parenthetical Phrase Could Change So Much

I sometimes miss the days when I was certain, when things were black and white, when I knew the answer *"because the Bible says so"* and when that felt like enough. I can't tell you the number of times in the past I pulled the, *"This is what the Bible says about x, y, or z so that's that"* card, thinking that would somehow cause someone to see the light in that moment. As I reflect back, the only person this method seemed to help was myself. Now, after many years journeying with people filled with doubt and intersecting with a big share of my own, I notice how much damage my original expectations have inflicted on people. The idea that we must maintain 100% certainty in the biblical interpretation of a passage has infiltrated many areas of the Christian faith. Many are sure they can state that, *"This is precisely, exactly what God meant. See, it says it right here."*

Years ago I had a parting of ways with a close friend over this issue. It still makes me sad. She began to move toward a more conservative denomination, which I respect. Sadly, when she discovered I was considering going to seminary for a counseling degree, she said that it was *"unbiblical and worldly"* and that the only thing she believed in was *"biblical counseling, or applying scripture to people's problems."* The biblical counseling course she was taking at her church was grounded in *"truth."*

I challenged her by saying, "Really, you are only learning what the author of the class you are taking says about certain passages. It's his interpretation, his best shot, and there are other people out there who see that exact scripture completely different from him and believe just as emphatically that they are right, too." She could not for the life of her let go of her conviction that this particular way of interpreting scripture was right.

I understand people's instinctive desire for certainty. We want something that is firm and solid. But the call to faith assumes the presence of doubt. It sits in the tension of the other person's view without demonizing it.

Certainty has created a lot of trouble for Christians with the rest of the world. We rarely, if ever, add one simple parenthetical phrase to the words that we share. Phrases like *"Here's how I see this passage,"* or *"This is what I think this passage could possibly mean,"* or *"I am not sure exactly what this means, but I've heard some people interpret it as...."* or *"I could be wrong but...I don't truly know, but...Yeah, it doesn't really make sense, but..."* are rarely added.

We can honor people's doubt better if we take ownership of our own interpretations, instead of pulling the absolute interpretation card as a cover. We actually have to trust there is something bigger at work—God's Spirit alive and well, unexplainable, mysterious, giving life to the black and red words on white pages.

My friend, Amelia, likes to say, *"We've slipped off the slope but actually found our faith."* A Christian youth leader for years, Amelia began experiencing a spiritual shifting, noticing that she was no longer comfortable with some of the language used for ministry. She, too, had hit the wall.

The exclusivity and focus on the pretty and the powerful instead of the least and the last started to get under Amelia's skin. Many things she used to believe started to unravel, and friends around her thought she was sliding down the slippery slope into the non-Christian abyss. Instead, she is intersecting with Jesus in ways like never before; she is in the trenches with the poor, the lonely and the outcasts, and she sees beauty everywhere she looks. She says:

> *"It is kind of weird sometimes, how much I've changed. So much of what I cared about seems really unimportant. I'm trying to focus on loving people with no strings attached. The doctrines and belief statements I used to cling to now seem silly to me. What matters more is being open and aware of the needs around me. It's freeing to be present to the people around me, regardless of what they believe. It's so much easier to not be caught up with looking for the right words or magic solution."*

Amelia found that when she started moving out of all she knew, she started moving into much of what she longed for—a tangible, active faith that centered around the least and the last, not only the pretty and most popular. We often think that if we have doubt, we don't have faith. In reality, they are inextricably tied to each other in the human experience, each one helping make the other more real. The presence of doubt doesn't mean we've lost our faith. It creates the space to actually find it.

The Refuge facilitated a challenging series of conversations surrounding doubt and faith. Some of the things we processed together included these themes:

- **Certainty does not equal faith.**

- **Faith is strengthened by doubt.**

- God fills in the cracks in wild and mysterious ways that dogma can't.

- God's love is more freely experienced in this place of wrestling and doubting than when we had all the answers.

- The idea of billions of God's creations burning in hell because they haven't accepted Jesus the proper way is awfully unsettling.

- We can boldly interact with God with our questions and our faith can survive.

There must be safe places to explore these questions out loud instead of alone or in some secret conversation over coffee with another potentially heretical friend.

In many of my church experiences and countless Bible studies I attended, I had been taught, both subtly and directly, *"Doubt means you're not trusting God enough."* Armed with this message, I would bear down and confess my lack of trust; I would pray that my questions and honest fears would go away, but they didn't. The good thing is God didn't go away either.

I think part of my spiritual reformation happened when I stopped listening to "the powers that be"—whether it's pastors, leaders, authors, or anyone else who was a little too certain, too sure, and used the word "should" too often. I started looking to the relationships I was in and respecting how valuable conflict was to strengthening our connection. Throughout this process, I saw that a true relationship can hack tension, but a superficial one can't.

God and I are still together. I have released some of my need to know and my need to be certain when it comes to doctrine and dogma. I liken certainty to a clenched fist—there's not much room for anything to come in and it's usually used for a fight. As I've loosened my grip and released what I used to hold tightly in my hand, as well as my heart and life, I have opened myself to new ideas, the mystery of God, and what is possible. I have also learned that an open hand to receive usually doesn't hurt anybody.

I often reflect on the story of the father who brings his demon-possessed boy to Jesus to heal him in Mark 9. The father cries out to Jesus, *"I do believe; help me in my unbelief!"* (Mark 9:24). In the past, this passage was used against me, and in some odd twisted way I used it against myself too. It wasn't, *"Help me believe, see, taste, know, and experience the real, untempered and unmanaged God."* Instead it was, *"Help me believe what they are saying to me about what I'm supposed to believe."* Those are two radically different things. The first one is where I want to live.

> *"Blessed are the pure in heart, for they will see God."*
> *Matthew 5:6*

Doubt and faith need each other; any faith that can't hold up to doubt isn't faith at all. I still believe in "what is unseen" and have faith despite my questions. I still believe a statement best expressed in one of my favorite lines from the movie, *Rudy: "There's a God and I'm not him."*[18] Life isn't some kind of twisted cosmic experiment. It's God telling a beautiful story through people.

Jesus is not a side-note but somehow the center. I'm not supposed to "know" everything, which releases me to focus on love and to walk in mercy, justice and humility. Jesus' spirit and example are alive, well and worth following. God doesn't seem to mind. He probably even kind of likes all my, "I don't knows." In all things, I am fairly sure his ways are higher than mine, anyway.

As we let go, we can learn to let even the most uncomfortable parts of life teach us.

Unhooking Belief from Faith

One of my favorite passages in Scripture is from James. And no matter where I go, it has always stirred up trouble. And I love it. The verse explores the tension between faith and works.

> *"What good is it, dear brothers and sisters, if you say you have faith but don't show it by your actions? Can that kind of faith save anyone? Suppose you see a brother or sister who has no food or clothing, and you say, 'Good-bye and have a good day; stay warm and eat well'—but then you don't give that person any food or clothing. What good does that do? So you see, faith by itself isn't enough. Unless it produces good deeds, it is dead and useless. Now someone may argue, 'Some people have faith; others have good deeds.' But I say, 'How can you show me your faith if you don't have good deeds? I will show you my faith by my good deeds.' You say you have faith, for you believe that there is one God. Good for you! Even the demons believe this, and they tremble in terror. How foolish! Can't you see that faith without good deeds is useless?" - James 2:14-20, NLT*

When we processed this verse together in The Refuge we had a wide range of responses ranging from initial feelings of shame and guilt for "not doing enough," to feelings of motivation and encouragement that we have a responsibility as Christians to actually live out our faith in a concrete way, so that our faith can increase.

In these moments of honest Bible reflection, I am always reminded how sad I am that the Bible has become distorted for so many. It has often been used as a tool of shame instead of encouragement and movement. One of the tasks on the downward descent is to reclaim the beauty, mystery, and challenge of the Bible, without setting people up for the, "I am a miserable wretch and can never pull this off" mentality that is terribly pervasive and often paralyzing.

In fleshing out the idea of an active faith, one of the things that emerged is how we often carry an unrealistic view of some simple things to which God calls us. We associate "belief" with "faith" and assume that if we believe the right things, that somehow we have faith. We might have already concluded that believing the "right" things doesn't end up amounting to the kind of wild, adventurous, transformational life Jesus radically offers.

Faith is cultivated by the act of love, not just beliefs.

As we wrestled with the passage in James, three important words arose from our community's conversation: *trust, courage and obedience.* These are challenging words. For those who might be wrestling with issues of faith, they may make us cringe because they have been over-used in ways that create shame. Many have probably felt or currently feel that somehow we don't have enough trust, courage, or obedience. We feel a sense of shame when we don't have enough "believing thoughts." We don't feel faith exactly the way we have been told we are supposed to. It is as if we have to save ourselves by thinking or believing in precisely the right way. Desperate to resolve our doubt, we often spend energy trying to figure out faith in ways that are in our heads and not in our hearts, feet, or hands.

One of my best friends is a therapist who works with people in all stages of their walk of faith. Many of her clients are trapped in a perpetual cycle of trying to "think" their way out of their feelings. She says we need to "change the channel" to get off the circular treadmill of getting stuck in our heads. Usually changing the channel requires action—we need to actively *do* something different instead of just trying *to think* something different.

Another element of downward living is unhooking "belief" from "faith." Belief is often seen as having all the right answers, where faith is sitting in a space of trust even when we don't. I have stopped being so hard on myself for not trusting enough, being courageous enough, or obeying enough. Instead, I am learning to step toward an active, risky, often unclear faith that requires a crazy, beautiful, yet not so big it's completely overwhelming, amount of trust, courage, and obedience. My intent is that it is slowly and surely being reflected in my actions and the ways I move toward love.

For me, I used to think these words meant unwavering trust, making-a-huge-bold-move kind of courage, and first-time obedience. Because these kinds of sweeping words are hard to live out, I often ended up stuck, paralyzed, and mad at myself for not having faith like I thought I should. It's easy to assume perfection is the only standard God will accept. A lot of examples given to us from the Bible can make it even worse, primarily because of the way we've been taught in Sunday school and many churches. It has been fed to us what trust, courage, and obedience are supposed to look like, and it's often intimidating and induces shame.

What if love is the space that actively reveals our faith?

I strongly believe that our faith is revealed when we put our butts on the line in real, active, scary, tangible relationship with God and other people in small ways. Like stepping out and acting on a stirring that God has put on our heart, love happens when we offer a cup of cold water to someone who's thirsty or when we receive a cup of cold water from someone who knows we **are, too.**

Faith increases when we offer forgiveness—even for just that day—even **when** **every** **part** **of** **us** **screams,** *"No way; that's impossible."* **Faith also** multiplies when we show up instead of hide and when we quit being passive or only centered on our own "personal and intimate relationship with Jesus." Faith multiplies when we choose to turn our focus instead to God's wild, crazy relationship with the world and consider how we can offer love, mercy, and justice in practical ways, on his behalf.

Faith does require trust, courage and obedience. These words don't scare **me as much as they once did. I want more of all three in my life, but I am** recognizing that the only thing I can hope for is a little more for today and **not worry so much about tomorrow. A friend shared a magnet with me that** reads, *"Courage doesn't always roar. Sometimes courage is the little voice at the end of the day that says, 'I'll try again tomorrow.'"*

In the work that I do alongside doubters and strugglers, I see people practicing these three elements in different ways that would usually never "count" in **many circles as real trust, courage, or obedience, because so many of the** "right words" or "right beliefs" or even typical "right actions" aren't associated with them. Some of my friends don't read the Bible, but they live the Bible all the time by sharing food and gas with their neighbors that have none, sitting with people at the hospital when they are sick, or hugging a hurting person but never saying a word. One thing I'm quite certain of is that their faith is not dead, and they are helping mine come more alive. They increase my desire to trust God's big story, to be more courageous, to move instead of staying still, and to do hard things I don't really want to do but that I know will be good for me in the end.

Where is God in the Midst of the $*!&!^!()#@

There is a lot of bad $*!&*@#! that happens in this world. We need to respect and recognize this reality and not just push it aside. Kids get horribly abused. People we love die. Entire cities are wiped out by floods. Houses burn down. Jobs get lost. Mental illness wreaks havoc. Horrid injustices are being carried out against innocent and beautiful creations of God. If we start listing them and let their painful reality get too far under our skin, it can easily overwhelm us and cause us to doubt. If we dwell on the negative, it's easy to doubt why **we would even believe in a God who is good and really cares, protects, and is in control.**

My thoughts about God being in control have radically shifted over the years. Now, when I hear people say things like, "God must know what he is doing," it turns me into a nutty person. Tell that to the little girl who was sexually abused from the time she was three years old. We need to be more honest that there are certain things that we can't reconcile into a rational construct **unless we apply really bad theology. Because we are human beings who want** to make sense of what we don't understand, we grasp at things that comfort in one sense but can also do great harm to people's faith in another.

My friend Mitchell has been a pastor and nonprofit leader for years. Recalling **a funeral he facilitated a few years ago, he said,**

> *"I finally had to address the oft repeated: 'God has a reason for everything.' I basically told everyone I thought that was a load of crap. It's easy to say when it's not your son, dad, mom, etc. who is laying here, dead. The bottom line for me was two beautiful teenage sisters who died together in an*

automobile accident. God had a reason for that? If so, God has little respect and value for life, is a sadist or worse.

*This is like saying God **caused** this tragic and senseless death to make a point. Look their dad in the eyes and tell him that. I dare you.*

*No. The fact is that the bumper sticker is right: Sh*t happens. To everyone, no matter what they believe or how much they think God likes them. How we live through the sh*t, once it's hit the fan and splattered itself all over our lives, is the difference that God makes in the tragedy. It rains on the just and the unjust alike. God **is** good (all the time), but he doesn't kill people to make a point to the lucky survivors. He is good enough to help those of us who survive learn how to live with the pain...and beyond it. "*

Mitchell realized that trite answers just don't work in the low places of people's experiences. In fact, they can make matters worse.

The promise of faith is that God is with us and will not leave us or forsake **us, even in the low places.** Faith is not rational, but I also don't think it's irrational; it lives in between, in paradox. To define everything by cause and effect, with God as the supreme micro-manager, is dangerous ground. It can end up placing blame on the victim and tearing down the faith of the afflicted. To believe that God will make us whatever we want if we just have enough faith is magical thinking, and not what God promises, either. The mystery and reality of God cannot be contained in our own feeble attempts to give reasons **for everything.**

I do not understand why certain things happen and certain things don't. Why one friend finds a partner and another lives their life alone. Why one child **dies and another goes to college. Why one has mental illness and another** doesn't. Why a girl is painfully abused in one home and another girl lives in a safe, loving one. Why one couple makes it and another ends up in a nasty divorce. Why a tsunami rushes through one town and not another. The list could go on, but I don't think we'd get any closer to understanding. We need to learn to be more honest: there's so much we don't understand.

Each of these questions leaves us wondering where God is in the midst of pain and suffering. If our questions draw us away from faith in God, we will never sit in the midst of that pain and suffering long enough to discover that God is **actually there. Real trust, courage and obedience occur when we sit in the** midst of our questions long enough to realize our faith.

I rest firmly on the reality that we live in a broken, messed up world, and trying to get our heads around "why" isn't the idea. What if faith is more like asking ourselves these questions:

- How do we become part of God's redemption in the midst of such a mess?

- Will we accept our lack of ability to reconcile what we so desperately want to make sense of in our own lives, and in the lives of others?

- **Will we taste a bit of hope and pass it on to someone else?**

- **Can we let go of what we want and accept the goodness in what we have?**

- Can we respect that this world is hard, bitter, and often cruel but Jesus is alive and well in the darkest of places in ways that our limited minds and hearts often can't even begin to understand?

- Will we strain to see the light through the pitch black?

- Can we respect that others often can't see it and it's not our job to tell them they are supposed to; instead can we quietly and tangibly love them in their darkness?

- Will we let others help us when we are in the same boat and can't see **the forest through the trees?**

- **Will we open our ears, hearts, and minds to the ways God is present** that we might not easily notice?

When we step back into the pain and suffering, we become part of the solution. We become part of revealing God's love. We reveal a Kingdom that says, *"It doesn't have to be like this."*

I often cry out to God in deep and sometimes terrifying ways. When you are around a lot of pain day in and day out, it can get pretty rough sometimes. *"God, are you out there? Where are you? Show up, why don't you!"*

Then I hear of someone going over to be with a friend in an hour of dire need; I see the texts, phone calls, and emails that are being passed between fellow strugglers. I see friends going to recovery meetings together. I see food being brought to fill empty cupboards. I see hugs, tears, and honest anger at God. I see people saying, *"Yeah, it sucks sometimes, but I choose to have faith."* I see people taking their next breath and staying in when every part of them wants to flee. I see glimpses of hope and small, wacky miracles that don't seem more than little kindnesses here and there but actually have the power to sustain life.

God, help us trust that you are big enough for our doubts and help us be people courageous enough for the doubts of others.

I hope we can try in our own simple, rough and unedited ways to live more honestly, to wrestle with God, to live in the tension of what we do not know and stay focused on what we do: *God's love, hope, and kindness in dark places always seems to prevail.*

As we get more comfortable with the idea that the presence of doubt is not the absence of faith, we can help people learn to live in the tension along with us. We can affirm that real people have a wide range of feelings, emotions and responses that shift and change over time. A beautiful gift we can give to others is the space to be wherever they are and trust that God is at work and doesn't always need our two cents added to the mix.

* * * * *

Personal Reflection:

1. What scares you about doubt?

2. How easy or difficult has it been for you to live in the tension of your own doubt?

3. What used to feel clear that now feels muddy?

4. Respond to the words "trust," "obedience," and "courage" in your journal. What feelings and thoughts do they stir up?

5. Finish these sentences:

   a. Even though I still believe _____, I sometimes doubt _____.

   b. Even though I doubt, I still believe _____.

Group Discussion:

1. How easy or hard is it for you to honor doubt in other people? What are the hardest things for you to hear?

2. When you are in a season of doubt, what have friends done for you that help? What have been some not-so-helpful things people have tried?

3. Work together to come up with a list of things that used to feel clear in life and faith. Now, make a list of what feels muddy. Discuss how it feels to realize others are wrestling with some of the same issues.

4. Think through the idea of certain phrases that help reduce certainty and improve safe communication with others. What parenthetical phrases do you try to use when communicating about the Bible or issues of faith?

5. Respond to the words "trust," "obedience," and "courage." What

kinds of feelings and thoughts do they evoke?

6. **Share with the group your responses to these sentences:**

    a. Even though I still believe _____, I sometimes doubt
        _____.

    b. Even though I doubt, I still believe _____.

Group Practice:

Read this Doubter's Prayer out loud together. Respond to any parts that move you:

A Doubter's Prayer

God, sometimes I'm not sure.

I don't understand. I can't understand. I don't know what I'm **supposed to understand.**

I am trying to let go. Trying to hold on.

Learning. Growing. Stretching. Leaving. Coming. Going.

What do I leave behind?

What do I move toward?

God, grow my faith, whatever that means.

Not in man, not in systems, not in what-someone-else-tells-me-I-am-supposed-to-believe.

But in you. The living God. The one who heals. The one who reveals. The one who restores. The one who turns the ways of this world upside down. The one who calls me to mercy and justice and love. The one who stirs us to move.

Yeah, that's all I really want. More of you in me. More of you in us.

Ways to Honor Doubt:

1. Practice not having to give an answer when someone starts to share questions, fears or struggles. Resist the urge to give advice and just listen.

2. Create spaces for lament. This could look like a special gathering, a guided spiritual reflection, or a sacred space to let people vent, cry out to God, and let out what's deep within.

3. Get good at the phrases "I am not sure, but..." and "The way I understand it is...."

4. Write out areas of struggle in relation to doubt/faith and when you are done, seal and date your letter. Create a reminder to open the envelope in a year and acknowledge how things have shifted or remained the same over time. Honor those changes.

5. **Consider reading** *Evolving in Monkey Town* by Rachel Held Evans, an excellent book centered on doubt and faith. Find ways to process what it stirs up in you with a friend or small group.

Chapter 8

Diffusing Power

"Justice and power must be brought together, so that whatever is just may be powerful, and whatever is powerful may be just." - Blaise Pascal

Years ago I was on a church staff with a lot of extremely unhealthy dynamics. Many of my teammates were amazing people with sincere and dedicated hearts to serve God. At the same time, when our lead pastor stepped down **due to a moral failure, a power vacuum was created that opened up the** perfect opportunity for havoc. Before we knew it, the person closest to the lead stepped in and began abusing his power. It started a season of back-room conversations, hacking into people's emails, pitting people on the team against each other and all kinds of other craziness.

I was the pastor on the leadership team with the least amount of power. The only woman, the one who didn't need to keep my job in order to feed my family, and also the lowest paid. Maybe because of those things, it gave me **the most courage to say some hard things that needed to be said (or maybe** I just went a little crazy). But I started to call out the abuse of power and destructive dynamics and challenge the elders and other pastors to consider ways to share power differently. Within weeks, I was on the outside, the one who was being talked about in back-room conversations. Within a month another teammate and I, who was also questioning the blatant abuse of power and process, ended up losing our jobs. All the work I had done on behalf of caring for people didn't matter anymore; what mattered was that I was questioning the power.

Since the beginning of time, humanity has struggled with our need for power. We do whatever we can do to create it, keep it, serve it, and make other people serve it. We've all heard the saying, *"The love of money is the root of all evil."* **Because money is about power, I believe the pursuit of power is the deeper root of much evil.** This side of heaven we will always live with the tension of our tendency to pursue and keep power.

The problem I have with power issues related to the church and Christ-followers, though, is that we are supposed to be strangely different from the world. The Kingdom principles that Jesus shares in the Sermon on the Mount aren't just good ideas he shared for the fun of it. He made it clear that the **ways of the Kingdom require a radically counter-cultural way of living.**

This requires giving up our power and diffusing what we have so that those who don't naturally have any will also get some. It means giving up what we have held dear, making ourselves incredibly vulnerable, and humbling ourselves to be wildly reliant on God. This happens by sharing instead of hoarding, and lowering ourselves instead of seeking only to elevate our status.

The main problem, however, is that we, as people and communities, are **generally addicted to power. We are strangely drawn to it. We tend to want more of it ourselves or to surround ourselves with those who have it.** We are far too eager to grant power to those who abuse it. Whether we like it or not, we will have to continually reckon with issues of power until the end of time.

Once we open our eyes to issues of power, we begin to see things we formerly might have missed. My husband is Hispanic, and I have witnessed first-hand what White Privilege looks like and how it affects his family and friends with dark skin. English is their second language, and my in-laws are sometimes targets that get taken advantage of. They often receive unnecessary charges **on their bills and are mistreated by doctors or other professionals.** When my father-in-law calls to get information, he gets brushed off. When I call, doors open and problems get solved. It feels bad to be treated well after watching **someone I love being oppressed.**

This crosses into many advocacy relationships I am in. Friends are often mistreated because of lack of resources, education, or social status. But

when I step in or go with them to appointments, they are treated much more respectfully. Unfortunately, I have also seen the dominance of men not only in organizations or churches, but also in abusive relationships where women "have their place" and lack value, voice and dignity. I have seen who gets promoted and who doesn't when the only difference was gender. Issues of power are prevalent when we look for them.

I have seen what perpetrators can do to victims by abusing their power in wicked ways. I have nursed many wounds of those hurt by the church and am continually disgusted by the things people do, say and get away with in **the name of God.**

The thirst for power and control is deeply engrained in the human DNA, and it continues to cause damage in almost every strata of society. Power in the real world is a given. Even though I am an idealist and wish they weren't, I expect corporations to be power-hungry. They don't exist to save the world; they exist to make money. The problem is when the church inadvertently adopts the world's thirst for power into our culture, our homes, and the fabric of our lives. The upside-down message of Jesus is radically lost and we are sucked **into the same fuel the world thrives upon.**

I work with a lot of abused women, those who have been stripped of their dignity because of sexual, emotional, or physical abuse. These women on **the margins are in desperate need of empowerment. But I will be honest:** sometimes "the church" feels like the worst place for them because it can often be another place they are undervalued and disempowered. I have sat across the table from all kinds of amazing, beautiful, courageous women who finally have gained the strength to come out from under an abusive relationship and try to find their voice and pursue freedom. As I hear them talk about their passion for God and their desire to serve, lead and give, I sometimes get that feeling in the pit of my stomach because I know that many of the churches they are part of will not let them freely speak or fan their giftedness into flame because of their gender.

I have a dear friend who was married to an abusive pastor and finally left. She has struggled with finding a church that doesn't keep tapping into the same **pain, basically telling her,** *"You can only do this or that here because that's a woman's place."* These limitations silence her strong and powerful voice. And this time is it not her husband but the body of Christ, which is supposed to be a reflection of Jesus himself. Jesus continually called people out of oppression **and into freedom, drawing out their value and dignity.**

When I use the word "power," I think of these words: *leadership, value and voice.* One of my dreams is that we would learn what it means to diffuse power – *to give away leadership, value and voice as much as possible, and as deeply and creatively as possible.* This is incredibly counter-intuitive to what **so many have been taught in terms of leadership.**

A life of descent invites us to give away power as much as possible. We can't **ignore that the church is a place of power. But when power is controlled by** a select few—when the poor, hurting, and lost have no leadership, value, and voice—it is not true power diffusion. Genuine power diffusion means giving it away to people who aren't typically influential. The least. The last. The marginalized. The oppressed. The not quite as pretty, talented, educated, or **socially accepted individuals.**

If we examine the Beatitudes, power in its typical, hierarchical form doesn't fit. Jesus continually challenges us to a counter-cultural life, and in a merciful, gentle, kind, humble life issues of power aren't about one-upping, hoarding, **or lording. When Jesus was being tempted by Satan to use his power to** turn the stone into bread or jump off a mountain and save himself, Jesus **refused. When he was on the cross, he stayed on it instead of stepping down,** sacrificing his power for the sake of others. He washed his disciples' feet instead of expecting them to wash his. He used his power on behalf of others and shared it freely with the disciples, empowering them to heal the sick and free the captives in the same way he had. Jesus continually gave away power instead of keeping it all for himself.

Jesus clearly empowered us, too, encouraging us to emulate his ways of love and hope. In many Christian circles there's a lot of talk about being the priesthood of believers (1 Peter 2:9); the reality, though, is that many of our systems prevent it from being lived out in all its fullness. The priesthood of **believers means we are all important and fully empowered by Jesus. We all** have something to bring. We all have value, not just the ones with seminary degrees, charisma, preaching talent, or visionary leadership. The beautiful part of Jesus' message is that he consistently looked toward the margins, to

those with the least power, instead of toward only the powerful.

In the wider evangelical church world, I am marginalized because I am a female lead pastor. Sometimes, when my teammate and co-pastor, Karl, and I are together in certain circles, people will automatically assume I am his assistant. Also, although I don't believe anyone overtly says, "Let's not include her," I am often not invited to all kinds of gatherings that male pastors share together. They pray and support one another, network over golf and sponsor events together. I had a colleague who was coordinating a networking project with most of our city's local churches, all pastored by men. He didn't invite me, which is very typical. I often hear about these kinds of things after the fact. These pastors already hold a lot of power in their own churches; combined, they hold a lot of power in the wider church. In that circle, I just don't have **much power.**

In The Refuge that is not the case. I am not on the fringes, but instead, fully included and empowered to lead. It's funny because sometimes friends from my community will hear me talk about a weird story in which people haven't recognized my role as a pastor and they respond with, "Really, you're kidding me, that really happens to you?" They don't see me any other way. I am thankful for the freedom I have to co-pastor The Refuge. I am also aware that because of the power I do have there, I need to be careful with it. My team and I are deeply committed to giving away as much power as we can. It is hard sometimes because I have a lot of energy and a lot of dreams. While some of my dreams are important, the dreams of my friends are just as important. Sometimes I have to give up some of mine to accommodate some of theirs. This requires real relationship and sacrifice.

If the people I am in community with are simply bodies—those who can fulfill certain roles and perform certain duties to increase the effectiveness of our mission—then it decreases the importance of caring about their dreams. This mentality creates a subtle expectation that, *"There's work to be done, and we just need to figure out a way to make it happen!"*

What if giving away power is actually the more effective thing to do? I have seen horrible things done to people, "for the sake of the Kingdom." Now, that phrase tacked onto things really scares me. What if giving away power is **actually the only way to destroy its power over us?**

Real relationship and incarnational community means that I care so deeply about my sisters and brothers that I continually make room for them to use their leadership, value and voice, whatever that looks like. By creating a space **for others and by giving away my power, I increase the value of the community.**

Sabio encountered what power diffusion can look like. He says:

> *"After being at The Refuge for a year or so, I thought I'd test the waters of influencing what we did here, since the invitation had continually been made that we could all contribute. I remember going to the pastors with my idea, with expectations that it would be critically judged, run through some secret committee, and then either implemented by them or sucked into the institutional black hole where ideas go to die. What happened instead was very disorienting.*
>
> *They said to go for it, and that if I wanted it, I had to lead it, structure it and do the work or at least find others to help me. In finding others to help me, I ended up hearing their opinions and needed to include their visions, as well, to be partners. There was no grand committee arbitrating everything, but that also meant that there was also no power structure to conveniently make everything happen for me, either. With freedom comes responsibility. In The Refuge, this means the opportunity to simultaneously learn to lead while also learning to listen to and include others."*

Sabio took the risk to step into responsibility, but his idea was increased and his influence was increased, when he gave away his power.

Hoarding power won't work on the downward descent. We will have to learn to diffuse power, which sometimes looks like giving it away, but sometimes looks like stepping into the responsibility of it. Diffusing power means inviting others to share leadership, value and voice. Diffusing power means moving away from one leader and hero worship, to finding ways to include and make room for others, and continually fan into flame people's gifts and passions.

Respecting Power Differentials

Giving away power first requires recognizing our own power. A few years ago I spoke at a conference about the issue of women in leadership. I was **really excited to have the chance to be part of this event and felt honored** to be one of the main session speakers. I also realized many of my friends would probably never get the chance to speak at an event like this and that often whoever has the microphone also has the power. These friends have **incredible stories about ways they are stepping into their leadership, value,** and voice but don't have a clear platform for sharing.

I decided to include them as part of the session, giving each a chance to

"Blessed are the meek, for they will inherit the earth."

Matthew 5:5

play a part; I tried as best I could in that circumstance to use the power I had to pass it on to others. There's no question, **in that moment there was less of me than there would have been if I had used the** entire time by myself, but personally I think that's a good thing. It also strengthened a **core value I have when it comes to power:** *Whenever I have it I want to practice giving it to others.*

My guess is if you are reading this book, **you probably have some extra power that** many don't possess. You know how to read, you have enough money to **buy luxury items and you probably have been involved in some form of faith** community along the way. Right there, you have power where some don't. Some of you have been leaders for years; every leader has a tremendous amount of power, more than we may think.

Diffusing power begins with respecting that it exists. The first place to start is by recognizing one's own power. In the world I used to run in, I don't think I even realized how much natural privilege I had because of my education, income and outside appearance. I came from a fairly poor, broken family, but I was determined to do whatever I could to shift that cycle by working harder and climbing the corporate (and ministry!) ladder to somehow garnish **as much power as I could get.**

As I began to engage a downward path, I was struck by how many people don't have power and how much I have, automatically. Socioeconomics, race, mental illness, disability, lack of education, gender and life circumstances that have kept people paralyzed all rob people of their leadership, value and voice.

As we learn to respect power differentials, we also need to recognize how we continue to perpetuate systems that abuse or hoard power. We need to ask ourselves: *"How am I helping perpetuate systems of power where the underdog, the devalued, the least and the last aren't ever treated as equals in terms of leadership, value, or voice?"*

"When we give away power, we reveal the true value each person has to the community, to God, and to the world."

It is easy to be complicit with systems that suppress women, minorities, and those with no resources. It's easy to separate the "recovery people" from the neat and tidy powerful ones. It's easy when leaders never hang out with anyone except other people like them, where lack of diversity is never questioned, and where racial, sexual and gender innuendos and jokes are commonplace. We're often so desensitized, we don't even notice how screwed up it really is.

When we have power, it's hard to give it away because we assume we'll lose it. But in the Kingdom of God, giving away power is one of the most meaningful things we can do. When we give away power, we reveal the true value each person has to the community, to God and to the world. We create the space for people to develop and flourish their God-given talents.

A huge shift will take place in the world, in Christianity, when those who have automatically held power for generations start to recognize the ways it has intentionally or unintentionally kept people oppressed. The scales must fall off our eyes and our hearts in order to see injustice the way Jesus does.

Shoot the Sheriff

My friends in Portland planted a church over 12 years ago called The Bridge. They shared leadership from the start; at first they had two co-pastors and then they widened it to three. Many people told them that it couldn't be done, that they were a "three-headed monster" and ultimately one person had to make certain decisions so it had better be clear who was the final authority from the start. Although no one has accused The Refuge of being a three-headed monster, many have expressed concern about the lack of one voice at the top—one final decision maker when push comes to shove. This is **one of the more common concerns about an egalitarian marriage, too.**

It's funny to me how strongly people doubt that mutual submission is possible. The Bridge has had to make some painfully difficult decisions over the life of their community; so have we. Here's how we make them: *We listen to each other, we pray and we submit to one another.* **No one gets to power up and tell the rest of the team,** *"This is what we are going to do."* We each pull strongly and share our own perspectives but no one has the ability to trump everyone else just because they are on top. It takes longer to make some decisions. It requires patience, humility, and trust that we're not often used **to in leadership. It also challenges us to step into the responsibility we do have instead of hiding behind a** *"Well, I just do what I'm told"* **mentality. Shared** leadership not only protects the communities we serve; it also protects its **leaders.**

Throughout history, humanity has consistently been drawn to giving power to those who already had it. We're attracted to having someone rule over us so they can somehow make everything right in the world. In the biblical exodus when the Israelites left Egypt, many couldn't accept their freedom and longed to go back. Even though they were slaves, they knew what to expect and it seemed safer. For generations the Israelites waited for their Messiah.

They got what they never expected—the long awaited king of all kings was an average guy with a crazy message. The first would be last and the last would be first. Power, religion and knowledge meant nothing in contrast to **the simple and radical ways of love and generosity. Instead of powering up, Jesus powered down to the lowest of places.**

Chris Hawes, co-author with Shane Claiborne of the popular book, *Jesus for President*[19], came to speak in Denver when the book was first released. He shared how it took three days for the Israelites to get out of Egypt, but it took a lifetime to get Egypt out of them. The structure, the subservience and the predictability of someone oppressively ruling over them got into their skin. I think it got into ours, too.

The truth is it's easier to give away our power to those we think can handle it, even when they can't. We bestow an incredible amount of power onto Christian leaders, celebrity figures, and the talented and strong. Our tendency is to keep them securely on a pedestal. It takes the pressure off us and places it on them.

The problem is that absolute power corrupts the imagination. We're not really designed to rule over other people. We can't control what other people do, so we can't control their outcomes. We're designed to rule over ourselves. When we give away that rule to someone else, we're avoiding our own responsibility and empowering other people to oppress us.

In general, having only one leader seems to be a bad idea when it comes to issues of power. It is hard when some people are genuinely strong and gifted because it's tempting to put too much weight on their shoulders and give them more power than we should. I call it hero worship—we elevate certain people to a god-like status, robbing them of their humanness and robbing others of their dignity. It's not good for them, and it's not good for us.

Unfortunately, this is still the most prevalent model in most churches. Shifting away from this power structure is a two-way responsibility—the responsibility of people to not duplicate models of one leader over all and the responsibility of leaders to resist taking sole power and consider different forms of intentional sharing.

My friend, Karl, and I always say we know how to shrink a church. The very first thing to do is *shoot the sheriff*. It is guaranteed to radically shift what most people are used to—looking up to and following one powerful charismatic leader. When leadership is shared, power is diffused.

Diffusing power is more natural for women; we are used to collaborative leadership models and love to partner with others. But since many of the current structures of church have men at the top, diffusing power will require a concerted effort on the part of men. For men, sometimes the desire is there but the grooves in the systems they live in are so deep, it's nearly impossible **to change.**

I have the utmost respect for men I know who have given up powerful roles for the sake of sharing. I also want to remind us there are plenty of women "on top" of organizations and structures who aren't great at diffusing power, either. The temptation is to think that once we've arrived we need to stay on top. As we continue to wrestle with Jesus' ways, we will need to seriously consider how we are replicating systems that keep power on top and many **people on the margins.**

A Culture of Inclusion

People engaging a life of descent give power to those who have never had it before in noticeable, concrete ways. They live with a courageous spirit of inclusion instead of exclusion. They recognize that in the Kingdom of God there is room for everyone. What's critically important, though, is that we make sure we give it to people different from us.

It's easy to pass power to people who think, act, and live as we do. Those on the downward descent give it to people who normally don't have any as well as people who see things differently and might even get on our nerves, and **people who are learning instead of only those who have mastered certain** skills.

A central idea in diffusing power is providing avenues for as many voices as possible, in as many ways as possible. I think this is where the greatest spiritual transformation might take place—when we give away power instead of taking it away, when we serve instead of demand service, when we offer space and **voice to the typically unheard instead of demanding the microphone. When** we bend our knee instead of expecting others to bend theirs. When we give instead of take. A true community, no matter how small or big, is made up of different voices. They are all important, powerful and deserve to be heard. Voice is not just words but also creativity, dreams, passion and purpose.

I think every group of people – whether it's two or three folks, or hundreds of people – need to figure out avenues for each and every person who is part of that group, to be seen, valued and nurtured to use their voice, whatever that looks like. This creates a culture of inclusion instead of exclusion.

The Refuge continues to press out what this looks like, but it starts with ensuring there's no "us and them." This great divide perpetuates power like none other. In practical ways, we continuously make room for dialogue, creating a natural space for everyone, we rotate facilitation to ensure many voices are heard instead of only one, and we work to uncover each person's gifts, even if they don't think they have any, and we intentionally ask as many different people as possible to contribute.

My friends, Kevin and Linsey, were part of our original planting team at The Refuge. Having been part of countless churches and organizations over the years, they were passionate about shared leadership and pushed us further than we would have gone had we been left on our own. Early on, we could always come up with reasons why we should control certain aspects of our life together. Each and every time, they'd respond with "Why?" Their questions forced us to confront our own fears, so we could overcome them.

Power stems from a desperate desire to control. Control feeds off insecurity and fear. Kevin and Linsey pushed us to trust in a way that scared a few of us half to death, because we had never seen it before in the models we came from. Open microphones, allowing anyone the freedom to share whatever they wanted, however they wanted, weren't popular in the extremely controlled ministry environments we were used to.

Every time they shared I had almost the same emotion: fear. It's scary to diffuse power, but the downward ways of Jesus lead us to a deeper understanding of community, relationship, and growth. They draw us to a sacrificial kind of living where we give up control and submit ourselves to God and others. They invite us to a level of trust that is terrifying while at the same time incredibly freeing.

In Alcoholics Anonymous there's a famous cliché that has a lot of power. It says, *"Let go and let God."* I am seeing what happens when we let go—a texture of beauty and belonging is created that can never be cultivated when power is held by only a chosen few.

Light Someone Else's Fire

Embedded in the idea of giving away power is a simple possibility. When we give it away we unleash the beauty that is already present but lies dormant. Letting go of power allows us the room to fan the flame of people's God-given giftedness, even if it has nothing to do with extending the precise ministry or mission of a particular church. This is a hot topic for me because I know that the people that get the most attention are usually the ones who will advance the vision that has been chosen by whoever is on top. What about nurturing dreams, no matter who gets the benefit because of a brother or sister with dreams that deserve nurturing?

I know many lovely people with diverse and beautiful gifts to offer the world, who are shriveling up and stifling their creativity because their dreams are not deemed important to the ministry at hand. I also know a countless number of people who don't think they have anything to contribute.

The marginalized, oppressed and discarded are rarely invited to the party; they are likely busy surviving and have time to nurture their natural giftedness or hidden passions. Inviting and including other people's vision into community results in increased diversity, beauty, opportunity and chaos. It creates an overall spiritual ecology that no one could come up with alone.

To do this, we need to intentionally create space at the table for people who aren't used to sitting there. There's plenty of room. The table is big enough. Just keep putting in as many extra leaves as you need. The question is whether we are humble and brave enough to keep pulling up more chairs and inviting new people to sit in them.

An amazing thing happens when we ask. Countless times I have asked someone who is not used to being asked to contribute, and almost every time I get a *"Really? You mean you really want me?"* response. Every time I want to cry. How could they have gone this long with no one seeing all their buried beauty that needs a space and place to rise to the surface?

The temptation is to think that everything must run smoothly in order for the mission to be accomplished. But when we invite people to the table and give them a voice, we validate who they are as human beings. We restore dignity. Yes, it often produces a strange chaos, but isn't this the mission of the church—*to step into the chaos and to breathe the love of God into people's lives?*

Almost nine years ago, that was me, the one saying, *"Really? Like you really want me?"* When a friend called to ask me to join his church staff as a Care Pastor, I initially thought he was calling to see if I knew anyone who might be interested. Never in a million years would I have expected that he'd want me; **it was embedded in me that the ministry I was doing was small potatoes and** that "pastors" were always men.

I still remember the moment he called. I thought it was going to be a quick networking conversation; when I realized what he was asking, I ended up sliding down to the kitchen floor and sitting there in shock. I wasn't sure if I heard him correctly. To feel valued, wanted and pursued in an area that I was most passionate about—healing community—was extremely powerful. That moment was pivotal for me in terms of beginning to really step into leadership. I was one of those people who knew deep down that I wanted a chance at freely leading but felt so disempowered that it didn't seem like something more was an option. I am grateful he lit that spark in me.

The most powerful people in the room are the ones who can give power away.

Since then, I try to play whatever tiny part I can in helping someone else fan their passion into flame, even if they don't yet know what it is. I really didn't know this call to love was inside me so strongly, but my friend saw what I couldn't. Likewise, I sometimes see beauty and passion in others of which **they are unaware. Part of my role as a leader and follower of Jesus is to see** what others can't see and then use whatever power I have to call it out, give **it space, and nurture and challenge it to emerge.**

Being on both sides of power has given me a different perspective. I now notice **how many strong, wise women live with this same feeling of powerlessness** and purposelessness. We know we have something to bring, that there's more to be lived out, but because of engrained systems of power, we often feel helpless or ambivalent, unable to believe that things can be different. I **see this because I experienced that same sense of disempowerment.**

I also meet many men who feel similar feelings for different reasons. What makes someone "powerful" can be very confusing; what feels quite clear, however, is the kind of power Jesus emulates—freeing people, serving others, including instead of excluding, sacrificing his time, heart and ultimately his life—is not very popular in modern culture.

Apologies Help

A few years ago, the government of Australia made a public apology to the Aborigines for the ways they oppressed, marginalized and stripped them of their dignity and culture. After generations of disempowerment the government took the critical first step toward restoration—admitting they had wronged them. Denial is a human defense mechanism, a way of closing ourselves off to the magnitude of the pain we have caused. Breaking out of denial requires humility; the Australian government humbled itself and took responsibility for something they themselves hadn't even started. They essentially declared, "We are sorry for the wrongs done by those who went before us and are committed to do what we can to change this." Their bravery didn't make the mainstream news, but it made a big impact on me.

It came on the heels of a women's event I spoke at where a man stood up, unplanned, and publicly expressed how sorry he was for the ways we as women had been abused, used and oppressed instead of valued, treasured and empowered. Like the Australian government, he wasn't responsible for the whole of female oppression. There are many that have contributed to it long before he was born. He was simply apologizing for the way he had contributed to the cycle and sharing his desire to play an active part in pursuing change on behalf of women. There wasn't a dry eye in the room.

When we recognize and call out the oppressive systems of power, including how we participated in it, we make a significant difference. Apologies help. They call out the reality of what is broken. They recognize the dignity of those who have been oppressed, as well as the dignity of the oppressor.

I know I have used my power to hurt people along the way. For that, I am truly sorry. Because I respect how easy it is to misuse power, it's easy to offer grace to others when they humbly ask for it. Typically, though, apologies are rare. I hope over time we can change that, transforming into people and systems that are humble and reflective about ways we may use or have used power to damage others. There's so much healing that can happen when someone in power actually apologizes in an attempt to make amends.

Part of making what could be a reality includes becoming people and communities who are keenly aware of our power and the powerlessness **of others, both inside and outside of systems we live in.** If we have it, we must do everything we can to give it away, cultivate new voices and make room at the table for those who normally wouldn't have a seat. If we don't have it, may we find courage to step into it, whether we're asked to or not.

Power is complicated but it's not impossible to behold. The less aware we are of our **own power, the more damage we can do.** **As human beings and as Christ-followers,** we can use the power we have to influence, **help, love and serve those without it.** As we continue the downward descent, we must learn to respect power differentials, acknowledge the implications of our own **power, and address the powerlessness of others. Sharing power causes us to step into our own power, while at the** same time giving it away, thereby making **room for others to step into theirs.** As we acknowledge the ways power has harmed others and make amends when we need to, the Kingdom of God begins to reflect God's image of humility, sacrificial love and equality.

God, help us be power diffusers, to be humble and courageous enough to take any power you give us and give it away.

* * * * *

Personal Reflection:

1. Reflect on your own leadership, value and voice right now. Do you feel empowered or disempowered in these areas? How?

2. How have you been affected by unjust power structures?

3. What kind of power do you possess that you might be unaware of?

4. How do you feel about your own power? Is it hard or easy to step into it? Why?

5. What could power diffusion look like for you in the systems you live and work in? Reflect on ways you may have either knowingly or unknowingly disempowered others. Are there steps you could take toward apologizing? Reflect on ways you may have been disempowered by others. How are these past experiences affecting you now?

Group Discussion Questions:

1. How can we reconcile the word "power" with the Beatitudes? What does that really mean?

2. Is it easy or difficult for you to step into your leadership, value or voice? Why or why not?

3. Brainstorm together the costs and also the benefits to power diffusion. Consider both sides—those with the power giving it away and those who may not have power receiving more of it.

4. Imagine what it would look like if you "shot the sheriff" in some of the systems you live or work in. Think through its implications and benefits.

5. Share with the group ways you may have either knowingly or unknowingly disempowered others.

Ways to Diffuse Power:

1. Engage in honest dialogue with people you know who may be under empowered. Find out how they feel and try to not just listen, but **also understand.**

2. If you have power, find ways to give it away. Look for someone who might have less than you and invite them into the work that you are doing, realizing sometimes it will take more time and effort, but that in the end, it's worth it.

3. If you know you have somehow participated in disempowering others, consider an apology or a making of amends.

4. Invite others to the table when you are working on a project or initiative and seek their input and collaboration. Try to include **people who might not normally be included.**

Chapter 9

Practicing Equality

*"There is no more beautiful art than to see a person, a man,
a woman, a child, crafted in God's image and living as fully
into that image of God that only they can fill. It not only
makes them more beautiful, it makes God more beautiful."*
- Christa Romig-Leavitt[20]

The seminary I went to had a very strong emphasis on training and mentoring; every student was required to take a comprehensive battery of tests that assessed giftedness and passion and then meet with an employment counselor. I will always remember the counselor's words to me after discovering that my top two gifts were #1 Leadership and #2 Mercy. He said, *"Kathy, you will be bored as a therapist. You like to lead and build things. But I have one important word of advice that feels extremely clear after meeting with you—whatever you do, don't work for a church. They will not know what to do with you!"* I remember laughing in the moment, not taking his words too seriously. Little did I realize that just a few years later I would be on a church staff, his prophetic words ringing in my ears.

When I entered full-time ministry, I jumped into the deep end as a female pastor on a lead team of eight other male pastors. At first, I was proud that I was able to sit at the leadership table. It didn't take long, though, to see that even though I was at the table, I didn't have an equal voice. My team was good to me in many ways but ultimately, all of the power resided in their connection to each other and their positions as male pastors entrenched in ministry, and as being the ones who actually made the decisions when push came to shove.

I am extraordinarily thankful that I am now part of a community that fully embraces equality for everyone, where women are highly valued. A few years ago I met my friend, Stacy, online. She had been reading my blog and felt connected to the dream of finding a place to lead and use her gifts. She had lost hope that would happen in the church and began focusing her energies on cultivating her professional life instead. I remember the first time I met her, thinking she was similar to many other strong women I know—*there are just not that many places for them in the church.*

She ended up moving to Denver and now, after almost two years, she is an integral part of our community, empowered to lead freely and actively shape our community. What's different about her experience and my former experience is clear—she isn't a "token woman" on our team while all of the power is held somewhere else. She is a full and integral part of the work that we are doing. Her leadership, value and voice count as much as the rest of ours.

Downward mobility means becoming people that create places where equality is practiced. Equality and power are intimately entwined. Like diffusion of power, equality means that everyone has an important voice that needs to be heard and are welcome at the table.

"True equality is restoring the dignity of those who have had it stripped from them and living in mutual submission, one to another, in community."

Equality crosses more than just gender. Gender is sometimes the most obvious piece of equality to focus on, but gender equality dovetails into other divides such socioeconomics, race, education and life circumstances. Practicing equality requires incredible intention, understanding of our own prejudices and a modeling of "this is what it can look like" that is normal and **natural instead of forced or demanded.**

The beautiful, wild body of Christ is supposed to be the one place where the playing field is leveled and all are equal. The Apostle Paul reminds us, *"There is no longer Jew or gentile, slave or free, male and female. All are one in Christ Jesus"* (Galatians 3:28).

My friend, Pat, went from what most would think was a wonderful life, to **losing his wife, house, ministry leadership and lifestyle. Now he struggles** financially and is in the category of the "working poor" where one day of missed work can make it impossible to pay his bills that month. What's wonderful about Pat is that he sees the Kingdom of God like never before in his new job as a bus driver for the elderly and people with special needs.

He's dedicated to true equality—restoring the dignity of those who have had **it stripped from them and living in mutual submission, one to another, in** community. He says:

> *"True Christian leadership is corporation-based leadership turned on its head. Some call it equality. The Bible calls it servant leadership where 'the first will be the last.' The idea of 'the last' means a lot to me right now. When you really experience this equality it is in a community of friends that look to you for support and guidance while, at the same time, you desperately need the same from them. Until we give up the 'lead, follow, or get out of the way' choices offered by the typical corporate Christian model, I don't think we can really, truly, in the deepest place in our hearts, be 'free in Christ.'"*

Equality means freedom from labels, distinctions, assumptions and preferences that look like us. It begins with seeing the other as God sees them, as human beings created with a distinct and unique image. When one is put underneath another in a consistent up-down position, it means that one party's power is always diminished. Equality is mutual submission, the kind that often gets overlooked: *"Submit to one another out of reverence for Christ"* (Ephesians 5:21).

Love is the Great Equalizer

The Webster's definition of egalitarian is: "asserting, resulting from, or characterized by belief in the equality of all people, especially in political, economic or social life."[21]   It stemmed from the word "equalitarian." I wish they had kept it that way because it would probably make more sense for people. Many share a core belief that everyone is equal and that one should never be subjugated underneath another. This issue is a hot button in many Christian circles but a non-issue in many others.

Personally, I stay away from theological arguments centered on gender (typically stated as "equal in value, different in role"). I strongly disagree that women can only do certain things and men can do others, and the notion that **we are supposed to build our lives and ministries upon that principle. I also** respect that many interpret scripture differently.

For me, women being regarded as less than men damages the foundation of the value of in a way that affects not only women but also the under-represented, voiceless, powerless and marginalized. If the two primary groups in humanity—men and women—aren't treated equally, then it is a much greater stretch to expect other forms of equality. In living out Jesus' ways and creating equality-infused communities, some critical questions need to be asked in each community.

- **Where can I begin to embrace equality?**

- How can we really live out the value of equality and what does doing so look like?

- How do power and equality mix together?

- How can we work to ensure that the pull toward typical hierarchical power structures doesn't happen?

Practicing gender equality, like every other Kingdom principle, is not an easy task. It will take brave men and women who are willing to go against the grain of the systems and cultures they live in to take a stand on behalf of a better way.

One of The Refuge's greatest strengths is how we handle the male-female issue. We are learning how men and women can work alongside each other, take out the typical destructive power dynamics, and be friends, equals, and partners in ministry. It is glorious, and we continue to work our tails off to **protect it.**

However, what is more important to us is that we try to extend equality far beyond only gender. There are also characteristics that separate people, including race, socioeconomics, politics, sexual orientation, education and age. We **include those who are young, old, married, divorced, educated,** unschooled, charismatic, not-so-charismatic, excited about God, mad at God, artsy, not-so-artsy, brown, black, white, Democrat, Republican, making good money and living at the poverty level. People representing all of those categories, and therefore the wider community, are part of The Refuge. **Diversity helps with equality because it begins with what we have in common: our humanity. We are all human beings made in** the image of God, each reflecting our own unique gifts and contributions. Without diversity, **the value of equality cannot be fully expressed.**

"Praciticing equality is mostly about praciticing humility."

Mixing up gender, socioeconomics, education and theological differences is tricky. Homogeneous relationships and groups are, indeed, easier to manage. When those involved represent a wide range of the population and are dedicated to equality, it is a lot trickier. It means going back to the guiding principle of "there is no us or them." It means we all have dignity and value, no matter our background or the gifts that we bring. It means that leadership **is not about a role but rather a way of living. It means love comes first.**

My friend, Dylan, says it this way.

> *"I don't think much in terms of equality, but rather of love. These work together toward the same thing, life in the Kingdom of God. It's a way of life; practicing equality is mostly about practicing humility. The kind of humility which allows beautiful and sometimes odd relationships to flourish,*

in service to the Kingdom. It seems like almost every part of downward living points toward humility. Without humility and sacrificial love, equality is not possible."

Unleashing The Caged Animal

A crucial part of practicing equality requires intentionally encouraging women, minorities and other underrepresented friends to step up and contribute fully. Yet, we can never underestimate how foreign this is for many who have not ever had an equal voice before. Most are a little gun-shy. I liken it to a **caged animal that has never experienced freedom. We would expect that** once the cage is opened, they would jump out and into freedom; but often, **they remain inside, scared to emerge.**

I have heard many people with power say, *"Well, we made room for so and so but they didn't want to be part."* To engage people in their own freedom, we will have to ask over and over again, nurturing and affirming people's contributions in small and big ways, respecting that disempowered people **need a lot of encouragement to really step up and out.**

Making room for equality sometimes means we have to let go of our tendency toward perfectionism. Many ministry leaders are obsessed with perfection and being "the best." I completely understand our traditional desires for wanting to give God our best, individually or corporately. At the same time I don't think God is interested in perfection, especially when it comes at the **expense of people.**

I know this can make some strong, charismatic leaders twitch, but I believe you can't have true equality and a culture of perfectionism. When the person who can't sing very well is given an equal shot at participating, the music won't sound as good. When the person who stumbles over their words and isn't smooth at communicating is speaking, it will make some people feel uncomfortable. When people who actually do tasks better hold back so that other people who aren't as good at them get a chance, the "quality" **decreases.**

Letting go of perfectionism takes time, and I know that it drives some people a little crazy; many long for someone to step in and clean it all up. The reason we at The Refuge don't, and won't, is that the core Refuge DNA includes the value we always want to protect—that everyone who is part of our community is equal. Sure, individuals do certain things better than others, but instead of controlling and managing them, we give everyone a chance to participate as much as possible, even though this may mean taking a hit on "appearance." It **is my favorite part of our community.**

This is also why The Refuge is small! Inside many people are expectations of performance and perfection, and churches have done a fine job cementing this idea over the past few centuries. We also don't have the advantages of efficiency that come from making things happen in a top-down sort of way, where institutional help, power and money flow down from the hierarchy in order to make things work.

When we give up our notions of perfection for the sake of equality, the cost-benefit is more than worth it, especially when you notice beautiful things **transforming underneath the surface. When we give people equality, they** reveal something beautiful: the present image of God.

Recently, we invited my friend, Jessica, to led communion at our weekend gathering. Jessica is a former drug-user with a powerful story of transformation and redemption. Love exudes from her despite many difficult circumstances, including raising a granddaughter and navigating day-to-day with two grown children who have a host of severe addiction issues.

Jessica is not a typical leader, but we value her voice and experience and asked **her to facilitate communion and share a bit of her story. When she went to the** front to set up communion, all the lights went off. At first I thought something was wrong with the power, but then I heard her voice in the darkness. She had crafted a beautiful monologue, a crying out to God that gave me chills. It wasn't polished. It wasn't professional. She stumbled over her words here **and there.**

But here's what was so amazing— she had the space to share it. No one edited her work or previewed it beforehand. No one evaluated her personal life and deemed her worthy or unworthy of contributing. Instead, she was fully empowered to bring her gift to our community and freely share it. She is not a project or a less-than because of her past or struggles in the present.

She is an equal, valuable part of our story...God's story.

Although I talk a lot about equality in systems, the same idea applies to individual relationships. Equality means we see ourselves on an equal with others, even though their lives may be completely different from our own. Judgment is deeply embedded in us; it's why Jesus continually reminded people to work against it. If we believe we are somehow better than other **people, we cannot see each other as truly equal brothers and sisters, on the** same journey.

Practicing equality requires recognizing our own prejudices and fears. No matter how progressive, we all have them. Part of changing the face of Christianity will include reckoning our prejudices about all kinds of things. Sexism, racism, classism and dogmatism plague us. When asked, most will **nod and say that everyone has a fair shot and we see people equally, but the** truth is that such equality is rarely, if ever, truly practiced.

Equality requires intention because there is a natural propensity toward inequality. Like the gravitational pull towards comfort, we can be deeply prejudiced toward talent, charisma, ability and power. We will be drawn to people who are educated, good communicators and charismatic leaders. I'm not dismissing their importance. However, we have to be careful that we don't rely on only those people and then subtly separate them from the many others who may then be seen as "underlings"—the less pretty, not as smart, **or not as squared-away.**

Prejudices and fear have an insidious way of ruining equality and keeping people marginalized both directly and indirectly. We will have to talk about our prejudices out loud, in community, with safe friends and to deal with our tendency to judge, ignore, dismiss and rob equality in our relationships, as well as our communities.

A while back I had a dear friend who is part of The Refuge come to me and ask for forgiveness. Not realizing anything had been between us, I asked, *"For what?"* He said, *"For judging you for being a woman pastor. I didn't think I could listen to you. I thought you were violating the Bible by leading. I am so sorry."* I will never forget that moment when my friend reckoned with his prejudice and had the guts to admit it.

Making it Normal

A while back a mega-church in our area had a female guest speaker come for weekend services. I can't count the number of people who felt the need to tell me, *"Isn't that so cool?"* I was incredulous, honestly. As much as I see a subtle shift happening, I couldn't think that having a female guest speaker once a year immediately changes their view of women. It's a beginning, but we have a long way to go. The only way to make equality normal is to make these practices normal, to do them over and over again, until we don't need to mention it.

It's not hard to imagine a world where equality is the norm. We just have to dream a little. We have to see the world from God's perspective, a world in which each of us is valuable and worth it. Each of us has a deeply embedded sense of dignity, regardless of gender, race, nationality or creed. With a sense of the intrinsic value of people at the core, we can begin to create a better reality.

"Blessed are the peacemakers, for they will be called children of God."

Matthew 5:9

Unfortunately, equality is not the norm. My friend, Lily, married a youth and worship pastor at a growing church. Lily was a strong and creative woman with a wide range of gifts and abilities, but she never really felt like she was able to fully contribute in the churches she attended. She experienced what many women married to pastors sometimes feel—the church ends up getting a "two-fer," both him and her for the price of him. It is so obvious, when meeting Lily, that she is a gifted and talented leader.

We don't talk about equality much at The Refuge. It's just a part of who we are and what we do. When Lily came to The Refuge, we saw her giftedness and immediately called it out. Here's what she said, after living in our community for a while and then engaging with the wider church where inequality is more the norm:

"I was at what I call a 'normal' church just a couple of weeks ago with my husband, who was leading worship for one of the church's services. A man walked into the room during the sound check; it was clear he was 'someone,' as he strode in with confidence and walked up to the stage to talk to my husband.

He made eye contact with me, and as he drew near I stood up to introduce myself to him; it was clear by his expression and quick introduction that he in no way intended to actually introduce himself to me, let alone talk with me.

Later before the service there was a time of prayer and as I stood to join the other leaders I noticed I was the only woman. This made me realize how much equality I have every time I meet with my Refuge friends. I have wanted this equality for a long time; in some situations I have experienced it within a framework of theatre or work or marriage but never have I experienced it within faith. Doing so has been lovely and empowering and scary and beautiful.

I never asked The Refuge to consider me equal—they just did. I never asked The Refuge to consider me for more than women's or children's ministry— they just did. I have been given a gift that I was hesitant to open, scared of what it might mean to have myself fully able and fully acceptable in this place of faith. But what a gift it's been! To see myself through the eyes of equality and to see others through eyes that are more focused. To sift through the veil of gender, age, color, sex, financial status, etc. and to peer through to the heart and mind of a child of God."

Until the barriers are broken down between men and women in the body of **Christ, a chasm of lost experience and wholeness will always be present in** our relationships and communities. We can never underestimate how much healing and spiritual transformation can happen when men and women learn to live alongside each other in equal, loving relationship.

Throughout my entire faith journey I have never experienced this many men and women doing life together the way we are trying at The Refuge. We are **learning to be brothers, sisters, mothers, fathers, daughters, sons, friends and co-laborers with each other.** We are learning to fight for (and with) each **other, to serve together, to give, receive and believe in each other, and to** point each other toward Jesus' hope and redemption.

God, help us notice inequality and strive to be practitioners of equality in our individual realtionships and our communities, in risky, new and creative ways.

When we foster a culture of equality it instinctively removes our fear of being **undervalued. I am learning how to be** more comfortable in my own skin, use my voice, make mistakes, let my friends see my bad side, risk, put myself out there, and **humbly share how much I need them when** everything inside of me screams, "I do not need anyone!"

Intention requires practice. We need practice in order to learn how to naturally work, live and love alongside each other as **brothers and sisters in the family of God.** More healing will happen when we take sex, **race, economics and power out of the** equation and model the radical equality that Jesus brings to a world filled with inequality, injustice and oppression.

We don't have equality mastered at The Refuge; inequality is the norm in the wider cultures we live in, so we're constantly brushing up against it. But we're choosing to practice, learn, try and experiment. It's not easy, but it's good. There are many additional ways we can infuse our life together with the value **of equality, so that each person feels as valuable as the next, regardless of** gender, giftedness, contribution, or life circumstance.

In the past few years I have become much more passionate about this issue, since everywhere I look I see power systems that directly conflict with the

Kingdom value of equality. As pioneers continuing to stake out new ground, my hope is that everyone who is dreaming of nurturing a new missional community, experimenting, or living out their faith more intentionally would keep asking themselves, *"What does equality look like for us and how can we do everything we can to preserve, promote and nurture it."*

Equality is beautiful. Equality is possible. When practiced, it reflects the **Kingdom of God in the here and now. Part of living into the downward** descent means that we become courageous people, willing to reckon with our prejudices and take radical risks to practice equality across gender, **race, socio-economical and any other categories that create inequality and prevent us from seeing and loving one another as brothers and sisters in Christ.**

* * * * *

Personal Reflection

1. When considering the topic of equality, what are some feelings that are stirred up in you?

2. How have you personally experienced inequality in your spiritual journey? How have you contributed toward the inequality of others?

3. If you have been on the receiving end of inequality, connect to the image of the caged animal with an open door. How easy or hard has it been for you to come out of the cage? Why?

4. Take some time to pour out your feelings about equality in your journal. Write it in a letter to the church, someone you hope reconsiders their position on it, or someone who treated you poorly. Use it as a tool to simply express your feelings, knowing you won't be sending it.

Group Discussion

1. Discuss why focusing on the issue of diversity and the unique image of God reflected in people is far more important than focusing on only gender or other characteristics of inequality.

2. What do you think about the thought that practicing equality is essentially practicing humility?

3. How have you personally experienced inequality in your spiritual journey? How have you contributed toward the inequality of others?

4. Think of the systems you are currently part of; how can you contribute toward making equality more "normal" there. Make a list together.

Ways to Practice Equality

1. Include, include and include. Invite and include as many diverse people to the table to sit alongside each other and learn from one another.

2. Respect that many underrepresented people will need to not only be asked but also strongly encouraged to participate. Understand that only opening the cage door isn't enough.

3. Talk openly about prejudices and fears of living in equal relationship with each other. Share what you're learning along the way; what is hard, or easy, for you?

4. If you have held the power, do what you can to give some of your power to others who haven't had it. If you haven't held the power, when asked, try to step into it instead of avoid it.

5. Find a group that is that is out of your comfort zone, in terms of race, culture, political belief, etc. (Meetup.com is a good option). Consider attending a meeting. Recognize what is stirred up inside of you.

6. Ask someone different from you (gender, culture, race, etc.) to engage in an open conversation about the challenges that you each face in being the "other."

Chapter 10

Pursuing Justice

"Justice is what love looks like in public."
- Professor Cornell West, in the documentary Call +
Response[22]

When I was a senior in high school I was a self-proclaimed liberal activist, longing to go to Cal Berkeley so I could change the world. Through an odd turn of events, gears shifted and I ended up at a conservative Christian college where some of that passion waned. I loved the school; it was filled with fantastic friends and challenging experiences, but it set me on a spiritual path **that was far more focused on a personal spirituality than a corporate one. I was into God for** *me,* **but I wasn't that concerned about God for** *the world* **(beyond spiritual conversion).**

Over the past few years, that old spark of justice ignited in me a renewed interest in the suffering of others.

As I began to explore the idea of justice in my life, the traditional definitions in the dictionary were not very appealing. It included words like "administering of punishment," "rightfulness" and "lawfulness."[23] **But when I viewed it** through the lens of Jesus, justice seemed to become much more robust and life-giving. Jesus was not about punishment, but about restoration. He called to us to bring the Kingdom of God here, now, by acting on the words of the **Prophet Isaiah:** *"Seek justice, encourage the oppressed, defend the cause of the fatherless, plead the case of the widow"* **(Isaiah 1:17).**

Jesus defined justice as a sense of equality. Justice was about going down and finding solidarity with the poor and oppressed. When Jesus was declaring the "woes" to the Pharisees in Matthew 23, he made it fairly clear they had done **all the religious things**: *"…But you have neglected the more important matters of the law—justice, mercy, faithfulness…"* (Matthew 23:23).   Jesus actually saw justice and mercy as more important than the traditional religious duties.

For some, justice is not a new topic; many in the church have been standing on behalf of the oppressed for years. Others are experiencing a shift from a more individual, personal faith, toward a strong desire for justice and equality for those on the margins, and want to dedicate themselves to practicing what that means in real life. Regardless of where we are on our journey, there's always more to learn as we enter the fray of injustice personally, locally and **globally.**

At the heart of justice is the fundamental assumption of human dignity. Each **human being bears the image of God and has inherent value. When that** dignity is stripped, ignored or oppressed, there is injustice.

As we engage downward mobility, life begins to magnify the issues of justice **in ways that living on the ascent never will. Eyes become open, hearts begin** to feel and anger begins to stir on behalf of the marginalized, oppressed and victims of injustice. Part of our responsibility as Christ-followers is to pursue justice on behalf of those who are being treated unjustly—to risk our hearts, time, money and position to stand up for the underdog, however we can.

Part of our brokenness as humans includes a corporate, natural propensity toward injustice. A piece of our humanity is deeply rooted in a desire for power and control. We long for safety by grasping for power. Injustice always leans toward taking advantage of the poor, marginalized, oppressed, and those perceived as less-than. Because injustice is intensely rooted in almost **every culture, it is quite easy to say,** *"There's not much we can do about it; it's just the way of the world."* However, Jesus says the Kingdom of God is at **hand, in the here and now (Luke 21:31)."**

As **Christ-followers, we are supposed to model the image of God to the world,** in order to restore the world. In Micah 6:8, God expresses what is required of us: *To seek justice, love mercy, and to walk humbly.* I love the words "seek" and "pursue" because they imply something very important: *they won't come naturally.* We will have to work, advocate and sacrifice for it. Part of life on the journey down is pursuing justice on behalf of those being treated unjustly. In seeking justice and fighting for it, we give it meaning and value.

To become pursuers of justice, we must first listen to those marginalized in relationship. Hearing stories and knowing real people helps make these issues far more real, rather than an abstract notion we read about in the newspaper. As issues of injustice become more apparent to us, we will be challenged to act, recognizing there is never an easy time to jump in. We must respect that turning the tides of injustice will always rock the status quo, creating tension and conflict. Once we see injustice and gain courage to stand against it, then **we can use our voices on behalf of others in a spirit of advocacy.**

Justice Starts with Listening and Understanding

Pursuing justice begins with listening to and trying to understand each other. At The Refuge we host challenging topics and process them together at our community gatherings. Last year, we facilitated a series of conversations on justice. One of the panels had a mix of people who were marginalized, oppressed, or treated poorly for one reason or another—a single mom, a parent with a disabled child, a Latina, and a homosexual. I was reminded that restorative justice begins with relationship.

As each of my friends shared, I was struck by the power of their stories. Even though I know them all personally and have heard their struggles and **circumstances, as I listened to their sharing I was reminded in a much deeper** way what day to day life is really like for them. It's not easy. Every day they experience injustice; shame, struggle, and always being treated as "less than" **is part of their ordinary experience. A sense of anger and compassion rose** inside of me as they shared and I realized, yet again, how easy it is to stay safely protected from the realities of injustice.

Without listening, understanding and actually knowing each other will be unable to move toward any kind of restoration together. It's also why we need a mix of diverse people from various walks of life, experiences, theologies, socioeconomic backgrounds, political views, colors, and shapes and sizes all in the same room, at the same table, engaging each other.

At the same time, hearing and listening are two different things. When I hear someone, I only hear the words they have to say. When I listen, it means that I enter into a deeper experience and understanding of where that person is coming from. This is vital when it comes to issues of injustice. It is easy for those of us who may not be from the same place or share a similar experience to say, *"What's their problem? It's not like that...they just need to get over it."* Unless we have walked in another person's shoes, we will never understand. The only way we can develop a sense of empathy is to listen—really listen. Relationship transforms understanding.

Gandhi said, *"When we are silent we stand on the side of the oppressor."*[24] Even though we might want it to be, silence is not neutral. Silence empowers injustice. Speaking up doesn't solve every problem, but it is the way to start.

When we allow our brothers and sisters to have their dignity stripped, to be constantly silenced and pushed down, we allow them to be oppressed. When we see discrimination because of race, class, or gender, and do nothing, it means we are actually agreeing with the system that oppresses them.

I understand why people don't want to take the journey down. It opens our eyes to a world that we will no longer be able to ignore. It's why close relationship with the marginalized and oppressed is so important. When it's my friend who I eat with, share life with and really know that is being oppressed, I can not stay silent.

A few years ago one of my gay friends was doing her laundry at my house while we had company. An old friend brought a new guy she was dating over for dinner. Sonia was quietly doing her laundry in the other room while we were hanging out in the kitchen. The date happened to hold very conservative views about a lot of things related to church and life and somehow made the assumption that we naturally agreed with him. I was doing everything I could to be kind and my husband was giving me that look that said *"Kathy, please, honey, be nice. The night's almost over; we're almost done."*

However, when this guy started in on homosexuality, the dam broke. My dear friend was in the other room folding clothes and he was basically condemning her from the kitchen! I strongly interrupted him, saying, *"You are talking about some of my friends and that is hard for me to hear, especially in this house which is a safe spot. It's a lot easier to sit in that seat and be really sure. Things change when it's your friend, someone you love, someone who loves you, too."* In that moment, it would have been easier to gloss over what he was saying and scurry him out the door, but I needed to be able to look Sonia in the eyes and have her know that we would never leave her hanging.

After they left, Jose and I had a long conversation with her. She didn't hear his comment, thankfully, but was grateful we stuck up for her. I am glad too, because it was a tiny way I could stand on her behalf. *When we are truly friends with the marginalized and oppressed, we can't stay silent.*

I know people who strongly believe in **women in leadership, yet remain silent** in the churches they attend because they don't want to rock the boat, stir up dissent, or lose their communities over it. Their **silence means that they are agreeing** with an oppressive system. The same is **true for a racist comment made toward** a co-worker. Silence in that moment means we are subtly siding with the joke-teller because we didn't have the guts to *say, "That's wrong."* It's always easier to remain silent than say something. It's also easier when we're not in the shoes of the one being oppressed.

> *"When we are truly friends with the marginalized and oppressed, we can't stay silent."*

Learning to See and Smell Injustice

Injustice is easy to miss if we're not looking for it. When we have power and life is pretty good, it's easy to miss what's going on in worlds different from ours. In my immediate neighborhood, most everyone has good jobs, fairly nice houses and a life of stability. It's not that my neighbors don't struggle—they do—but they possess a life of privilege that is starkly different from the lives of friends who live 10 miles east. Very rarely do these two worlds intersect. Sometimes when I am at games for my kids I talk to parents about things related to injustice and pain that I encounter in my daily life. They are completely surprised that people who live only a few miles away don't have **insurance, cars, or beds for their children.**

We begin to notice injustice in three ways. The first is when we actively look for it. It's not hard to see if we're looking. The second is when we experience injustice ourselves. The feeling lingers in our system long after the event happens. The third is when we are in relationship with people who are marginalized in any shape or form. We feel their oppression because we care **about them.**

To confront injustice, we've got to learn to see it first. As we engage in relationship with the oppressed and marginalized, seeing the world through their eyes, we begin to recognize it more clearly. Confronting injustice then means getting active, entering in relationships with the poor, physically disabled, mentally ill, underrepresented, or uneducated. Jesus continually points us to the margins because these are the people on whom injustice **preys.**

For the past few years I have been in contact with so much injustice that it sometimes seems that's all I ever talk about. But my husband, Jose, who is a great listener and puts up with my swearing and ranting, couldn't always see the brokenness of the system. Now that he is a practicing attorney at a legal aid clinic working with the poor and marginalized—primarily women—he's the one swearing and ranting.

A few years ago I saw the film *The Great Debaters* with Denzel Washington, the true story of an all-black college debate team in the 1930's that was the first to compete against students from white colleges. Our family loves these kinds of movies—the ones that stir up great conversation and a desire to make a difference. There's a powerful moment in the film when one of the debate team members, Samantha Booke, is arguing for the immorality of segregation. Her opponent shouts, *"The world's just not ready yet for integration."*[25] Samantha immediately roars back with, *"So when is the time? When will there be a right time?"*

I cried throughout the entire movie. I saw Samantha's struggle and courage to keep standing up for what was right despite the loneliness and difficulties, and

I was even more inspired to pursue change. I was sitting next to my daughter, Julia, as I was watching, which made it even more motivating because I don't want her to be stuck in an oppressive system that does not properly value **her as a female. Julia, along with all the other girls of the world, needs us** to take action now, on their behalf, instead of waiting and hoping but never being willing to actually work toward a different way. If I keep waiting for the right time, the perfect conditions, and the gates to magically open to the marginalized and oppressed, it will never come.

The world needs people who recognize the time is now. If Rosa Parks never got on the bus, if the Freedom Riders never took their first bus trip, or if the first black student didn't walk through the door of a white college, segregation would still exist. Why?

Because there's never a right time for unjust systems to magically fall. It doesn't work that way.

Years ago, this exact statement was said to me after I taught at a large church. I was the first woman to preach there, and afterward, a few men with deep pockets and conservative convictions asked the question, *"What is our stance on women teaching?"* It stirred up a hornet's nest of back door conversations. This is what the conclusion was: *"We believe in Kathy. But we're just not ready for it yet. It's not the right time."*

A few years ago a Bible study tool I co-wrote got published. The number one Christian retailer of Bible studies refused to sell it in their stores because I'm one of the "lead" pastors at The Refuge, and they hold the belief that women should not be in top positions of leadership. I was told, *"They're just not ready yet. "* Do you know how many women I know who are gifted and talented communicators, pastors, innovators and leaders who are waiting around for the "right time?"

On a global scale there are horrific injustices being waged against women and children, where extreme power differentials are the norm and inequality is deeply engrained into the fabric of many cultures. It's easy to look at the magnitude of those injustices, while minimizing others. However, all injustice has the same thread; the status quo becomes accepted, and we believe that we don't have the power to make a difference. Unjust systems are allowed to perpetuate themselves because it's never the right time to change.

There will never be the right time for people to suddenly accept what has never been accepted before, but it's always the right time to stand up against **something that is oppressive.**

I also recognize that there are vast differences between what issues people view as unjust and wrong; each person needs to listen to their own convictions, but it's worth remembering that Jesus did not side with the powerful and strong. Instead, again and again, he aligned with the accused, sick, rejected, oppressed and neglected. When we take the side of the status quo, we run the risk of finding ourselves on the opposite **side of where Jesus calls us to stand.**

"Blessed are those who hunger and thirst for righteousness, for they will be filled."

Matthew 5:6

The status quo is always the path of least resistance. There's never a right time to go against the flow. The hard road, to a more just and Kingdom-infused society, is paved with years and years of crazy sacrifices, casualties and experiments.

As we connect more deeply with those on the margins and learn to see injustice, we will then have to sacrifice our time, pride, position and a host of other things to use **our voices to advocate one the behalf of others.**

Becoming Advocates

Intricately weaved into Kingdom living is the art of advocacy. My definition of **advocacy is** *helping give voice to the voiceless, and ensuring that the powerless don't get harmed.* Jesus was and is our advocate, and we are called to be like him. This looks like risking our position and pride for the sake of another, refusing to support systems that hurt our friends and neighbors, and actively **using the power we have to be a voice for the voiceless.**

As Christ-followers and advocates, we must sometimes speak out on the behalf of others. Right now, this is happening in unique ways around the world through reinvigorated movements against human slavery and trafficking, and for women's rights and advocacy for the poor in third world countries. While these big movements are gaining steam, we must remember that advocacy includes small, subtle ways we stand up for someone being taken advantage right next to us. These are the opportunities in our midst to call out injustice, instead of watching it happen and assuming there's nothing we can do about it.

I go to social service agencies a lot with friends who need to access community assistance. It is one of the most demoralizing, dignity-stripping experiences anyone can encounter. Each time I am there I wonder why the church isn't as present as it could be in these moments. In a truly just, integrated and connected community, there would be no need for social services. But that's a long way off in many of the communities in which we live, so we must become better advocates and journey more closely with those in need.

When it comes to accessing social services, no person should have to go there alone. It's too hard, humiliating and confusing to navigate. I have a graduate degree and consider myself to be fairly intelligent, but every time I intersect with the system it feels overwhelming and utterly confusing.

One time I was at a local government office and saw a veteran get so frustrated during the check-in process that he threw up his hands and stormed out the door. I wanted to run him down and cry out, *"Come back, I'll do this with you!"* but I was tied up holding a single mommy's hand as she had an anxiety attack at the thought of losing a chunk of her benefits. Every time I am in these agencies I think, *"Everyone here should have someone else with them to be a support and strength, an in-the-flesh advocate."*

Scripture is littered with calls to advocacy. In Luke 10, the story of the Good Samaritan challenges us to action, while James 1:27 reminds us that, *"Religion that God our Father accepts as pure and faultless is this: to look after orphans and widows in their distress..."* The psalmist in Psalm 140:12 says, *"I know that the Lord secures justice for the poor and upholds the cause of the needy."* The prophet Isaiah says, *"Is not this the kind of fasting I have chosen: to loose the chains of injustice and untie the cords of the yoke, to set the oppressed free and break every yoke?"* (Isaiah 58:6-7). Psalm 82:3-4 includes the cry,

"Defend the cause of the weak and fatherless; maintain the rights of the poor and oppressed. Rescue the weak and needy; deliver them from the hand of the wicked." **Although the psalmist is crying out to God, this verse is a call to advocacy.**

Over and over in scripture we see a call to justice. We are called to be reflections of God's image in the world by recognizing the value and dignity of those who have been oppressed. Similar to almost every aspect of living in the trenches with people, advocacy always starts with relationship. Friends don't let their friends do hard things alone. Without an in-the-flesh, face-to-face, heart-to-heart relationship, personal advocacy can't happen.

Advocacy also requires a willingness to step into the mess even when we don't have any answers. Contrary to what we might often think, advocates don't have to know much. We don't have to know the intricacies of the system or even what programs or resources are available. The only quality we need is a **willingness to be present and to say,** *"I'll stand with you even if we can't figure it out. You will not have to do it alone. You need to try to use your own voice and advocate for yourself, but if you can't, I will be there to help you."*

We also can't keep leaving advocacy to the professionals. We make assumptions all the time—*"I am not a professional; they need to figure it out with their caseworker, therapist, doctor, lawyer, or _____."* Yet sometimes all people need is help navigating connection with these professionals!

An advocate speaks for those who have lost their voice. This loss of voice takes many forms; it comes from shame, past abuse, deep insecurity, and fear of further injustice. Although it often helps, one counseling session a week with a professional isn't automatically going to recover someone's voice. Rather, we need people to coach and help us practice standing up for ourselves.

Roxanne is a perfect example of someone who could easily fall through the cracks. As a single, uneducated woman with a minimum wage job, she went over a year with no health insurance and a long list of physical ailments. The stress from no insurance or income was almost enough to kill her. When she needed to file for disability, I told her, *"I'll be there with you in case you need some help, but it's best that you try on your own first."* **She had always been a** faithful employee, but as time passed she could no longer meet the physical requirements of her job. We do our best to make sure someone goes with her to each of her appointments, guiding her through the process and helping her find her voice each time so she can practice self-advocacy.

She says,

> "If I hadn't had someone with me, there's no way I could have made it through the past few years. The entire process was so confusing; every time something came in the mail I had someone I could talk it through with and they could translate it for me. Then I would make the calls, take the next step. Every time someone is with me, I get treated better, things move faster, and somehow I can get what I need."

"Intricately weaved into Kingdom living is the art of advocacy."

I am not sure what would have happened to Roxanne if she hadn't had advocates alongside her, but I know this—she struggles to believe that God cares about her or believes in her. Through tangible advocacy, she gets a taste of God's support and provision, feels far less alone, and works on her own behalf against injustice.

Advocacy and the pursuit of justice require a commitment to the long haul. I realize that thought is overwhelming for some, but Christian community requires a much longer view of relationship than we typically try. We are called to be people's mothers, fathers, brothers and sisters for different seasons, and to strap in for the long haul. One of the reasons it is hard for hurting people to trust others is that they continually get ditched, making it difficult for them to trust. Life in the margins requires patience and endurance.

In reality, we all probably need an advocate now and then. When I went through an extremely difficult time exiting an unhealthy church staff, my husband, Jose, and a few friends advocated for me in a powerful way. I will never forget it. I had become voiceless, beaten down, but they stepped in and said a few things that needed to be said on my behalf.   Honestly, it felt like God sticking up for me when I needed help the most.   In this situation, I was incapable of asking for what I needed because I really didn't know. But that didn't stop them. Through their words and tangible actions on my behalf—I **felt less alone, more protected and valued.**

In those moments, I got a picture of God's heart for me. Young or old, educated or uneducated, shy or loud, there's always someone out there who needs us to stick up for them, to be a voice when they have none, to restore dignity, and to offer extra hope for the journey. That's advocacy. It's not going to just drop out of the sky. We have to actively participate in it.

Patience and Urgency

Becoming justice pursuers means that sometimes we will never taste the full fruit of our labor. However, the work we do now does affect the future. The civil rights movement in this country has taken decades and we're still not where we want to be. If we give up because we don't see results, change will not happen. The mustard seeds we plant now can grow into strong trees in the future, but sometimes it takes generations.

Living in the tension of patience and urgency is required when we pursue justice. We will have to work with passion and also trust that God is at work in ways we often can not see. Because injustice is the norm, if we stop lending our hand to the pursuit of justice, unhealthy and disparate systems will naturally tend to creep back to the status quo and the path of least resistance. That's why activists are painfully aware of their need to keep injustice in the forefront of people's minds; if they don't, it's too easy to forget.

To help our community practice confronting injustice, I facilitate a monthly advocacy group hosted by The Refuge. This group is a learning community for people who are interested in gaining training, skills and support to journey **alongside others in hard places. We invite a wide variety of guests to help** strengthen our experience. The majority of folks who attend are connected to The Refuge, but we have people from several other churches and agencies who also participate. Our logo is a superman symbol with an X marked **through it.**

When it comes to issues of justice, it is easy to develop an, *"I can save this person,"* or, *"I can save the world"* **mindset. It can tap into our deep desire to feel needed, important and someone who contributes to the greater good.** These feelings aren't inherently bad, but are very typical in Christian circles, where we are working hard on behalf of Jesus. It's quite easy to develop a savior complex while walking alongside someone who "needs" us. It can feed our ego when things are going well and destroy our confidence when things aren't going so well.

God, give us strength and courage to passionately and actively pursue justice on behalf of others.

There is a cost to confronting injustice. In Matthew 5:10, Jesus promised we'd be **persecuted if we followed these Kingdom principles here on earth. When we stand with the oppressed, we will be oppressed** too. When we advocate for justice, we will take a hit personally, professionally and sometimes even spiritually. When we intersect with injustice, it can rock our world and sometimes it can cause us to doubt God's plan because of his seeming **inability to right what is wrong.**

This is the tough part of pursuing justice. Are we willing to lose our jobs for it? Are we willing to sacrifice positions in church **for it? Are we willing to lose face with** groups of people we've been in relationship with for years and won't be too happy about our "bleeding hearts?" Are we willing to actually have people leave our communities (especially the ones who give lots of money) when we make decisions on behalf of justice, or fully welcome and love the world's **outcasts? Are we willing to roll up our sleeves and enter into the mess and** muck of another person's experience?

There are countless ways we can act on behalf of each other. Buying differently, advocating, marching, voting, speaking out, as well as offering our time, hearts and presence are all possibilities. It looks different for everyone, but the question on the journey downward is, *"How is God calling us to act on behalf of others?"* My hope is that we will become people and communities who are relentless pursuers of justice on behalf of those being treated unjustly, whether it be in the circles we live in or around the world, and that we'd risk our reputations, voices, time, resources and power to advocate for individuals and groups who can't advocate for themselves.

Pursuing justice begins with relationship and cultivating the ability to see power structures. Then, it requires us to advocate on behalf of others, using our voices, time and power. Pursuing justice takes a long view, requiring a tenuous balance between patience and urgency.

* * * * *

Personal Reflection:

1. Can you think of some examples of injustices that you have experienced in your own life or seen in the lives of close friends? What does that stir up in you?

2. What are some injustices your eyes have recently been opened to?

3. How have you advocated for someone else (or wanted to)?

4. Has someone ever advocated for you? What was that like for you? **What did you learn through that experience?**

5. Pour your heart out to God about the injustices you see. Tell God what it feels like for you and what you long for God to do in the midst of what's happening.

Group Discussion:

1. What are some injustices your eyes have recently been opened to?

2. How has knowing someone who is marginalized or oppressed made a difference in how you view justice?

3. Have you ever advocated for someone in a tangible way? What was it like for you?

4. Have you had someone else advocate for you in a tangible way? What was that like for you?

5. What are some of the hazards of pursuing justice?

6. Brainstorm together ways to pursue justice, individually and as a **community or group. Which of these can you possibly commit to as** a regular practice?

7. Consider a prayer I wrote called A Prayer for Justice together. Which parts jump out at you?

A Prayer for Justice:

God, may we be people of justice.

May we humble ourselves and be willing to learn from each other.

May we stand on the side of the oppressed.

May we not be silent.

May we call out Your Image in others.

May we be brave on behalf of our friends.

May we bring your Kingdom to earth, now.

May we be known as those-crazy-people-who-stick-up-for-the-underdog-even-when-people-think-we've-gone-off-the-deep-end.

May we let your Spirit compel us to act.

To love.

To learn.

To speak.

To move.

To sacrifice.

On behalf of our brothers and our sisters next to us today, on behalf of **those who have gone before us, and on behalf of those who will come** after us.

On your behalf, Jesus, as your ambassadors, with your humility, your **courage, your Spirit as our guide.**

Amen.

Ways to Pursue Justice:

1. Think of the relationships you are in and friends or people you know who are somehow marginalized or oppressed. Take time to listen to their story and hear what their needs are and what life is like for them.

2. When there is an opportunity to stand alongside a friend in a tangible way, risk your time, pride and heart and show up for them. Go to a doctor appointment when they are scared to go alone. March in a parade on behalf of a cause they are passionate about. Consider how you can support them by not supporting organizations that harm them somehow.

3. Check out local agencies in your area that advocate on behalf of poverty, homelessness, equality and community change and see how you can support their work.

4. Julie Clawson's book, *Everyday Justice*, is a great resource for tangible ways to live more justly in how we buy, eat, vote and love.

5. Consider developing a skill, learning a new language, or increasing your knowledge in a practical area, for the purpose of advocating for another. Find out ways you could use this to benefit a local agency or group.

Chapter 11

Cultivating Creativity

"God is heaven and art" - a 5-year old girl at a Refuge art event

Kids amaze me with their creativity. They come up with games on the fly, are inclined to express freedom, and often spend hours working on projects that light their fires. It's always fun to watch them doing what they love to do.

One of my twins has always been incredibly creative. Jared takes paper, pens and scissors to bed with him all the time. A while back he started creating these amazing books on the computer, stories he wrote along with elaborate illustrations. He printed them out and brought them to my husband and I. We were enthusiastic at first, until we realized how much color printing he had done. Jared had moved on to something else, and Jose and I were left in the kitchen where we started whispering to ourselves, *"You know these are really cool, but they use an awful lot of ink. Maybe we should tell him not to make anymore like this?"*

As soon as the words slipped out of our mouths, we both realized how ridiculous we sounded and started laughing at ourselves. We had the $10 to pay for an inkjet refill. Why were we focused on saving a few bucks instead of freely celebrating and honoring Jared's tenacity and creativity? We never said a word to Jared and he naturally moved on to other projects that weren't **quite as expensive, but** it brought to light our natural knee-jerk reaction to value what appears "practical" and how easy it is to stifle and shut down others' creativity.

Think about what happens when you or another creative person you know **tells their parents or friends,** *"I want to be an artist, musician, photographer, actress, actor, writer, etc."* Most people react with a little eye darting, maybe an even imperceptible wince, a throat clear, and then usually say something like, *"Umm...that's great, but make sure that you get a real degree first. Get something that you can fall back on. Art doesn't pay the bills."*

When I was in high school I had an excellent and unconventional English teacher. She inspired us. My senior year I was the Editor of our high school's Literary Magazine, and we created a volume filled with art, poetry and short stories. I am still awed by the beauty that emerged from an average bunch of 16-18 year olds. For me, creative writing was a way to express my feelings in ways I couldn't in my regular life. Thoughts and feelings flowed out of me **that I was unable to say audibly.**

When I graduated from high school and went to college some of this creativity persisted, but as time progressed it was slowly replaced by life's practicalities. Expressions of the more creative part of me began to feel frivolous and unnecessary. By the time I finished graduate school and got married I had stopped writing all together and focused my energy on becoming a good Christian wife and mother, taking care of my babies, going to bible studies, and trying to make it through the day. During those years I essentially closed myself off to creativity.

About five years ago I opened back up to it again—to being more willing to express myself creatively and risk being vulnerable in that way. It came in the form of not just writing but actually creating and nurturing The Refuge. It's been one of the deepest expressions of my heart; in many ways, cultivating **life together has been my art.**

Everyone's an artist. God, the most brilliant creative artist of all time, put his image in us from the very beginning. Creativity often gets buried beneath life, brokenness, circumstance, and negative messages. Eventually, if we fail to cultivate it, we lose connection with. One purpose of the body of Christ is to help uncover God's image in each other—to draw out the good, to call

people to be who they are created to be, and to restore dignity, beauty, and purpose in others' lives.

On the downward path, this becomes even more critical because of the amount of brokenness that's present in people; as I keep emphasizing, a central part of our role in relationship with each other is to become dignity-restorers. **We do this by helping people draw out and express their natural** creativity. To create is to directly connect with the image of God within. The Sufi poet Rumi says, *"Inside you is an artist you don't know about."*[26] *The creativity that is in each person is a natural reflection of God's creative image inside of us.* When it's stifled, buried, stuck, or ignored, not only do we miss out but the world misses out, too. When we have a space for creativity to flourish, we become more and more complete. Through creative expression, we are participating in God's ongoing work of redemption in this world.

Part of downward living is actively cultivating creativity and bringing more beauty to places in desperate need of it. Most people I meet are dreadfully disconnected from creativity. When I facilitate groups, discussions, or our weekend gatherings, I include exercises that help people tap into some of their hidden creative talents. Often, people moan and groan and roll their eyes. They chime in *"There she goes again, making us do hard or silly things we don't want to do."* I still do it, though, because the most unexpectedly beautiful things seem to get expressed. Every time those same people share **how deeply they were moved or how surprised they were by the experience,** I am consistently amazed by what's inside people that rarely has a chance to **come out.**

Subtly or directly many have been taught, *"We're not artists,"* or, *"We're not that good at creative things."* This usually isn't the original message we were taught as kids. For most of us, when we were younger, we probably didn't think twice about creating, making, trying, risking, and participating. Over time, though, we grew older, and we began to edit ourselves, hold back instead of participate, evaluate and critique ourselves instead of freely sharing. Slowly, many of us became closed to creativity.

Unfortunately, many church systems have directly perpetuated this kind of closed-door policy to creativity because they have adopted a professional, "*only the good ones get to play*" mentality. Often, average musicians don't get a chance. Pretty people are the ones who sing on stage. Art shows are reserved for the talented and screened for submissions. We've forgotten that the beauty that's in each other–whether it's deemed good enough, or not, by a man-made measuring stick–needs a place to be nurtured, a forum in which **to be revealed.**

One aspect of cultivating creativity as part of downward living is to stop measuring creativity as talent. Our human tendency to compare can be a great detriment to creative expression. As we do that we can expand our view of creativity. We have limited it to certain mediums and missed out on the vast possibilities for creative expression. Lastly, we must intentionally create safe spaces for a wide range of people to try various forms of creativity. This often does not come naturally and requires focus and continued practice.

Quit Measuring Creativity as Talent

As we engage our sense of creativity, it's important to examine what hinders it. One of the easiest temptations to fall into is comparison. When we compare ourselves to others, it often closes down what we are capable of doing. During the Advocates group at The Refuge, we always do some intentional work with **a spiritual director or therapist who helps guide us in nurturing care for our** souls. At a meeting last year the facilitator encouraged an artistic expression experience with pastels and markers.

One of my friends, who is a therapist and in the process of building a thriving private practice for grieving children, spent a lot of time focusing on her lack of artistic talent. She was in the same small group as an extremely gifted visual artist, and she got stuck in comparing her work. She completely forgot how brilliant she is when it comes to drawing out children's grief and connecting **with them in deep ways. She also dismissed the reality that she is bravely** building a counseling practice from scratch, and conveniently ignored that she has written several pieces for The Refuge blog, pieces that have touched **many hearts and lives.**

At first glance, Stacy does not think of those things as creative expression. Like so many of us, she limited her creativity to the arts–painting, music, photography, acting, writing, etc. But creative expression is that and so much more. Creativity is also a person trying something they've never tried before, using their voice in new ways, taking a step toward a dream, experimenting with something scary. As we quit measuring creativity as talent, we start to see the lovely ways each person is made and notice more of the gifts and **talents that are buried within them, crying to come out.**

Most people default toward self-criticism. When challenged to do something that requires creativity, people tend to put a disclaimer on it—*"This isn't that good; I am not that good of an artist; mine is not nearly as good as his or hers."* You name it and we can find a way to self-deprecate! What happened to Stacy is not unusual. We measure our creative talents against those who have spent years developing their expression. And instead of taking the time **to develop our talents, we never start.**

I tested this theory recently at a group experience facilitated by a friend. When she asked everyone to share their very simple pieces, the majority found ways to minimize, compare, or somehow put down their work. We have been programmed to measure and compare talent. Many ministries and churches perpetuate this idea is by perpetuating a showcase mentality. The best musicians, prettiest singers and the most talented artists are the ones who usually get the gigs. Think of how many budding singers and musicians know they will never get a shot at being part of these teams because they don't quite make the cut. They're not good enough, skinny enough, or confident enough. We cultivate creativity when we continually nurture people's passions, even when they are off-key or not as professional **as the rest.**

Widening our View of Creativity

As leaders and cultivators of life in the trenches, part of our responsibility is to help others use their God-given creativity more freely, to empower them to step up and into their creativity, whatever shape or form that may happen to be in. When we create a space for creativity and remove the obstacles that keep it from showing, we begin to widen people's view of what is possible.

I have another friend who loves to build houses from scratch, or even better, take an ugly existing mess and transform it into something beautiful. He also uses his construction expertise to help build wells and pumps that create clean water in third world countries. I have seen his work up-close and personal and it is remarkably creative, figuring out ways to build hand pumps that can be made from cheap, easily obtained materials in indigenous cultures. Honestly, he would never identify himself as an artist. He would say he's an engineer and a thinker. Yet, not only does he create something from nothing, his work **also strengthens the dignity and beauty in people who are in desperate need** of water and hope. There's no question he's an artist.

My friends Angie and Todd Fadel are pastors at The Bridge church in Portland and are deeply dedicated to opening the space for creativity and play in their community. They write songs together as part of their worship experience, **ensure everyone has an instrument, and create** ways **for people to paint,** write, or connect with what's going on in their heart. The way they ignite creativity creates equality. Their core tenet is inclusion—everyone is part of **the experience and has something to bring. It is incredibly healing and dignity-** restoring for everyone who participates.   Their ongoing encouragement to cultivate creativity has helped us stay the course and keep pressing the **envelope in our context.**

We have modeled inclusive creativity in The Refuge at a great cost and an even greater benefit. Part of practicing equality and diffusing power is ensuring there is room for everyone to express themselves, no matter how talented they are. Anyone can play, share, and be part of what we're doing. This has created fertile ground for creativity to be expressed. Over time, I have seen the least likely folks bloom.

Recently, we hosted a semi-regular gathering we call Beauty Night, an open space forum for people to share anything they have created. We do not edit, choose, or control who or what is shared. Several contributors are new to our community, living on the fringes of life and faith. Socially awkward, filled with fear, they graced us with a glimpse into their hearts through their creative pieces. The most gorgeous thing happened as they shared. For a few short **moments, they stepped out of their uncomfortable exteriors and let their** creativity flow out in the presence of people who warmly and kindly received **it.**

It makes me cry when I think of it, all that beauty suppressed inside finally given a safe space to come out. These moments capture everything I believe about Kingdom living—how the least likely people and the least likely moments are intimately connected with the deepest parts of the story of God. Calling out creativity is part of our responsibility to each other.

For our Beauty Night, it would be easy to make an assumption that anyone who wants to share will sign up. If that were the case, we would miss out on many wonderful gifts because often people don't even have the strength to put their name on a piece of paper signifying their willingness to participate. They need someone to call out what's in them, to beckon them to try by saying, *"We need your voice, please be part of tonight."*

They need someone to help them try.

Creativity is one of the hardest things to uncover in a person because people are often afraid and ashamed of it. Similar to practicing equality, we can't open the doors and expect that people will come rushing out, ready to create. Shame, fear and lack of confidence invade so many people's lives. Cultivating spaces for creativity to be expressed requires relationship and intentionality. I can't tell you the number of times I have discovered people's hidden creativity after hanging around them for a while.

"Cultivating spaces for creativity to be expressed requires relationship and intentionality."

I have a friend who is a single mom and struggles to emotionally make it through each and every day, but she is an incredible artist. She makes me things now and then. Although very reluctant to share, she has offered her work occasionally in our community; each time more glory is exposed. To uncover what's been buried requires each of us to learn to see what usually doesn't get seen, to spend time with each other and tap into places in our own and each other's hearts that are usually ignored.

Everything comes back to relationship. Unless we get close, we can't see what **is buried inside others, what only needs an opportunity to come out.** We will stay focused on outside appearances or circumstances and make many assumptions about people that might not be true. The margins are filled with creative, imaginative people who do not have the spaces, resources, or confidence to express themselves freely.

Create Safe Spaces to Try

Once we create the internal desire, we need to create the space for people to try to share in a safe space. I keep emphasizing that creativity isn't just art. It's trying things that we aren't used to trying. This means providing a venue for people to explore their passions for all kinds of things that normally wouldn't get tried due to fear or lack of support. As brothers and sisters, we can cultivate creativity in each other by coaching, encouraging, and cheerleading **new ideas into existence. In the past few years I have seen 501c-3's started,** ministry ideas implemented, art created, new careers pursued, and little and big dreams realized because of the consistent support of some faithful brothers and sisters. A little encouragement and a safe place to try go a long way.

The question is, how do we draw creativity out of people? The simplest thing to do is recognize what is already there. The image of God is already present... if we look. When we recognize people's dignity in the space of community, we call out what is meaningful inside. And when we call out people's dignity, **we begin to empower people with the capacity to nurture what is already** there. Essentially, our role in living this out is becoming cultivators of courage. **We nurture courage by encouraging people that they have an internal story worth embracing.**

Fear holds back creativity the most. Many are afraid to "fail," afraid to speak up, afraid to step out, afraid to put something on paper that looks "stupid," afraid to be vulnerable, afraid of what people will think.

My friend, Lori, is a beautiful writer. She works a day job as an administrative assistant, but in the evening, an incredible talent flows out of her through words. A few years ago, several friends and I started a creative expression initiative for women called Voca Femina. Tired of seeing creativity often tied only to professional artists and people who could somehow sell their work, we wanted to create an open and encouraging platform for women to share their creative expressions, no matter the medium. Lori became a regular at our quarterly gatherings. She had been writing quietly and secretly for years, but she never had a place to actually share some of her work out loud. She shared a "letter" with me that she had written to a friend that was a poignant and hysterically funny piece. I asked her to please share it at one of our Voca Femina parties. Here's what she says about this first experience:

"I was shaking for days with fear of letting myself be so exposed and vulnerable. But when my name was called and I started sharing, I looked up when I was crying and some were sad with me. When I was laughing, they were, too. A transformation took place that night. I felt more courageous, more connected not only to the joy and pain in my story but also to the beauty that was shared with me through the other people there."

Lori became part of Voca Femina's core here in Denver. Over the years, I saw her continue to blossom, experiment, and try to let some of what was in her, out. She just needed a safe place to try.

Every time I am at one of these events, the beauty that emerges gives me a deep sense of awe. Married, single, poor, rich, old, young, educated, uneducated—the floor is open to anyone who wants to try. Sure, some are more talented or eloquent than others, but often the roughest, least-polished pieces tend to be the ones that bring the most joy to me because I know the back-story. I know that woman struggles with mental illness and lives in a constant state of shame. I know this woman is still reeling from a painful divorce. I know that young girl has so much potential if she can just have **enough support and love to remind her to use her voice as freely and strongly as she can.**

Several times we have hosted Voca Femina share parties at Joshua Station, a ministry in Denver that provides transformational housing for homeless families in our city. Their lives are hard. They are working their butts off to change and turn things around on behalf of their kids. Harshness, not beauty, has permeated much of their experience. At the share parties, the residents shared some of their work—spoken word, photography, poems, paintings, collages, and a mix of other mediums. Those moments were holy moments, God's image reflected in raw, stunning, and unexpected ways—homeless **women and their daughters sharing incredible beauty and depth in a free and** safe place. In that moment, dignity is restored and the playing field is equal. They are not homeless women, abused women or addicted women; *they are just women created in the image of God, letting some of that reflection out.*

God, help us to tap into your creativity and courage in our lives, and intentionally nurture others.

This wouldn't have happened naturally. We needed to intentionally cultivate a safe space and then encourage them to try.

To create spaces where creativity can be freely expressed, we have to ask people **to engage with boldness and courage,** step out of their comfort zones, and tap **into the deeper places in their hearts.** We also need to risk failure. I do not know **what God is nudging every person to do,** consider, try, and explore, but my guess is often we may be too afraid to listen. To cultivate creativity on the downward path, we will have to ask God to give each of us **an incredible amount of courage.**

Creativity and courage are linked together in Kingdom living. Uncovering God's creativity inside each of us is a life-long, never-ending process. We will need each other to do it. We'll need to quit worrying about practical things like how much ink we're wasting in the printer and who will sound the best up **front.**

We will need to widen our view of creative expression and resist our tendency to measure creativity as talent. We will also have to work intentionally to give people a safe place to try. My hope for us as people and communities is that we'd be people and places who actively help one another discover the creativity buried deep inside of us and provide venues and encouragement **that call out beauty, wildness, and freedom.**

* * * * *

Personal Reflection:

1. What is God stirring up in you through this idea of cultivating creativity as a part of downward living?

2. Do you consider yourself an artist? Why or why not?

3. What are some of the obstacles for you related to creative expression?

4. How has "measuring creativity as talent" affected you personally?

5. Think through the idea of widening our view of creativity. What is your "art?"

6. Have you had some safe spaces for you to try to express yourself creatively? What was that like for you?

Group Discussion:

1. Reflect together on how easy it is to self-critique anything that we create. How does that protect us?

2. What would shift in your personal or corporate experiences if you "quit measuring creativity as talent?"

3. Consider together how widening our view of creativity can be helpful. How would it expand creative expression in the communities you live and work in?

4. **Share with the group some of your personal experiences with having** a "safe space to try." What was that like for you?

5. Brainstorm together a practical list of "blocks to cultivating creativity" and "possible ways to cultivate creativity."

Ways to Cultivate Creativity:

1. Create a safe space to try, whatever that might look in your context. It might be an evening of sharing creative expression in your small group, a special event, or an art exercise at a gathering.

2. Carve out some time for yourself to actually create: written word, mixed media, a musical piece, or something else. Try not judge your work. See if you can identify what is beautiful in the work.

3. Individually or together in a group, sift through a magazine, find a picture or word that represents what you are feeling or experiencing right now and use it as a launching point to write, draw, or even sing something.

4. Do a free-writing exercise: Write about everything you are feeling about church, life, relationships, etc. Don't worry about correcting spelling, grammar, or punctuation.

5. Through authentic relationship with people, discover their gifts and passions, especially those that may have been buried for many years. Actively nurture them and encourage them to let some of it out.

6. In any places creative expression is welcome, make sure everyone is encouraged to try—not just the best musicians or the one with the most talent but rather anyone with a willingness to take part.

7. Ask people intentionally to share their work—not only those who identify as artists. Find ways to give them a space to share.

8. If you are nurturing creativity in a faith community, check out the resources on Love is Concrete (www.loveisconcrete.com) for ideas.

Chapter 12

Celebrating Freedom

"The Spirit of the Lord is on me, because he has anointed me to preach good news to the poor. He has sent me to proclaim freedom for the prisoners and recovery of sight for the blind, to release the oppressed, to proclaim the year of the Lord's favor." - Luke 4:18-19

As we practice a life of downward mobility, we can't ignore that Jesus came to set people free, to rescue us from spiritual and emotional captivity despite our circumstances. Freedom has a wide range of facets. There is a freedom that comes from entering into the mysterious and powerful walk with Jesus. It also comes as we recognize the Spirit's work in our lives. At the same time, **there is a consistent need for ongoing freedom as we grow as human beings, sons and daughters of God.**

All of the practices we've been journeying through together so far—extending love, mercy, and compassion, welcoming pain, honoring doubt, diffusing power, practicing equality, pursuing justice, and cultivating creativity—open the space for restoration and change in our own lives and in the lives of others. Since each of these practices are deeply rooted in relationship, it's **nearly impossible to not see lives somehow change. Each of these central aspects of downward living point directly to the big idea of a Jesus-infused life:** *freedom*.

In the downward life, freedom comes from engaging God's healing by shedding the things that hinder and rob us of life, relationship and love. Most everyone's hope is to somehow experience greater freedom in their lives. In Christian living, our hope is that those around us experience greater freedom, too. This is not a new thought. However, I believe it can be easy for us to **get so focused on doing, building, growing and reaching that we distract** ourselves from what is right before us—our own and others people's real stories, unfolding in beautiful ways.

Freedom looks different for everyone and cannot be measured by human eyes that tend to focus on words like "progress" and "behavior change." Sometimes freedom and healing mean that nothing shifts on a circumstantial level, but our hearts, relationships and view of God and ourselves somehow do. Captivity and bondage produce death, while healing and freedom produce **life.**

Often, even though we don't want a life of captivity or bondage, it is sometimes easier. It's predictable and comfortable. When the Israelites left Egypt, their first reaction in Exodus 16 was, *"We want to go back; at least we had food there."* Change is hard. The path of least resistance is always to stay the same, to stay stuck. There's a natural pull toward the status quo. But God calls people to something more; he calls us to freedom.

Years ago, when I first started the healing journey, freedom felt very elusive. It **was a word that people tossed around that I interpreted as meaning I would** not feel pain, anger, or anything negative but instead would live in a state of weird bliss, disconnected from the things of this world. I know that may sound a bit like an exaggeration, but it was indeed a message passed on to **me through church and Bible study. I believed I was falling short because I** never felt completely free. I wish I had some better models for downward living earlier on—honest, authentic people who helped me understand that freedom shows up in different shapes and forms and who would have **embraced and honored any movement that I experienced because it came** from God's spirit at work in my life.

A while back, someone on the fringes of The Refuge become frustrated that we honored sobriety from drugs but didn't actively discourage them from stopping smoking, too. She basically said, *"We're all excited that they gave up one addiction, but the truth is that another one is still actively roaring and we pretend like that doesn't matter."* **I responded strongly,** *"Hey, I'll take any freedom we can get and do absolutely anything we can to celebrate and honor it, no matter how long the line of other addictions are."* **Any movement** is better than none. Expecting people to make the leap from A to Z in a flash is completely unrealistic; in fact, unless we celebrate the small steps, often people won't ever make it around the first corner, let alone the long path.

It might be easy to dismiss this person's statement as an example of someone **being crass, but the truth is that many of us share that same mentality** when it comes to transformation in our own lives and the lives of others. Like the greedy Veruca in *Charlie and the Chocolate Factory*[27], **we want healing and we** want it now! We want change, and we want it now! We want it all, and we want it all now!

We get impatient with ourselves and with those on the journey with us and we lose sight that God is always at work, always redeeming and restoring, above and below the surface and in unexplainable ways that often make it difficult to measure or even explain. In John 9, the Pharisees were trying to figure out how to explain why a blind man whose sight was restored by Jesus was born blind. They were haggling back and forth to try to make sense of it all and discredit Jesus at the same time. The man who was healed said that he really didn't know the ins and outs of Jesus, but he did know this, *"...I was blind, but now I see"* **(John 9:25).**

I was thinking about this verse the other day and how most people I know in real life on the downward journey don't spend much time picking apart and defending systematic theology. Actually, most people I hang out with these days don't really know what that term means. These friends don't care about what this or that verse is supposed to mean or scriptural technicalities that people seem to spend a lot of time volleying around. What many of my friends seem to care about is what I think most people actually care about **when we get right down to it:** *Where is God in my real life?*

I love this story of the man Jesus healed because, while the Pharisees were trying to figure out a methodical way of explaining what had happened, and **all the reasons why it was wrong for Jesus to heal him on the Sabbath, the man** exclaims, *"I don't know...but I know this: I was blind, and now I can see."* *(John 9:25).*

Regardless of all the ways we dot our i's and cross our t's, the gospel prevails. Justice and mercy for the poor and oppressed, the message of death, resurrection and new life and the ways of Jesus' love and grace always seem to remain. The kind of healing Jesus offered in that moment to the blind man is available through us now. Because Jesus is incarnate in us, we can bring what was dead back to life. We can be part of restoring sight and of bringing hope and light to the darkest of places. *We can slowly and surely become part of setting people free.*

"In the downward life, freedom comes from engaging God's healing by shedding the things that hinder and rob us of life, relationship, and love."

It's also important to remember that freedom costs something. In my own life, this is apparent. Over the years as I emerged as a pastor and leader and found my voice, many others weren't happy about my new-found freedom. It was threatening. It rocked the boat and made some people feel uncomfortable. They weren't used to me disagreeing and preferred it when I was quieter and more compliant. On a much wider scale, the same thing happens when we gain sobriety over addictions or change unhealthy patterns in relationship with others—*people don't know quite how to relate to us anymore.* It can be confusing. And threatening. When we change, other people may be challenged to change, too. Many people don't like change.

This is part of the high cost to becoming a disciple of Jesus.

We need others to celebrate freedom with us and remind us that the cost is worth it. Freedom seems to come when mercy, love and compassion are extended to us and we step into a new way of seeing ourselves. Part of life on the downward path includes celebrating freedom and honoring change in our own and others' lives. Like each of the other characteristics **of life in the trenches, freedom is not measured by the typical standards but rather by something far deeper that can only come from strongly connected** relationship.

Celebrating freedom includes honoring change in people's lives no matter how big or small, by seeing what they might not see, finding ways to celebrate milestones on the journey, and getting really good at throwing a lot of parties.

See What Others Don't See

My good friend, James, a brother on the journey, is healing from childhood and marital abuse, as well as substance abuse and sexual addictions. When I first met James he was angry and harsh; insecurities and shame were infused into every part of his life. Over the years he has forged a few safe, healing relationships, and I see more kindness and love emerging. In a phone conversation I reminded him of the changes that I have seen. *"Really, you can tell?"* he asked, wondering if it was really possible. For him, it's hard to see **the change, but because a few of us have been along for the ride we can see** the shifts. He, like so many of us, needs tangible reminding.

It can be easy to downplay freedom—to compare, minimize, or assume that because people are struggling in other ways that any small shifts we make aren't meaningful enough to celebrate. We must resist our tendency to minimize or measure freedom. Every little bit of change is worth honoring! One day of sobriety, one hard conversation that someone was willing to engage in, one asking of another person for help instead of isolating, one bill paid on time, one job kept, one sliver of forgiveness offered against all odds, one stepping out of our comfort zone to serve another person, one moment of real laughter after a season of depression—*all are worth honoring because they point to faith, courage and change.* Each one is a gift and a glimmer of hope, healing, and freedom, no matter how small it seems.

This is a different way of thinking for many who have been part of certain Christian circles where change is measured in a very particular way. Freedom stories tend to be pauper-to-prince kind of stories where someone was living in disaster, found Jesus, and is now doing great. I don't want to minimize these kinds of stories because they really do happen, but if those are the only tales deemed "successful," those of us living in the low places of life with people will remain extremely discouraged. Most stories I intersect with are not glamorous or exciting; instead, they are simple examples of change that could easily go unnoticed if no one cared. Kingdom living cultivates eyes to see small, almost imperceptible changes in others and draw them out so these shifts can be celebrated.

We need help seeing and noticing change because we become blind to what God is doing in our own lives. It's one of the reasons we need each other so desperately. Community gives us a different set of eyes. I can see in others what I often can't see in myself. Part of our responsibility as brothers and sisters on the journey is to point out, acknowledge, and notice changes we see in each other--the large and small shifts. The seemingly imperceptible ways that we notice God healing, restoring, and changing us are easily overlooked; **we must be bold, call it out, draw it out, and remind others what we see. In the same way, if someone is telling us what they see, we need to be humble** enough to try and receive their gift of encouragement and love.

Celebrating freedom is not easy, especially when we know we have more work to do. I have a dear friend who is reckoning with some painful parts of her past that she stuffed down deep for years. She recently entered a very intentional healing process and has an amazing support system. No matter how supportive her friends are, though, she's the one who has to do the work, and it has been brutal. In such a short time, I have already seen changes in **her. She is less defensive, more vulnerable and more present. I told her the** other day that I could really see and feel this shift in her, and that I felt more connected to her than I ever had before. Like James, her first reaction was, *"Really? You can see change?"* To her, she only sees her life falling apart and **a long road of pain ahead. We can already see freedom emerging.**

The only way we can notice these kinds of movements is if we are in loving relationship with people who have developed eyes to see change. Most of the people I know who work in the trenches realize that from the outside looking in, it usually appears that we're not really doing much. That's because freedom is often gradually developed over time. Sometimes people still can't pay their bills, may still be using drugs, grieving over the loss of their marriage or parent, still struggle with mental illness, or seem to not have made much movement. Yet, because we are in close relationship, we know that for the first time in their lives they have felt loved and accepted, even if the feeling comes and goes. They are trying to hold onto a sense of love when they normally would give up. They are giving to others instead of only taking. They are crying instead of stuffing their pain. They are experiencing less shame this **year than last year.**

None of this movement is perceptible to the un-Jesus-trained eye. If we rely on the world's measures or on the need for 180-degree change success stories, we will be sadly disappointed. However, if we remain so intertwined with people's hearts and stories that we notice each shift toward good instead of evil, light instead of darkness, hope instead of despair, we will find reason after reason to celebrate. The more we celebrate, the more God-at-work we seem to notice.

Let Others In On It

A while back at a Refuge concert to benefit our advocacy fund someone slipped me a note and asked me to read it. I snuck away to a back room and opened the envelope. Inside was a letter and a small check made out to The Refuge. To most, this would probably seem an uneventful moment; people write checks all the time. But to my friend—a single mom who is now raising her granddaughter—this was the first check she had ever written in her entire life. Yes, her entire life.

With a long history of trauma, abuse, and addiction, she had never been financially stable. Through a series of steps to build a new foundation, she filed bankruptcy with the help of the legal clinic that my husband works for and now has her very first checking account. I asked if I could share her letter with our community; we hooted, hollered and celebrated with her. Even now, two years later, when I think about it I still can't help but smile. I feel incredibly blessed because I get to experience these kinds of stories, up close and personal, week after week. Part of my role as a leader in this community **is to help others get to share in the hope of these stories, too, instead of** keeping them to myself.

Freedom is intoxicating. When we find it, we want more of it. Part of my **responsibility is to help people let others in on it so that their freedom can** help others on the journey, too. It's important to cultivate cultures and **spaces where we say,** *"Can we share this out loud so hope for freedom also gets passed on to others?"* This takes courage for people and requires safe spaces where every story is welcomed and honored. The more it is weaved **naturally into our way of being and living the easier it becomes.**

The Bible is full of celebrations to honor God at work. In the Old Testament there are festivals to honor the first harvest, the freeing of God's people from captivity in Egypt, provision during the exodus, and the forgiveness of debts. Each celebration was focused on remembering what God had done and centered on a spirit of gratitude and humility.

The recovery community is savvy about measuring small steps. They have systems in place to honor sobriety, creating a place each week at meetings for folks to humbly and thankfully share their progress. As each story is **shared, it helps others remember what God has done and can do. We have** adapted their model into the culture of The Refuge, celebrating sobriety birthdays at our gatherings. We don't limit sobriety to drugs or alcohol, but also include abstinence from other things that harm us like cutting or abusive relationships. We aren't rote about it but rather adapt celebrations to each person's story and personality. Some may want a bigger more public party while others may only want a few close friends to be part. The important **thing to us is that somehow the freedom our friends are experiencing is celebrated.**

After a lifelong addiction to cocaine, my friend, Janice, finally made it to one year, clean and sober, then two years, then three years, then four years; she is now at five years. It's been a bumpy road with many ups and downs but the **part that seems the most clear is that people are her lifeline to God. When** we **honor her courage and the slow, hard-fought freedom she is experiencing,** it gives her the strength to keep going. It inspires others to keep going, too.

Get Really Good at Throwing Parties

I have always loved parties. I believe that Christ-followers should become the best party throwers in town, people who spend a lot of time celebrating what God is doing in lives. Ever since I was young I was always the one planning the get-together, hosting the shower, or gathering people to celebrate something or other. It wasn't until the past few years that I recognized that parties and celebrations were actually a spiritual discipline, a practice that strengthens our faith.

It seems that most people love a reason to gather, to get together with other people and "honor" life somehow. It could be a birthday, a sobriety or healing milestone, anniversary, graduation, retirement, promotion, post-memorial service reception, moving in open house, a moving on farewell, or a host of other causes to celebrate. These kinds of moments are sacred spaces no matter how fancy or unintentional. They are a set-apart time to celebrate God's movement in our lives and the lives of others. Over time I have seen the value of creating spaces for celebrating freedom in unique ways.

I had a friend who had been through an extremely painful season, journeying through a difficult divorce and losing his job. He entered into healing community and began to gain hope for what could be. As he approached his sixtieth birthday, we facilitated an intentional celebration that enabled him to reflect on the past by sharing his story and also look forward with hope to the next stage of his life with encouraging support from loving friends. His journey is far from done, but this moment is one that he can draw strength from as he continues on his way. It called out the reality of how far he had come. We celebrated the freedom he had been experiencing along the way, instead of saying *"you're not quite there yet."*

I am reminded of the powerful parables that Jesus tells about the lost coin, lost sheep, and lost son in Luke 15. In each story, it could be easy to discard the missing item as a lost cause, unimportant, or not worth pursuing, but God is relentless in pursuit, and each of these parables end with some form of party and rejoicing. In the stories of the lost coin and sheep, the finder exclaims, *"Rejoice with me, I have found my lost sheep...my lost coin!"* (Luke 15:6,9). The scriptures also say that not only does the celebration happen on earth, it happens in heaven, too, with great rejoicing at the finding of what was lost. In the story of the lost son, the father, delighted at the return of his son, takes the rejoicing even further: *"...Bring the best robe and put it on him.*

Put a ring on his finger and sandals on his feet. Bring the fattened calf and kill it. Let's have a feast and celebrate. For this son of mine was dead and is alive again; he was lost and is found..." (Luke 15:22-24).

Many people living on the margins do not feel valued. Instead, they often feel unimportant, unworthy or lost. We model God's persistence when we celebrate change no matter how big or small and rejoice over transformation in people's lives in intentional ways. Jesus seemed to love parties and get-togethers. I wonder if it was for some of the same reasons. Throughout the history of Israel, God even commands the people to celebrate with a festival, to go all out, and recognize what is good and valuable. God builds into the community a way of celebrating.

Each party or celebration we are part of is a sacred form of communion, a celebrating of life, an infusion of the spirit of God into our hearts individually and collectively. Parties and celebrations are an integral part of community life together on the downward path, and a significant place to notice God-at-work.

God, help us embrace your freedom and celebrate it in others.

To become people who celebrate freedom, we need to recognize that the cost of freedom is worth it because it is God working in our lives, transforming and healing us. The downward descent requires that we develop eyes to notice freedom and healing in our own lives and the lives of those around us. We need people to see in us what we can not see. At the same time, we must call out what we see in others, too, and celebrate it. We also need to become amazing party throwers, constantly honoring God's movement in people, no matter how big or small it may seem.

* * * * *

Personal Reflection:

1. How are you experiencing greater freedom in your life right now? What changes are happening in your personal and spiritual journey?

2. Is it easy or hard for you to celebrate freedom in your life? Why?

3. Is it easy or hard for you to see movement toward greater freedom in others lives? Why?

4. What are some movements toward freedom you need to consider celebrating in your own life? In the lives of others around you? What are some ideas to honor and celebrate them?

5. Take some time in your journal to thank God for the work he's doing in your life right now and the freedom you are experiencing, no matter how big or small. Consider this practice an act of humility and gratitude.

Group Discussion:

1. Connect with the story in John 9:13-25 about the man who was born blind. How have you seen freedom minimized because it didn't follow a specific spiritual guideline?

2. Share with the group how easy or hard it is for you to celebrate freedom in your own life.

3. What are some movements toward freedom you need to consider celebrating right now in your own life? In the lives of others around you? What are some ideas to honor and celebrate them?

4. What are some fun celebrations or parties you could consider building into your group's culture, to honor freedom and God's work in your lives?

Ways to Celebrate Freedom:

1. Whenever you notice change in someone's life, tell them. Share it in a card, an email, or a face-to-face encounter. Don't leave it unsaid or assume they can see it, too.

2. Find what specific kinds of freedom celebrations might work for your particular family, community, or context where you live or work. Build the practice of celebrating these markers together and consider integrating certain rituals or practices that help tangibly mark the moment. Be creative!

3. Throw parties for any reason you can. These can be small, intimate gatherings or large parties. The key is to find ways to gather people together and celebrate movement and freedom.

4. Think in advance of something that you would like to celebrate in your own life, big or small. The beginning of a new plan for health, 30 days with a counselor, path to work through anger, etc. Tell your friends that you would like to start the practice of celebrating the steps each of you are taking toward more wholeness and freedom.

Some Final Thoughts on Section Two: *A Life Centered on Action*

Extending love, mercy and compassion, welcoming pain, honoring doubt, diffusing power, practicing equality, pursuing justice, cultivating creativity, and celebrating freedom—these are essential practices of Kingdom living. Active, challenging, and inspired by the Beatitudes, these practices are embodied in **the life of Jesus, who told us to follow him on the downward descent so that** we might find life—*real life.*   Sure, the world—and sometimes the church— tugs at us, whispers to us and often screams at us, to go up, not down. But once we've tasted life down here, it's hard to go back.

Foundational on this downward journey is the practice of love. Jesus embodied love, mercy and compassion and calls us to the same. As we learn to receive these three things from God and others, we become more able to tangibly extend it to others, too. Deeply dedicated to seeking out the hurting, marginalized, oppressed and lost, we become people who go to others instead of expecting them to come to us, who leave the Ninety-nine to find the One. Through love, dignity is restored where it once was lost.

Fueled by a spirit of love, mercy, and compassion, we also become safer people who can welcome pain. We learn to embrace our own stories instead of run from them and accept brokenness as part of the human experience. As **we learn how to honor pain in our own lives, we are also able to hold pain** better for others. We respect that real people doubt. We understand that **doubt can strengthen our faith rather than be a detriment to it and learn to** hold certainties less tightly. This creates a space for people on the fringes of **life and faith to feel more comfortable sharing their real struggles with God.**

Inspired by Jesus' example, we are challenged to become sacrificial people who use our power—our leadership, value, and voice—on behalf of others, diffusing it in tangible and God-honoring ways. We intentionally nurture **a culture of inclusion that draws out the dignity and value of those who have been crushed under the weight of misused power. We also become** active practitioners of equality, a central component of Jesus' love that sets all captives free. We intentionally invite the marginalized, oppressed, and **neglected to the table so that we can be a more whole, integrated Body** together, and a more accurate reflection of the image of God than when we **are segregated and divided.**

Diffusing power and practicing equality are core aspects of pursuing justice on behalf of others. To pursue justice, we must first learn how to listen well and understand the needs and feelings of those experiencing injustice. As we **hear their stories and our lives become intertwined, our eyes are opened to** unjust systems and we naturally find ways to advocate for others.

There's often a human resistance toward expressing creativity and making ourselves vulnerable, but since we know that God's image is in us to be expressed, we become good at finding ways for people to cultivate creativity. We widen our view of creativity and resist the urge to measure creativity as talent, which keeps many from expressing what's deep within. Creating safe spaces to try to share creative expression opens up places in people's hearts and experiences that expand God's reflection in all kinds of ways. Because kingdom living is about transformation, part of life down here means we will celebrate freedom any way we can. No matter how big or small, any movement away from darkness and bondage and toward life and freedom is worth celebrating. As we notice the changes we see in our own lives and the lives of others, we celebrate them with parties and celebrations that honor God's restoration at work.

The downward life is centered on these eight practices. They give us an opportunity to participate in God's redeeming work instead of sit on the sidelines. They open up our world in ways that resonate deeply with the longings in our heart as Christ-followers desiring a life of practice instead of **theory.**

Our journey through them here is far from exhaustive. It takes a lifetime to both embrace and engage them. These elements have the potential to stir up a wide variety of challenging conversations on how they intersect with your personal story, the stories of the communities you live in, and the dreams you **have for the future.** *My hope is that each of you considers what they might look like in action in each of your particular contexts.*

It is quite easy to nod our head in agreement about their value; however living them out in daily practice is entirely different. Where and how are you seeing these values lived out? Which ones seem far away from your experience but resonate deeply in your heart?

Like most of Jesus' ways, no one is able to master these ideas. However, I do think it's possible to get better at some of them over time with practice, focus, and the wind of the Holy Spirit at work in and through us. We're all in different places. We each have diverse strengths and weaknesses. Our faith journeys are being challenged in different ways. The important questions are: *1) What is God stirring up in each of us? and 2) How can we gain courage to try them in our own unique ways?*

SECTION THREE
STAYING THE COURSE

"So in everything, do to others what you would have them do to you, for this sums up the Law and the Prophets. Enter through the narrow gate. For wide is the gate and broad is the road that leads to destruction, and many enter through it. But small is the gate and narrow the road that leads to life, and only a few find it." - Matthew 7:12-14

Living into the wild ways of Jesus is dangerous. Some days I wake up and plot **my way up and out of this downward way of life into a more comfortable,** secure place that doesn't require so much of my heart, life, flesh, or blood. There's no time clock to punch down here, where I magically turn off the "work" and focus on "real life." This is my real life. These are my real friends. There's no turning back or putting all the stories, messes and beauty that have been unraveling over the past chunk of years into a little box that makes **it feel more manageable.**

I admit, sometimes I'm very jealous of my therapist friends who have the luxury of once a week for 50-minute sessions and get paid an awful lot more than I ever will. I also think of what I aspired to when I first went to college and then graduate school and how vastly different things turned out for me. *This is definitely not what I pictured my life to be when I was in my 40's.* I pictured a few more zeroes on my paycheck and a personal assistant who made my life easier. Now, when I'm sitting in the lobby at the Social Security office holding my friend's hand while she's applying for help, I kind of shake **my head and laugh.**

I also get tired of pain and poverty. I get tired of trauma. I get tired of the needs being exponentially higher than the resources, especially when there is a multitude of money and people pouring into the church down the street with the best show in town. I get jealous. I get mad. I whine and complain, but I always come back to this—*life for Jesus-followers is not supposed to be easy, cushy, or predictable.* That was never the idea. He said it was going to be hard, and I am more confident than ever that he really meant it. But he also said it was a path to life...real life. So after I have wasted a few hours searching for jobs on Monster.com, I usually come to my senses and remember how beautiful life down here is, how much I'm learning about God, myself, and others that I would never learn if I took the easier path back up. No matter how hard I try to run away, I realize I'm ruined. I've tasted the Kingdom of God and now, nothing else will satisfy. My guess is that in all kinds of good ways, you may be ruined, too. If that's the case, then we have no choice but to keep on going, to stay the course and cultivate patience, endurance, and courage to continue to try and live out these hazardous, wild **ways of downward living.**

Jesus seemed to think living the downward path was not the occasional jaunt, but rather, a way of life. And it wasn't a nice scenic route, but the better, **bumpier path. It led to life. Unfortunately, only a few would choose it. I get** that. To live down here takes perseverance and courage.

To stay the course, we must consistently develop Jesus-trained eyes to see what the world often can't see, the divine image of God that resides in each human being. Putting the value of people above everything else is beautiful, but also hazardous because of the messiness of relationships and real life **together.   We will also need to give up typical measures of success and be** willing to be perceived as crazy or ineffectual. Jesus was not "successful" in the world's eyes. If we're really doing what he said to do, we probably won't be, either. Lastly, we will need to find strength from other brothers and sisters **deeply dedicated to life in the trenches to help sustain us along the way.** Otherwise, life down here is just too lonely.

Chapter 13

Beautiful and Hazardous

"Blessed are the eyes that see what you see." - Luke 10:23

I occasionally have weeks where I want to throw in the towel and run for the hills. And other weeks I have interaction after interaction that remind me of how thankful I am to get to do what I love to do. It is a privilege to engage in the low, dark, ugly places of people's lives and see God's grace and healing **bloom there.**

As much as it's nice to have money, it is also a gift not to have the confines of money, power and control guiding the life of our community. Many other innovators and in the trenches people I know are finding their way, too, offering love and hope outside of traditional church systems. Their actions **and perseverance help remind me what is possible.**

A while ago, on a particularly difficult week, I got a text message from a dear friend and brother from The Refuge. He knew I was blue and sent a text of encouragement, reminding me that we're not stupid, but what we are doing is "beautiful and hazardous."

Beautiful. Hazardous.

These two words resonated deeply. I see incredible beauty in the weirdest, darkest, strangest places. I see the good news of the gospel in living color. **I see hope emerge from hopelessness. I see voices used that were once** silenced. I see dignity restored. I see the cycle of addiction broken. I see the **unloved learn to love and be loved.**

Unfortunately, I often also get to see up close and personal how guided I still am by worldly (and sometimes religious) thinking. Deep down, I often want all the beauty and none of the hazards. **I want to live in the low places but I** don't want to let go of the things that keep me from getting there. I want to **do hard things during the day but have my comforts at night. I want smooth sailing in the middle of a wild and unpredictable ocean. I want to have my** cake and eat it, too.

I chose this downwardly mobile life. I chose to leave the old and embrace the new. No one forced me. I am a willing, though sometimes reluctant, participant in this glorious mess. Sometimes I need to be reminded that despite its beauty it is, indeed, hazardous.

Kingdom living is hazardous. Giving up the predictable confines of "church where you get to just sit and listen" is hazardous. Intersecting with people's real and painful stories is hazardous. Mixing with people who believe completely different things from us is hazardous. Living honestly is hazardous. Letting others love us is hazardous. The gospel is dangerous, scary, wild, hazardous and beautiful.

To live down here we will need to develop resolve, a deep sense of knowing that even though it's hard, it's worth it.

I was with some friends the other day that I hadn't seen in a few years, and they were asking a lot of questions about The Refuge. We have similar hearts **for the church but we rarely get the chance to connect. I shared a story about Christmas dinner at our house this year and how glorious it is to see those who feel orphaned by life and faith begin to feel connected to people in a** deep, dignity-restoring way. To hear someone, who less than year ago tried to kill herself, say that this was the best Christmas she had ever had, made **everything we do worth it.**

As I was **telling my friends these recent stories of hope, I felt my eyes well up** with tears. It is very easy for me to get overwhelmed by all of the ways The Refuge appears inefficient, confusing, or unsuccessful. We gather weekly as a large group in an old, ugly meeting hall in the run-down part of town that's hard to find. All of the leaders are in the messy process of healing just like everyone else. People interrupt us while we're facilitating and leave in the middle to smoke a cigarette. Some show up faithfully at every party and gathering and others drop by now and then. Sometimes our offering plate has less than 20 bucks in it. There are far more questions than answers. There are more awkward, holy moments than I can count and an overall spirit of never quite knowing what you're going to get.

However, when I tell the stories, I always get reminded that the Kingdom of God first appears inefficient, confusing, and unsuccessful. It is not a well-oiled machine, designed to produce a consistent outcome. If we're really living out the wild ways of Jesus we will never be efficient. It's just not possible, *because people and relationships—the most important part of Kingdom living—are always going to be messy, unpredictable, and hard.*

"To live down here we will need to develop resolve, a deep sense of knowing that even though it's hard, it's worth it."

Yet, in the midst of it all, it is important to develop a story that compels us to continue. We need a reason to stay in the trenches when it's hard, when life invites us to quit, and when we just don't want to continue. When we sit in the midst of conflict, and allow God's Spirit to work in our midst, when we get out of the way yet participate in what God is already doing, it's beautiful. It makes sense. It's not pretty but it's glorious.

It's too hard to live down here if we continue to see life and people through the eyes of the world (or even church, as usual). So many of these principles of downward living are not measurable and are often extremely difficult to see in the thick of our own and other people's real lives. It is important to acknowledge the costs and hazards of this kind of living. If we only focus on the costs, though, we'll miss that a better story is being told in us, through us, and around us. It is a gift to be part of God's restoration in this broken and hurting world. Through life down here, not only are others' lives being transformed, but ours are, too.

Life Down Here is Expensive

My friend and teammate, Mike, sometimes says, *"This is the most expensive damn church I've ever been part of."* He's a retiree on a limited income, but the truth is he has more money and resource than many others in our community. He shares his resources, time and love in so many ways, giving of his heart freely and purely. He pays for friends' counseling so they can get extra healing under their belts. He buys books for people when they really need encouragement. He takes people out to movies and dinner, and passes on simple acts of loving kindness in wonderful ways. The truth is, even though we joke about the financial cost, they are comparatively minimal. The real cost we're all paying is something far deeper.

It's the cost of discovering that a dear friend is back in the mental hospital after having another breakdown, after having been better for months. It's the cost of knowing that other friends are losing their house and there's nothing we can really do about it except hold their hand when they cry and help them move their things to a storage unit for a while. It's the cost of pouring and pouring love into people and finding that even after years, none of it has really stuck.

Those costs are painfully expensive because they engage our hearts, not our wallets.

And they are part of the cost of living down here.

A few years ago I intersected with one of the most painful moments of life in the trenches with people. I journeyed closely with a young woman with deep pain from her past, as well as some of her church experiences. I was glad she was part of our community because I knew the potential was high for her to find love, acceptance and belonging here. We loved her as well as we knew how to love her. But it wasn't enough. It just wasn't. I almost quit over it. After pouring out so much, for so long, and then finding that we were back at square one, I honestly was overwhelmed with sadness and shame. I felt like a failure. I felt used. I felt stupid. I felt angry at God for his supposed lack of healing. And I felt mad at myself for giving so much of myself for so long, thinking that somehow we'd turn a corner any day. We never turned a corner. We hit a dead end.

My back went out, literally, and I couldn't get off the couch for days. It actually was the catalyst for a year and a half of back problems, culminating with surgery this past year. It's not her fault. It's not God's fault. It's not The Refuge's fault. It's not my fault. Sure, we could all do some things differently, **but the more we have prayed and processed through it, the more convinced** I am it's just part of the hazards of living in the low places of people's experiences. Sometimes, it just takes a toll.

I've continued to learn a lot through this difficult season, but the biggest lesson is that I'd still much rather err on the side of love and mercy. In the midst of pain and suffering, we chose to love. And in choosing to love, we became the space for love to reside. No one can ever take that away from us. The value of being love for someone is not that they will change. Love is unconditional. The value of being love is that we get to experience loving **people. We stayed in a lot longer than many people might have because we** saw what Jesus saw—beauty, value, dignity that was buried very deep and **needed to be uncovered. So we gave it our all, the best we could, with all our** limitations and all our strengths.

It definitely didn't turn out the way we hoped. When we look back, sure, we made some mistakes we can learn from, but on the whole we would probably **do the same thing all over again. We would try. We would reach out. We** would love freely and without condition. We would show up as best we could. We would listen. We would offer a safe space to just be. We would trust more deeply in the knowledge that sometimes, no matter what we do, it might not turn out the way we hoped. It doesn't mean we are failures, didn't listen properly to God, had some wrong agenda or were somehow out of synch with God's will. *It just means that real life is messy and we're human.*

I have a good friend who got some excellent advice from a therapist about the importance of four simple things that can be very empowering in relationship **with people. She says part of loving well is learning how to: 1. Show up. 2.** Tell the truth. 3. Trust God. 4. Let go of the outcome.

The first two are skills based. They are focused on learning how to be present, **vulnerable, honest, and engaged with people in meaningful ways instead** of sitting on the sidelines. The second two are faith based. They require a **movement of God, something beyond us, and a peace that can only come** from the supernatural work of the Holy Spirit in our hearts and minds. I think these second two are the most difficult ingredients of life down here.

Trusting God and letting go of the outcome are risky propositions.

But isn't that the point. It's about developing the faith to stay in the space of love. **When we get out of the way, when we trust God and let go, we can** begin to see how God is redeeming the world. In letting go of the outcome, **God is able to do extraordinary things in us and through us.**

> *"Blessed are those who are persecuted for righteousness, for theirs is the kingdom of heaven."*
>
> *Matthew 5:10*

It makes me think of the cross Jesus died on and how at first things didn't turn out the way we had originally hoped. Through the gospels we see how Jesus showed up, told the truth, trusted God, and in so many ways let go of the outcome. In his last moments, even though he begged for this cup of suffering to pass from him and endured extreme pain and agony, he submitted to that trust, creating a far different outcome than anyone expected.

Jesus' example on the cross is central to life down here.

Real love hurts.

It costs something.

It doesn't always turn out the way we had planned, but in typical Jesus style, the story turns out better than we planned.

It's Also Priceless

A few weeks ago, while I was immersed in finishing this book and healing from back surgery, I received a painful email with some disturbing news. The orphanage we have been supporting in Africa was not legitimate. It is such a **sad story because of the supposedly real friendships we formed over the past** three years and how violating it is to discover such a deep betrayal.

We have been processing this together as a community in the past several weeks and the part that we always seem to come to is this: *We're glad we loved.* My son Jamison, who is 15 years old and was part of the mission team said it best: "No matter how things turned out in the end, we did the right thing. We loved." He's right. It is better to love than not to love. Despite the hazards, it was worth investing in the people who hurt us. It reminded us that **our choice to love could not be dependent upon the outcome.**

On the night he was arrested, Jesus still served the friend who was going to **betray him later that day, washing his feet, serving him food, and sharing his** heart with him. His farewell message to the disciples that evening centered on love. He said, *"...Love each other as I have loved you. Greater love has no one than this, that he lay down his life for his friends...this is my command: Love each other"* (John 15:12-13, 17). As the evening progresses, he was arrested and stopped talking about love, instead showing them what it really looks like. Love is the way of the cross. It is a way of sacrifice. It is the way of pain, and also the way of resurrection.

If we never love, we never get to experience the benefits of love. Sure, it's easier not to love. But it's also so much lonelier and emptier. Sitting on the sidelines at church every week, going through the motions, keeping our **hearts and lives protected is, indeed, easier and safer. It means less hassle** and less hurt. But it also means less love. The only way to experience love is to dive into it and be willing to risk getting hurt.

Our African friends hurt us, but every team member who recently traveled there agrees—it was worth it because we loved well. We became the space **where love resided. We gave our hearts as purely and as fully as we could.** Each person believes that despite the painful ending, there's a better story **being told in us and through us.**

Jesus is a story of love.

He loved well. And that love wasn't always well received. In fact, it ended up leading to his death. The part that I relish about the resurrection story, though, is that it seemed like all hope was lost when he took those last breaths on the cross. The promised Messiah was gone, just like that. But three days later, the story radically shifted. All was not lost; in fact, it was beautifully

redeemed.

In the trenches, loving others, we have to continually anchor ourselves to the bigger story. That love is worth it. That Jesus redeems. That what we see **here is not all there is.**

Jesus tells the disciples, "*I have told you these things so that in me you may have peace. In this world you will have trouble, but take heart! I have overcome the world*" (John 16:33). The Apostle Paul reminds us that, "*...if indeed we share in his sufferings in order that we may also share in his glory*" (**Romans 8:17**).

Suffering leads to experiencing God's glory. Yes, I have some hard stories with unhappy endings. At the same time, I also see lives change in a way that is priceless. I get to see the work of God in people's lives in the here and now. I get to see miraculous healings and resurrection happen in people. I get to see single moms gain the confidence to go back to school and get their degrees so they can support their kids. I get to see the way a loving community can surround a person who is sure they are unlovable, creates transformation. I get to see a new, solid faith emerge after a long season of deconstruction and doubt. I get to see sobriety after years of addiction. I get to see voices being used and gifts being shared where they once had been stifled. I get to see **people being set free from the pain of their past and passing that freedom on to others by sharing their stories openly and honestly.**

In the midst of other people's life changes, I am being transformed, too. I **am learning how to receive love instead of only give it. I am learning to feel** not only pain and suffering at deeper levels but also joy, hope and love. I am **learning to step into my leadership, value and voice in ways I never thought** possible. I am learning to listen better. I am learning to speak up more. I am learning to have patience. I am learning to grieve. I am learning how to trust **God, others and myself in ways that scare me half to death. I am in essence** learning what it means to be human...to be like Jesus.

I can't put a price on the benefits of living down here, but I know that once you've tasted it, it's really hard to go back. My friends and I often share how, after living down here, we're ruined for anything else. Once you've eaten this bread and tasted this wine, nothing else will really satisfy. It makes me think of Isaiah 55:1-3.

> *"Come, all you who are thirsty, come to the waters; and you who have no money, come, buy and eat! Come, buy wine and milk without money and without cost. Why spend money on what is not bread, and your labor on what does not satisfy? Listen, listen to me, and eat what is good, and you will delight in the richest of fare. Give ear and come to me; hear me, that your soul may live."*

The biggest benefit of life down here is life. When Jesus said, *"I came that they may have life, and have it to the full" (John 10:10),* I have a feeling this is part of what he meant.

I've never hurt this much, struggled this much, or prayed this much in my whole life. I've also never experienced more joy, beauty, love and hope.

The hazards are costly. Our hearts will be broken and we are sure to be hurt. The benefits are beautiful; seeing life change up close and personal, no matter how big or small, makes the journey worth it. The way to stay the course is to keep telling the stories of what God is doing in us, and in others, through life down here. They aren't all going to be success stories, but I have a feeling they will all be transformation stories—stories of changing, learning and growing. These stories will sustain us, feed us and give us strength to keep going. We will need that strength, especially with many forces working against us.

* * * * *

Personal Reflection:

1. What are some of the personal costs of downward living you are experiencing?

2. What are some of the benefits?

3. What is sustaining you and keeping you going? What is transforming in you during this season of your journey? What are you learning about yourself? God? Others?

Group Discussion

1. What are some of the costs of downward living?

2. What are some of the benefits?

3. What sustains you and keeps you going?

4. Stories can really help sustain us. Share with the group a short story that brings you hope or inspiration; this can be a personal story or something you've seen or observed.

5. Share with the group what is transforming in you through this season of your journey. Walk through these three areas together— What are you learning about yourself? God? Others?

Chapter 14

We May Look Like Losers

"So the last will be first, and the first will be last." - Mathew
20:16

By the world's standards, Jesus looked like a loser. When he left earth, he didn't seem to have much to show for it. Sure, people had been healed, and he had collected quite a following. But he didn't build an empire or overthrow the government like people expected. He didn't conquer the competition. He was supposed to save the day but was instead betrayed by his friend and unjustly executed on a cross. Then, most of his rag-tag band of followers **ended up dying cruel deaths on behalf of their faith.**

Regardless of the pretty packages people try to wrap Jesus up in, following him has never been a "successful" proposition. Even though Jesus tells us that to gain our life we will lose it, and that the first will be last and the last will be first, much contemporary Christian culture has packaged a much cleaner, **results-oriented faith.**

My friend and blogger Pam Hogeweide writes on the power of being small, **simple and ordinary. She says:**

> *"In the Western mindset, big accomplishments that create*
> *economic or social power equals greatness. For sure, there*
> *are many who prosper at what they do. Thank God for*
> *the inventors and creatives who go out on a limb to try*
> *something innovative. But in the kingdom of God, greatness*

is not measured this way. God's kingdom is an upside-down kingdom where the smallest becomes the biggest and the greatest citizens are its invisible sons and daughters.[28]"

When we choose this path, we will likely be seen as stupid, slow, non-strategic and crazy. Jesus reminded us we will take hits for loving the unlovely, when loving the lovely gets much bigger bang for its buck. We'll never have enough money, security or all of the things that would probably make us, and our loved ones, feel a lot better but will no longer satisfy. We embrace the words of Jesus because we've tasted and experienced the mess and glory of humanity and divinity mixed together, and we can never turn back.

> *"Incarnational relationships can't be measured."*

The downward journey includes shedding **the tendency to measure ourselves by the** world's standards and embracing the fact that we may often look like losers. This looks like breaking our addiction to the unhealthy pursuit of "excellence", letting go of how strategic associations make us look successful, and developing extreme patience by respecting that *incarnational relationships can't be measured.* This is terribly difficult to do, especially in a culture that is obsessed with measures, results, and worldly definitions of success.

Jesus Wasn't "Excellent"

In today's world of church ministry and planting, it's very easy to hear the word "excellence" thrown around. In our search for what works, we've learned **to mix growing and building the Kingdom of God with business models, and** not always to great effect. When I read the gospels and see the ministry of Jesus, "excellence" is not a word I would connect to him, at least not in the definitions we seem to use.

For most leaders, "excellence" means: *top-notch, focused, seamless, entertaining, powerful, inspirational, compelling, squared-away, and strategic.* We want our events organized, our gatherings structured, and our teams prepared. "Excellence" sells. People are strangely drawn to it. The bar keeps getting higher and the need for performance and perfection keeps **increasing.**

No one means bad by it, but we must be aware of how much damage the pursuit of "excellence" can cause to humanity. It often creates a false sense of what's really important in the Christian life, makes the not as perfect feel **unworthy and invalidated, and perpetuates power and strength instead of** humility and sacrifice. As we stay the course on a downwardly mobile life, we will have to reckon with the tug toward pursuing a false excellence as being a **sign of success.**

Seeking after "excellence" feeds our egos in provocative ways. It magnifies the "us vs. them" divide. It often reflects our desire for perfection rather than the good of God's Kingdom. It drives us to create performance standards that can be very unforgiving. It's easy to miss grace in a world centered on demanding expectations.

An unhealthy striving for "excellence" has permeated typical Christian culture more than we might even want to believe. The pressure for leaders and churches to "raise their game" and perpetuate perfection can't be underestimated; the competition is stiff and survival of the fittest requires the strongest swimmers to bring it, and bring it hard, for the purpose of taking **ministries, churches, and dreams to the next level.**

This kind of striving for perfection is a demanding taskmaster. It demands **certainty in a world of doubt. It demands performance in a world of pain.** It demands power and control in a world of chaos. It demands attention in a world of inequality. It demands punishment in a world of injustice. It demands only the best in a world of creativity.

By the world's standards, Jesus did not model "excellence"; in fact, he is the antithesis of many of the nutty things we build churches on. He chose the oddest, least likely, least qualified people to be in his inner circle, was completely unpredictable, continually interacted with the people everyone else looked down on, and was extremely confusing in much of his communication, teaching in parables. People looked to him to be the triumphant, powerful king, and he ended up hung on a cross like a mere criminal.

To sustain life down here, we will have to continually let go of our unhealthy striving for perfection and "excellence."

When I think of a Kingdom built on love, mercy and compassion, I don't think of performance or perfection. I think of equality, generosity, mercy, sacrifice, justice and freedom. I think of Jesus touching the leper and healing the lame. I think of reaching into the dark places and restoring someone's dignity.

Letting go of our addiction to perfection and worldly achievement is difficult but it leads to a very different discovery—relationship. A former pastor and friend of mine got tired of consumer church and longed to be part of a body that reflected Jesus, instead of focusing their energy on pursuing "excellence." In his search, he stumbled upon an aging mainline denominational community that looked radically different from most of his prior experiences. He said:

> *"There are maybe thirty people in a crappy little building, with music from a midi file off a laptop, bulletins with typos, no audio-visuals, no stage, no lighting, no greeters...nothing, and I mean **nothing** that added up to what I considered critical to being an excellent church in the past. Someone forgot to bring bread for communion, so they even had to use rainbow colored Goldfish crackers. I wept the entire way through my first visit, because it occurred to me that people aren't coming here because of all the stuff I thought was important enough to fire people over. They came because this was their family. Nothing else really seems to matter to them. They take Jesus very seriously. But they don't take themselves so seriously that the small stuff ever really bothers them. Good enough is all we really need."*

My friend could see that people weren't seeking performance or perfection **but instead desired true communion with God, each other and themselves.** They were seeking real relationship.

Every time I talk about this idea of an imbalanced perception of "excellence" there are always those who argue it should continue to be valued highly in the cultivation of God's ways. They claim, *"God calls us to our best."* **I do** not disagree with giving God our all, but we must remember everyone's "all" looks different. Also, the pursuit of perfection and "excellence" in ministry naturally tends to defer to strength and power instead of including the weak and vulnerable. Many people I know aren't perceived as "excellent" in the typical sense; where does this leave them? It leaves them on the outside with **nothing to contribute.**

"Excellence" can easily become an arbitrary standard of those in power. Kingdom living means sacrificially letting go of perfection and performance, in order to include and embrace the left-out and undervalued. It also means giving ourselves grace and room to let go of extremely high self-expectations that often only lead to shame. Letting go of this distorted focus on success increases the chances we will look like losers. But rest assured, Jesus was definitely a loser, and he changed the world because of it.

The Tortoise or the Hare

One of my favorite Aesop's Fables is *The Tortoise and the Hare*.[29] With five kids I have read my share of books over the years; the stories are timeless and profound. At a Wednesday evening House of Refuge gathering, the facilitator asked us to look through magazines and pull out pictures that represented where we were spiritually, emotionally, or practically. For some reason, a **picture of a tortoise and hare drew me in.**

I am a natural hare. I can work my tail off like there is no tomorrow. I am a sprinter and like to get to the good stuff as quickly as possible. Build, build, build. Faster, faster, faster. I set unrealistic goals that I can never meet. I have extremely high standards and am way too hard on myself. Over and over again, I restart my diet, my workout plan and my commitments to be more organized. The joke in my family is that when I die my headstone will say "Kathy Escobar – I'll start my diet Monday." I have been taught and trained that faster, quicker, bigger and smarter is always better.

Learning from the tortoise is difficult for hares like me. The tortoise is dedicated to one step at a time, slow and steady, with one foot in front of the other. A little movement is better than nothing. Chip away at it instead of trying to knock it all down at once. Do what you can to stay on the path. Celebrate any movement. Stay the course. Stop and smell the roses. You'll get there eventually. Small, stable, and simple is beautiful.

When I see that list of tortoise-like thoughts, I have a natural urge to say, *"Yeah, right, but that's not how things work."* That's not what wins games, awards, or the worldly things that make us feel good about ourselves. That's certainly not how church planters have been trained. That's not what most of the bestselling books tell us about life, relationships or reaching our goals.

Yet Jesus seems much more like a tortoise than a hare. When the wind is howling, Jesus is asleep. When the crowd is clamoring for his presence, he's nowhere to be found. When the Empire is ready to strike, Jesus is silent.

The hare-tortoise dichotomy shows up in many areas of our lives. Subtly, it becomes about "getting there, arriving and figuring it out" instead of enjoying the journey, noticing the beauty, embracing the ugly and hard when it comes up, and celebrating the process.

In downward living, tortoises win. Hares won't last. The hare will burn out, **become discouraged and frustrated, and get angry with God and themselves** for not "succeeding" in the way they thought they might. Tortoises will stay the course, weather the storms, and keep plodding along at a steady, slow pace. They will succeed by finding God in the midst of the journey, not just **at the end.**

When we planted The Refuge, my friends Ken and Deborah Loyd reminded me of the value of the slow course, and the fact that real community takes a frustratingly long time to develop. As I listened to their stories, I felt convicted by my urgency and frustration at the lack of support and stability that I desperately desired. They helped me recognize that this kind of living never equates to anything fast or stable—two qualities that I kept desperately seeking.

On one hand, their advice could have felt extremely discouraging for hares, leaving not much to look forward to or expect. Hares want things now. But it helped me to cut some ties that needed cutting—those that led to my need for efficiency and speed. It takes years, not months, to really cultivate these kinds of connected, interdependent relationships and a strong foundation for loving community. I knew this in my head, but hearing them share from their **years of living in the trenches with people, it began to translate into my heart.**

They didn't tell me what I wanted to hear, but they told me what I needed to **embrace.**

In the past, I would never say, *"Slow is good,"* but I'm beginning to lean into it. I am learning that nurturing and developing authentic, lasting community takes years upon years; there aren't any shortcuts. I am discovering that our traditional measures of success are arbitrary, man-made ideas, and have nothing to do with spiritual transformation. I am finding that when I slip and trip, I can get back up and put one foot in front of the other. I can keep walking instead of expecting myself to sprint to make up for my misstep. I am learning **to live in the paradoxes of my own life and the lives of others. I am developing** resiliency and the ability to bounce back from conflicts instead of letting them pull me under. I am slowly giving up the desperate quest for a quick God high, and am noticing the beauty and power of a day in and day out rhythm of a simple, no gimmicks spiritual walk on the downward path.

My friend, Karl, says that he is learning to take the amount of time he thinks it will take to produce change and multiply it by twenty, and that will possibly get us in the ballpark. He's not joking. That's a lot of time, a lot of patience, and an incredible amount of trust that God is at work even when it's hard to see.

Every day I look in the mirror I realize that hares can learn to embrace that **slow is good. Change is possible, even in me.**

New Measures of Success

Letting go of the false pursuit of "excellence" and gaining patience for the long haul paves the way for what is most important in downward living— relationships. When we redefine what is truly important, it creates a new **measurement for success.**

I sometimes tell friends that I wish I had "church amnesia" so that I could erase most of what I formerly learned about "success," "ministry," "leadership" and what makes things "viable." In my old circles, valid ministry means constantly "growing," "getting financially stable," and "building up new, stronger leaders." When I look at The Refuge against this list, I tend to get a little embarrassed. I hear the words of successful Christian leadership books and see how we are falling short. Sometimes it taps into my insecurity and woundedness, and my controlling instincts start to kick in. I then desperately try to prove that The Refuge is important, that what we're doing is valid, which quickly leads me to **becoming exhausted, overwhelmed and discouraged.**

Slowly but surely I am learning that none of the old rules apply. The Refuge is nurturing a way of living that is really only about one thing—relationships: **open-handedly and open-heartedly loving people in and outside of our** community in tangible ways. This requires an incredible amount of time, emotional and spiritual energy, and grace. The only way for me to be free is to completely throw out the old measures of success and look in one direction and one direction only—*where God's spirit is at work in the hearts and lives of the people right in front of me.*

It is incredibly easy to miss. I will never forget the words of someone who was visiting our community on our one-year anniversary dinner. We were in sad moods; it was a weird weekend and not as many people came as we expected. We **felt embarrassed and said to this guest,** *"Yeah, we're sorry, there are a lot of people missing tonight...we're kind of bummed."* That woman replied **strongly,** *"Well I'm here."*

I will forever remember the power of those simple words. *"I'm here."* It cut directly to the heart of the matter and was exactly what I needed to hear.

Downward living is about seeing what's right in front of us. Look at what we do have, not what we don't. Be thankful for the gift of today, instead of longing for tomorrow. Notice the beauty. Appreciate what is.

When we redefine success, it can easily drive away people who fund success. The Refuge is not rich by any means, but we are wealthy in ways that don't have anything to do with money. There are resources I long to have, but when I take a step back and look more carefully I see how many are actually right before me. They might not be big, shiny, clear, or exactly what I'm sure I really need but they are here, right before me. Small kernels of hope, reminders that God is taking good care of us, and showing us what it means to trust. I see tiny gifts of love, hope, peace and connection in places where there once was none, stalks of beauty seeping up from the ground, and small ways God says, *"I'm here, too."*

The people I know who are trying new forms of missional community and living into the wild ways of Jesus understand that we often don't know how to measure our impact in anything other than deepened relationships between people, God, and ourselves. We ask questions like:

- **Are people experiencing change, feeling more loved, and passing on more love to others?**

- **Are they less isolated and more connected?**

- **Are resources being shared between people in organic, natural ways?**

- **Are people's gifts and talents being drawn out of them and being used to grace and encourage others?**

- **Are voices being used that were once silenced?**

- **Are fear and shame lessening, losing their hold over people's lives?**

- **Are we seeing the image of God emerge from people in whom it once was buried?**

"Downward living is about seeing what's right in front of us, looking at what we do have, not what we don't."

Incarnational relationships are nearly impossible to measure, but they seem to align with Jesus' ways a lot more readily than what my friend and missional pastor, Rose Madrid-Swetman calls the three B's: budgets, butts, **and buildings.**[30] These are standard measures of success in most ministries **because they are tangible and easy to measure.**

At The Refuge, we have no money, building, put-togetherness, pat answers, or rising stars. We're just a hodge-podge of ordinary people trying to be **humble, open, caring, and dedicated to learning to be together and spread** love, mercy, and justice in whatever small ways we can. I think this is what is emerging in the next generation of church—a groundswell of people who look like losers to the powers that be, but are living out love instead of just talking about it, and who are becoming the Kingdom of God for one another instead of just thinking about it.

Downward living means embracing that we might look like losers. Jesus looked like a loser, too.

* * * * *

Personal Reflection:

1. How has a focus on perfection, performance and "excellence" affected you in terms of life and ministry?

2. Are you more of a tortoise or a hare? How?

3. What are some ways you measure change in your own life?

4. Consider the idea of "church amnesia" and trying to forget things you may have subtly or directly been taught about success. What are some of these messages you need to try to forget as you continue the downward journey? What are some new messages you need to remember?

Group Discussion:

1. Respond together to the word "excellence." What does it bring up for you?

2. Share with the group whether you feel more like the tortoise or the hare? Why?

3. Consider your own context and make a list together, with two columns. "The world (and sometimes "the church") says success is _____" and "In the Kingdom of God, success is _____." Brainstorm an unedited list and talk about it afterward.

4. Reflect on the list of questions at the end of this chapter that are better measures of change *(Are people experiencing change, feeling more loved, and passing on more love to others? Are they less isolated and more connected? Are resources being shared between people in organic, natural ways? Are people's gifts and talents being drawn out of them and being used to grace and encourage others? Are voices being used that were once silenced? Are fear and shame lessening, losing their hold over people's lives? Are we seeing the image of*

God emerge from people in whom it once was buried?). **Consider** the groups or ministries you are currently involved in. How are you seeing some of these shifts in people?

5. Consider together the idea of "church amnesia" and trying to forget things you may have subtly or directly been taught about success. What are some of these messages you need to try to forget as you continue the downward journey? What are some new messages you need to remember?

Chapter 15

We May Be Crazy But We're Not Alone

"But I don't want to be needy." - Almost everyone I know

This path of downward descent can be a lonely path. Often, we don't have great models for this kind of living so we can feel crazy, lonely, and sometimes **very discouraged. But the loneliness goes away when we are connected to** other friends who are passionate and crazy enough to risk their egos, pride, educations, salaries, time, hearts and lives to create spaces for others to love and be loved in. Finding and investing in that community is deeply important **to staying in the trenches.**

In the first six months of cultivating The Refuge I remember feeling completely stupid and was ready to give up. Stuck in the shadow of the thriving consumer church down the street from us, our efforts felt futile. I also knew very few female pastors and none who were experimenting with co-pastoring. I had lunch with a dear friend, Tracy Howe, who is a musical missionary and deeply dedicated to building bridges and encouraging others to find support. With tears flowing down my face, directly into my burrito, I told her I didn't know **if staying was possible. She reached across the table, put her hands on my** shoulders, looked me in the eyes and said, *"Kathy, you need to make some new friends."*

Tracy had given me a wise piece of advice. I needed to surround myself with **people who had been there before. I was the newbie and I needed people** who could speak into my life and remind me that it was possible. I couldn't do this kind of ministry alone. I needed people to walk with me as I thought out loud so we could learn from each other; I needed people who would provide **a warm shoulder to lean on when it was extra hard.**

To help me begin, Tracy introduced me to several men and women who were co-pastoring and who had been in the trenches, cultivating eclectic missional communities that looked different from our ministry, but had the same ethos and heartbeat. It took courage for me to make the calls, show up for some "blind dates," and intentionally meet new people. Beautiful, lasting **friendships emerged, and we have dedicated ourselves to learning as much as we can from each other, swapping stories, sharing tears, and clinging to each** other when we feel a little desperate.

An important aspect of sustaining life on the downward path is intentionally finding community with others who are passionate about living out their faith in similar ways. We don't have to have friends who are doing exactly the same work, but we must find connections with fellow sojourners who **understand how we feel, and who inspire and challenge us.** We also need to continually embrace a spirit of humility along the way. Life down here will naturally humble us; there's almost no way around it. However, leaning **into that humility and embracing it as a way of living is crucial to longevity.** Walking hand-in-hand with humility is the ongoing practice of relying on God, instead of ourselves. Like all parts of Kingdom living, this is easier said than **done, but we must always remember that God is the one who heals, restores** and redeems. We are only the vessels through which Christ's spirit flows.

Finding Community

When Tracy introduced me to those people, it opened up my world. I found **others who were trying to live out their faith in similar ways, leading, loving,** and learning along the way. Previous to those introductions, I did not have any friends in close proximity that really understood what we were doing. They assumed we were just "planting a church," with all of the same characteristics **of church they were used to. Even though I loved these friends, I could see** how we were comparing apples and oranges and it wasn't all that good for my soul. I'd leave some conversations feeling more lonely and discouraged **than when I arrived.**

Finding like-minded friends is not an easy task, especially if you live in rural areas or in places that frankly just don't have a lot of people practicing love in these ways. For me, the new, long distance relationships with like-minded men and women helped me build the foundation I needed to sustain the work. We committed to talking on Skype regularly and doing what we could to meet up at conferences or gatherings. It definitely didn't happen naturally. Because life down here is so full and often intense, there's not a lot of room for adding in "one more thing." I found, though, that making community connections a priority has been a necessity, not a luxury. I have moments where I desperately need to talk to someone outside of my immediate **community who understands what I am feeling.**

We have a better chance at healing the painful moments when we share **them. When I hear my friends in the trenches share their stories, I am infused** with hope. When I share my story, they are infused with hope. My friend, Donna, from The Bridge Church says:

> *"We talk at least once a month and are able to vent about life*
> *and our communities in a way that is encouraging and always*
> *leaves me feeling a bit more hopeful about what we're doing.*
> *These conversations assure me that I am not alone, and that*
> *the community I'm a part of is not alone, either. We are in*
> *different boats, so to speak, but the connection keeps me*
> *from being lost and scared in this huge ocean of church and*
> *community."*

Every time we connect, we learn we're not alone.

Even though I have been graced with amazing, in-the-flesh relationships over the past chunk of years, I have also found so much hope, community and connection through the online relationships I've formed. When I can't actually sit across the table from a friend over a cup of coffee, I can find love and encouragement through the Internet. There are many practitioners trying all kinds of beautiful and creative endeavors in missional living. Reading their stories and connecting with their journey helps expand my world and remember we are in good company on this downward path. My cyber-community is just as valuable as my face-to-face one.

Finding like-minded encouragers takes time and finesse. It requires stepping out of our comfort zones and asking people for help. The method that seems to work the best are natural connections that come from relationship. My friend, Tracy, knew me, what I was like and what I was about, so she was able to be an effective matchmaker, connecting me with others who shared a similar passion. Some don't have the luxury of these in-the-flesh connections. Many people are extremely isolated or don't know where to begin. Looking back, I would never have met Donna had I not picked up the phone. Attempting to connect through online networks and blogs is definitely worth considering, but it takes effort and risk.

Over the past several years, I have tested the waters with different networks to see which ones resonated more closely with my passion. Sometimes on the surface it might look like we have a lot in common, but if I find that underneath, there is an atmosphere of inequality, power, or people making a profit from it, I become skeptical. The appendix of this book includes some potential networks and resources to consider accessing to cultivate ongoing support and friendship. The bottom line is that every person is different. Each person needs to find what works for them, including ideas and solutions that are life giving.

Embracing Humility

Embracing a larger sense of community meant stepping into humility. Because I tend to be very independent and appear stronger than I really am, it took a lot out of me to seek input and admit how needy and lonely I often feel. At the core of downward living is the value of humility. Philippians 2:1-4 reminds us:

> *"Therefore if you have any encouragement from being united with Christ, if any comfort from his love, if any common sharing in the Spirit, if any tenderness and compassion, then make my joy complete by being like-minded, having the same love, being one in spirit and of one mind. Do nothing out of selfish ambition or vain conceit. Rather, in humility value others above yourselves, not looking to your own interests but each of you to the interests of the others."*

Even though the words resonate deeply, every time I am confronted with them, **it ignites a tension between what I believe and my own self-centeredness and** narcissism. Embracing humility meant I had to cultivate support, which meant I had to let go of my pride. It meant recognizing and acknowledging I couldn't do it alone. I could play the Lone Ranger, but it would kill me inside. I could pretend nothing was wrong or I could make the necessary calls to the people **who could help.**

Humility creates the space for God and our friends to speak into our lives. It requires admitting our weaknesses instead of pretending we have it all together, embracing the doubts of soft and open hearts, and letting go of being know-it-alls. It requires remembering we are no better than the person next to us, acknowledging our human tendency to control and aspire for power, and respecting and honoring our spiritual poverty and need for God. These characteristics are necessary for downward living but will also be counter-intuitive for many of us who don't like feeling needy.

Embracing humility allowed me to see some common threads woven through the lives of many people I know who have dedicated themselves to downward living. Three things feel clear:

1. **Finances are always an issue.**

2. We long to be connected with like-minded friends who encourage **and support us.**

3. **We consistently live with a feeling of inadequacy because the needs will always be greater than the available resources.**

Embracing humility means confronting difficult issues with finances. Most friends I know who do this work full-time are bi- or tri-vocational. The beauty of downward living, though, is that it doesn't have anything to do with full-time ministry or people with specific training. It has to do with a way of life that is available to everyone—*absolutely everyone*—not only those trained in seminary or with certain credentials.

At the same time, those of us who feel very committed to cultivating new communities and ministries as leaders will have to wrestle with the reality that there's no real money in this kind of work. Yes, we've wondered out loud, "*If we could only get a big donor,*" but that often means going back to a consumer, power-influenced model that can't be mixed with a Kingdom, power-diffused model. The result is that we will need to respect the difficulty of finances.

The needs in downward living seem to always be greater than the resources. When we first started The Refuge people outside our community would ask us how they could help us. I would always joke and say, *"Our prayer team is full. Send money."* It's not that I don't value everyone's prayers; it's the reality that there's never enough resource for the work that we do. Now, after five years of living like this, I think I'd add, *"Our prayer team is full. We always need money, but what we need more is you. We need more people willing to be in the muck and mire of real people's lives."* At some point we realized, real ministry happens when more people step into the pain and suffering in the world and reveal love. More money was good, but more people was great.

When we're struggling with needs exceeding resources it seems like the Serenity Prayer used in many recovery circles is a helpful reminder. The part many people know and recognize is the beginning:

> *"God, grant me the serenity to accept the things I cannot change, courage to change the things I can, and wisdom to know the difference." (Reinhold Niehbuhr).*

The rest of the prayer, added in 1953, goes like this:

> *Living one day at a time; Enjoying one moment at a time; Accepting hardship as a pathway to peace; Taking, as Jesus did, this sinful world as it is, not as I would have it; Trusting that He will make all things right if I surrender to His Will; That I may be reasonably happy in this life and supremely happy with Him. Forever in the next. Amen.*

Jesus told us this path was hard, that we would need to stop worrying about tomorrow and be thankful for provision, today. It is easy to talk about but **much harder to live. Daily, our faith is put to the test, and serenity in the midst** sometimes remains elusive. But testing our faith, allowing it to be developed, gives us resolve to stay when it's hard.

Addicts know that the path to freedom is living one day at a time and not getting too far ahead of ourselves. It's important to have dreams for the future; however, if we become tied into visions, strategies and plans, we can quickly lose peace when things aren't materializing as fast as we'd like or in the ways we think are best.   Cultivating a spirit of humility and patience is part of the journey.

Over the course of life in our community I have had to ask for money to help meet The Refuge's needs. It is always one of the **hardest things for me to do. We get by on a shoestring budget and our expenses are miniscule compared to many other** ministries, yet, every time, I feel bad asking for financial help. I think it triggers a deep **pain about not being valued enough and** sometimes sends me to a bad place of thinking of God's seeming lack of provision for us. I also see what having to ask teaches **me about humility and trust. At my core,** I don't like having to rely on others. I like giving, not receiving. **I have no doubt this is a character defect that God is transforming through my life down here. I am slowly and** painfully embracing that I need to practice humility and bravely ask others for help.

Now and then we partner with another church here in north Denver.   Their **resources far outweigh the needs and** every time I have asked for help for our

"To sustain life down here we need to intentionally find community with others, who are passionate about living out their faith in similar ways."

single moms, they have somehow come through. Asking does not come easy for me; I often hesitate before I hit the "send" button on an email, scaling through my options one last time to make sure I can't just figure it out on my **own. But inevitably, I always seem to come to the point where I have to be** courageous, press send, and ask for support. It's so humbling.

Who we ask, why we ask and how we ask looks different for each of us, depending on our own unique circumstances. The point, though, is that to live down here, we'll probably have to ask for extra support. **We will need to partner with other people, agencies, groups, ministries, professionals, and neighbors because the burden is too great otherwise.**

Stepping out of our comfort zones is not easy, but it is important. I personally am not too keen on feeling needy. I like to feel strong, confident and clear. What I continue to learn over time is that downward living requires me to step into the first Beatitude over and over again—*"Blessed are the poor in spirit.""* (Matthew 5:3). The New Living Translation of the Bible says it like this, *"God blesses those who are poor and realize their need for him."*   As much as I don't like it, I need God. There is so much down here that can't be **controlled or managed in the ways many of us are used to. It is a wild way of living, not a tame one, and requires a level of trust that can feel completely** foreign to those who are used to being able to rely on skills and abilities. Recognizing my need for God helps me remember that God is the one who produces healing. I'm just a messenger.

Relying on God and Each Other

I have some new friends who are cultivating a faith community in upstate New York called The Distillery. They are trying to live out Kingdom values in tangible ways and continue to bump into the same issues that most of us experience in these downward places. When we talk, I resonate with so much of what they are feeling. They sometimes feel tired, lonely and overwhelmed by the amount of needs and the lack of resources. They feel frustrated at "the system" and sometimes at other Christians' ambivalence toward the poor and marginalized. We try to share ideas and experiences, but the thing that seems to help the most is simply connecting together, in prayer and through **encouragement, reminding each other that this is what we signed up for, and,** given the choice, we wouldn't choose differently. Then we cry out to God on each other's behalf and ask God to give us strength and courage to keep going.

John Martinez, one of the founders of The Distillery, describes it like this:

> *"We send emails and texts and pray for each other and support each other by sharing resources together. It is like we*

have a true friend who is praying for us and cares about what happens to our little community. We no longer feel isolated and insular in our approach to church, and we are proud to say that we are members of the TransFORM Network (www. transformnetwork.org). We have met with other folks in the network across the country and continue to try and sit down for coffee or send an email in an attempt to be in each other's lives and learn from each other. We have come to realize that God is not only building a community here in Albany called The Distillery, but just as important God is building community on a much bigger scale, and we get to be a part of it. We are finding that we need others and others need us, too."

We are both learning that needing God and each other is good and necessary for our survival on this downward journey.

At the same time, one of the most dangerous traps we can step into as we **nurture these friendships in the wider community is comparing ourselves to** others. Comparison is human nature and we can easily get sucked into this kind of thinking when we are intersecting with others in the trenches. We can think that because it's working for them, we need to do it, too. We can feel less-than or like we aren't doing something quite right. I can't tell you the number of times when I read certain blogs or books I think, *"Why aren't we doing that? Maybe if we did we'd be more this or that."* Almost every time I need to remind myself—these are great ideas and they are worth considering, but I don't necessarily need to do them nor are we missing out by doing things differently. Part of gaining resolve and strength for the downward journey is embracing our uniqueness and learning to be comfortable in our skin, instead of trying to be someone we're not. We need God to help guide, strengthen and remind us to stay anchored in our unique contributions as people and communities.

The big and beautiful body of Christ has many unique expressions. Needing each other helps us respect and honor our differences and learn from each other. We are each making our own contributions to the Kingdom: our individual and collective expressions of faith that are unique, creative and necessary. Needing each other isn't becoming exactly like each other; rather, it is to value and learn from each other, celebrating our individuality and God at work in us and through us. Making these connections with a larger community has been deeply critical to seeing the Kingdom of God in the trenches. It helps me remember why I'm here.

"Needing each other isn't becoming exactly like one another; rather, it is to value and learn from each other, celebrating our individuality and God at work in us and through us."

When we tell our stories to others on the downward journey we are remembering why we are here in the first place and why we are compelled to stay. We can laugh at our insecurities and celebrate the victories. We can try to take ourselves less **seriously and remember that God is at** work, despite us. We can chuckle at our failures and honor the transformation that **is happening, not only in our own lives but also in the lives of our friends.**

Even though this kind of living is heavy, it is also light. We don't have to be bound up with all of the complications of organized, power-infused systems. We don't have to **be distracted by rules, doctrinal statements** and official policies. We don't have to be **burdened by the weight of big budgets and people clamoring for power. Instead, we are able to live more freely than ever** before, and it's important to honor and celebrate that gift.

Jesus turned the ways of religion on its head and challenged the status quo to consider a new way with love at the center. Groups and communities infused with the values expressed in the Beatitudes, no matter how big or small, can change the world and infect people and places with Christ's love and heart:

> *Blessed are communities who are poor in spirit, for theirs is the kingdom of heaven.*

Blessed are communities who mourn, for they will be comforted.

Blessed are communities who are meek, for they will inherit the earth.

Blessed are communities who hunger and thirst for righteousness, for they will be filled.

Blessed are communities that are merciful, for they will be shown mercy.

Blessed are communities that are pure in heart, for they will see God.

Blessed are communities that make peace for they will be called sons of God.

Blessed are communities who are persecuted because of righteousness, for theirs is the kingdom of heaven.

When we allow the Beatitudes and 12 Steps to speak deeply into our lives, we cannot help but come back to a radical need for God. It is impossible to live out these dreams without God's constant help, without other people incarnating Jesus, looking us in the eye and reminding us it is happening, it is possible, and we're not crazy (or maybe that we are crazy but at least we aren't alone).

* * * * *

Personal Reflection:

1. How have you felt lonely on this downward path?

2. What relationships are helping you sustain life down here?

3. What does it feel like for you to "need" others?

4. Embracing humility as a way of living is easier said than done. How are you learning humility right now?

5. Do you tend to compare yourself to others? How? What kinds of feelings does this usually stir up in you?

Group Discussion:

1. Share with the group how you may have felt lonely on this downward path. Share what you think might be missing for you in terms of support.

2. What is it like for you to "need" others?

3. Share with the group what embracing humility looks like for you right now. What are you learning about it and how is it transforming you and your faith?

4. Can you think of ways you have compared yourself to others and how it's affected you?

5. Read through the Beatitudes (Matthew 5:3-12) through the lens of communities. How does it feel to look at the Beatitudes through this lens?

Chapter 16

Born Again and Again

"I have come that they may have life, and have it to the full."
- John 10:10

In John 3, Nicodemus engages in a covert conversation with Jesus in the middle of the night. Jesus shares with Nicodemus what it means to be born again. I love this imagery—a religious ruler sneaking out of his house so no one would see him, because some wild and crazy guy named Jesus had gotten under his skin. Jesus' response to Nicodemus has become a pivotal expression in the history of Christianity—*"...no one can see the kingdom of God unless he is born again"* (John 3:3). **For most, it has come to represent the idea of going to heaven.** We see Kingdom of God and we instinctively think, "Up there... after we die."

But Jesus was very concerned about the here and now. What if Jesus was talking about right now, this moment, and even in each second? It's easy to see the idea of being born again as one single event. But what if Jesus is presenting an idea of continual renewal?

A different way of viewing this passage as meaning something beyond eternal salvation is the idea that Jesus was talking about embracing a practice of continually being born again. Each person has a story, and that story can easily get messed up by the garbage the world throws at us. To be born again is to let go of the old story, the one that says we're worthless and less than, so we can embrace a new story that says we are worth it. To be born again is to be willing to readjust our thinking, actions and heart as the Holy Spirit moves and changes us. Life experiences change, cultures shift and we grow up, out **and into places we never expected. With each twist and turn we are required** to re-examine our faith, listen for God, and be willing to be "born again."

Christianity is in the midst of a major, history-making shift. I would suggest it's trying to be "born again." As a mother of five, I know the birth process is painful. While beautiful in so many ways, it is also long and sometimes scary. It's hard, messy and really bloody.   Like birth, the only way to see something new is to keep pushing through, to get to the other side. There have been so many times along this re-birth process in my faith and practice that I have wanted to turn back and go back to the old. But like the birthing process, once it's started, the best way out is to lean into it, breathe, and keep pushing **through.**

The other part I learned through the birth of my children is to remember the pain doesn't last forever. Eventually, a baby is birthed, bringing with it its own **unique needs that will have to be nurtured and strengthened along the way.** So it is with the downward journey. As we give birth to new ways of living **out our life and faith, we will experience pain and struggle. But the pain and** struggle leads to something better, toward transformation, hope and being conformed more into Christ's likeness.

The church isn't the only thing that needs to be born again and again. We do, too. As we let the Holy Spirit work in our lives and infuse us with courage to keep walking this direction, we will continue to give birth to new hopes, dreams and practices.

Let us never underestimate the pull to resist change, to be satisfied with the status quo. Anyone can relate to the religious order of Jesus' time that said, *"Hey, we have this religious stuff buttoned down, so what do you mean we need to be 'born again?' We've been doing this for a long time, and it is working for us. Don't mess with it!"*

However, there was a whole other group of people that got a stirring in their heart they couldn't ignore, a taste of the wild ways of Jesus that actually produce life. Who could have imagined that wacky band of misfits would end **up being part of changing the course of history forever?**

We follow the wild ways of Jesus because it works. It's real. It produces **something of deep value that completely alters our life in ways that we could never have imagined, but could never live without. Life on this downward path includes the willingness to be uncomfortable and let go of what we have** always known and to continually be born again.

The best hope for our continued future is to become people who are willing to give up comfort and ease and continue the journey down. We will have to **shed things that hinder our ability to love our neighbor the way Christ calls us to.**

We will have to honestly answer some tough questions:

- What is God asking us to consider that we really don't want to do?

- **What needs to change?**

- **What do we need to let go of?**

- What do we have to risk?

- How can the true heart of Jesus be **expressed through us, individually** and as communities?

- What obstacles are holding us back?

- **What are we afraid of?**

"The only way to get to something new is to go."

As we process these questions in the quiet, our hearts or in the company of other brave friends, I hope we hang on to an important truth—**the only way to get to something new is to go.** To put one foot in front of the other and start walking in a new direction. Jesus didn't say, *"sit around for years and years talking about following me."* He said, *"Come, follow me."* Now.

The Need For Practice

Downward mobility is about a wider, more open-handed view—a more trusting view that God is bigger than we've maybe ever known. It doesn't remove the fear, but it does produce more freedom, a soft heart, willing

hands and feet, and an openness to go places that before might have scared us away.

I use the words "try" and "practice" a lot, and hope both get renewed emphasis as an integral part of Kingdom living. Like so many parts of the Bible, there's no convenient formula to follow or easy way to master Jesus' commands to practice love. To lean into love is a lifelong journey of successes and failures. We will always live in the tension of doing the best we can, finding ourselves in need of God's and others' grace, and waking up the next day to try again. Practice implies that we don't yet have something mastered. It implies we're learning and engaging a sense of humility. It implies that we're attempting something that we might not yet know how to do.

Years ago when I was homeschooling my oldest son, Josh, he got frustrated when he wouldn't get 100% on his assignments. He would get so angry at himself, and at me. I continually reminded him that school is for learning, and that we aren't supposed to know everything automatically. We can only learn through practice. The same is true for us as we fumble and stumble through tangibly living out our faith. We aren't being measured or graded. Love is an art, not a science, and no one is keeping score here. What does matter, **though, is that we have a willing, humble heart that is dedicated to trying.**

To stay down here in the low places, we will have to continue to nurture our resolve. The pull "upwards" will always be a strong one, and we will need God's help to resist our natural urges for a safer and more predictable life on the upward ascent. Despite the hazards of Kingdom living, if we can notice **the beauty along the way, we will be strengthened and encouraged. We** also need to remember that we will probably look like losers in the world's **eyes. Because love cannot be measured, we must let go of needing to prove** anything to anyone but settle into living and loving more freely and purely. Also, we will need to forge community with other like-minded friends who are just as crazy as us and continue to support, pray for and remind each other that this way of living is indeed, worth it. Most of all, we will need God's **breath to blow through us, strengthen us and show us the way.**

Down We Go

Over the course of this journey together, I hope our hearts and minds have been stirred and challenged. The desire for living into the wild ways of Jesus is contagious. At the same time, we know these ways don't come cheap or easy. As we allow our faith and practices to be reborn again and again, we will find new life—and fresh challenges—each and every time.

Centered on a theology of brokenness that honors the real places that people **live, downward mobility is about being in Jesus School, a place to learn and** practice the wild ways of Jesus in relationship with other people. With the Beatitudes as our inspirational text, we can also draw strength from the 12 **Steps, which point toward a spirit of humility and a desperate need for God.**

Life down here is messy, and it doesn't take long to discover that dreams are a lot prettier when they are just dreams. In the trenches relationships with people require us to do our part to break the great divide between "them" and "us," and to restore dignity where it's been lost through unhealthy power dynamics that keep people separated. We trade easier "to" and "for" missional relationships for transformational "with" relationships, where we learn to not only give but also receive. The Kingdom of God isn't going to just drop out of the sky, so we will have to resist the gravitational pull toward resource and comfort and be active participants in making our dreams for "what could be," a reality. This looks like creating little pockets of love in different shapes and forms, places to actively practice the ways of love and **grace.**

Life down here also includes certain core practices. These are at the center of downward living and create transformation not only in others' lives but also in our own. These practices—extending love, mercy, and compassion, as well as welcoming pain, honoring doubt, diffusing power, practicing equality, pursuing justice, cultivating creativity and celebrating freedom—challenge the status quo and give us a strong, tangible framework for practice. In the world of ascent, these practices won't make sense, but on the downward path they **strengthen our faith and ability to tangibly love God, others and ourselves. I** keep returning to these eight challenging ways of living to continually align me with the essentials of life down here.

I also continue to learn that in order to sustain life on the downward path I have to see life and people through Jesus' eyes and strain to see the beauty amidst the ugliness and hazards of real life. Forging friendships with others **dedicated to downward mobility helps strengthen and encourage us along** the way and remind us that even though we might look crazy or unsuccessful to others, we're certainly not alone.

As I meet new dreamers and intersect with other courageous friends on the journey, I remember that despite all its hazards there's no place I'd rather be. There's so much beauty down here, and honestly, I'm ruined. I've tasted life and nothing else will satisfy. Sure, sometimes the lure of the ascent tempts me; I plan my escape back up for a little while before I admit, yet again— there's no place I'd rather be, no direction I'd rather walk, no people I'd rather **be with.**

Despite the current shifts in Christianity, many are being drawn back to truly reflecting Jesus individually and corporately in the ways he lived out the Kingdom. To do this, we will have to reject the powerful systems, structures, pull toward legalism, and quick fixes that permeate our culture in the same way it infected religion in Jesus' time. We will have to courageously risk our pride, safety, security, money, and our reputations to stay on this downward path. We will have to let the marginalized guide us, use our imaginations, and **courageously lead other people down with us, too.**

Tim Keel, author, pastor, and cultivator of missional communities, says it well. He reminds us:

> *"We need men and women who have previously been on the margins to come forth and lead us. In focusing so exclusively on our cognitive capacities, we have lost our imaginations. We need mystics. We need poets. We need prophets. We need apostles. We need artists. We need a church drawn out of the margins, drawn from the places and filled with people and shaped with competencies formerly thought to be of little account. In fact, perhaps it is from such 'marginal' communities as these that influence will begin to spread outward into communities that have been domesticated in a modern world and thus rendered docile. We need a wild*

vine grafted into the branch. We need alternate takes on reality. We need a different kind of leader – one who can create environments to nurture and release the imagination of God's person."[31]

As we are born again and again and continue to practice the ways of love, may **new dreams emerge and new ways of living out our faith be birthed.**

Grace, peace, and courage to each of us as we continue walking this hard and beautiful path together.

May we go where Jesus goes, love as Jesus loves.

With love and hope at the center of all we do, down we go.

* * * * *

Personal Reflection:

The final reflection is a practice I use to remember the reasons I chose this path.

God, may we continually humble ourselves and acknowledge our weakness, insufficiencies, and spiritual poverty. May our hearts be soft, open, willing to be changed even at great cost to our security and pride.

God, may we radically include the forgotten, the rejected, the marginalized, and the oppressed as a reflection of your love. May our tables be open and welcoming, with Christ's spirit binding us all together, despite our differences. May men and women, black and white, rich and poor, gay and straight, educated and uneducated, single and married, and everything in between, live side-by-side and be equally loved, respected and included.

God, may we cultivate compassion in our hearts and our actions so that the hurting will feel your healing touch. May we never be too busy to love. May we be the people who stop, who care when no one else does, who listen, bandage wounds, carry folks to the hospital, and ooze mercy.

God, may we boldly enter into deep and challenging incarnational relationship with each other to keep practicing your ways of love. May we get tangled up with other people, sharing the good, bad and ugly. May we be dedicated to people who get on our nerves and drive us crazy. May we share resources, carry each other's burdens, and pray intensely for each other, remembering that how we love each other is how we love the world.

God, keep showing us the way, guiding us as we stumble, practice and try.

Give us courage to keep following you down.

Amen.

Group Discussion:

1. Consider the prayer in the Personal Reflection together. Which parts are you drawn to? Which parts are the most challenging to you?

2. Brainstorm some other ways to be "born again" than maybe you have previously considered? What's being re-born in you right now?

3. Share with the group some next steps you feel God might be encouraging you to consider as you continue the journey down.

4. What are some of your dreams for community? How do they look similar to the ways of decent? Do they differ? Share your vision of hope with the group, and dream big.

Suggested Resources

Networks and Collectives:

1. TransFORM Network (www.transformnetwork.org) - An international, trans-denominational, missional community formation network. The purpose of TransFORM is to bring together men and women who are on the verge of starting new communities or are already cultivating new communities and to give them the encouragement and resources **they need to get started and be sustainable.**

2. Parish Collective (www.parischcollective.org) - A growing collective of churches, missional communities and faith-based groups which are rooted in neighborhoods and linked across cities.

3. Love is Concrete (www.loveisconcrete.org) - **An online community** dedicated to rallying and developing community activists through **story, play and song.**

4. Christian Community Development Association (www.ccda.org) - The mission of CCDA is to inspire, train and connect Christians who seek **to bear witness to the Kingdom of God by reclaiming and restoring** under-resourced communities.

Books:

1. *Community and Growth*, Jean Vanier (1979, Paulist Press).

2. *Changes that Heal*, Henry Cloud (1993, Zondervan).

3. *Jesus Freak: Feeding, Healing, Raising the Dead*, Sara Miles (2010, **Jossey-Bass).**

4. *The Irresistible Revolution: Living as an Ordinary Radical,* **Shane Claiborne (2006, Zondervan).**

5. *Church on the Couch: Does the Church Need Therapy?* Elaine Martens

Hamilton (2008, Zondervan).

6. *The Secret Message of Jesus: Uncovering the Truth that Could Change Everything*, Brian McLaren (2007, Thomas Nelson).

7. *The Critical Journey: Stages in the Life of Faith*, Janet Hagberg and Robert Guelich (1989, Sheffield Publishing).

8. *Evolving in Monkey Town: How a Girl Who Knew All the Answers Learned to Ask the Questions*, Rachel Held Evans (2010, Zondervan)

9. *Everyday Justice: The Global Impact of Our Daily Choices* (2009, InterVarsity Press).

References

1   The Twelve Steps of Alcoholics Anonymous are reprinted with permission of Alcoholics Anonymous World Services, Inc. ("AAWS") Permission to reprint the Twelve Steps does not mean that AAWS has reviewed or approved the contents of this publication, or that AAWS necessarily agrees with the views expressed herein. A.A. is a program of recovery from alcoholism only - use of the Twelve Steps in connection with programs and activities which are patterned after A.A., but which address other problems, or in any other non-A.A. context, does not imply otherwise. Additionally, while A.A. is a spiritual program, A.A. is not a religious program. Thus, A.A. is not affiliated or allied with any sect, denomination, or specific religious belief.

2   King, Martin Luther, Jr. *"I Have a Dream."* March on Washington. Lincoln Memorial: Washington. 28 August 1963. Address.

3   Rohr, R. (2009). *The Naked Now: Learning to See as the Mystics See*. (p. 132). New York, NY: The Crossroad Publishing Company.

4   Vanier, J. (1979). *Community and Growth*. (p. 96). Mahwah, NJ: Paulist Press.

5   Center for Action and Contemplation, Emerging Church Conference, Albuquerque, NM August 2009

6   Rasmussen, R. Kent. (1997). *Mark Twain: His words, Wit, and Wisdom*. (p. 93). New York, NY: Random House.

7   Vanier, J. (1979). *Community and Growth*. (p. 28). Mahwah, NJ: Paulist Press.

8   Prabhu, R.K., & Rao, U.R. (Ed.). (1945). *The Mind of Mahatma Gandhi*. (p. 27). Austin, TX: Greenleaf Books.

9   Prabhu, & Rao, U.R., p. 27.

10   Mother Teresa. (2007). *Come Be My Light*. (p. 279). New York, NY: Doubleday Religion.

11   Miyazawa, K. (1972). Winds from Afar. (p. 51). Palo Alto, CA: Kodansha America; First US Edition edition.

12   Hagberg, J.O, & Guelich, R.A. (Ed.). (1995). *The Critical Journey, Stages in the Life of Faith*. Salem, WI: Sheffield Publishing Company.

13   Hagberg, & Guelich, p17.

14   Hagberg, & Guelich, p6-16.

15   Hagberg, J.O, & Guelich, p32-160.

16   Merriam-Webster, Incorporated. (2001) doubt. Merriam-Webster's Collegiate Dictionary.

17   Bolz-Weber, N. (2007, March 31). Doubt and Idolatry. Retrieved from http://sarcasticlutheran.typepad.com/sarcastic_lutheran/2007/03/index.html

18   Anspaugh, D (Director). (1993). *Rudy* [DVD].

19   Claiborne, S, & Haw, C. (2008). Jesus for President: Politics for Ordinary Radicals. Grand Rapids, MI: Zondervan.

20   Romig-Leavitt, C. (2008, December 12). What Could Be: Equality Practiced. Retrieved from http://kathyescobar.com/2008/12/12/what-could-be-equality-practiced/

21   Merriam-Webster, Incorporated. (2001) egalitarian. *Merriam-Webster's Collegiate Dictionary*

22   Dillon, J (Director). (2008). *Call + Response* [DVD].

23   Merriam-Webster, Incorporated. (2001) justice. *Merriam-Webster's Collegiate Dictionary*.

24   abhu, & Rao, U.R., p. 150.

25   Washington, D (Director). (2007). *The Great Debaters* [DVD].

26   al-Din Rumi , J. (Ed.). (1997). *The Essential Rumi.* (p. 102). London, England: Castle Books.

27   Stuart, M (Director). (1971). *Willy Wonka and the Chocolate Factory* [DVD].

28   Hogeweide, P. (2010, Feburary 4). Church of the One. Retrieved from http://godmessedmeup.blogspot.com/2010/02/church-of-one-html.

29   Aesop. (2003). The Tortoise and the Hare. In D.L. Ashliman (Ed.), Aesop's Fables. New York: Penguin Group

30   Madrid-Swetman, R. (2008, July 19). Building to Serve Others Part 1. Retrieved from http://rosemadridswetman.com/2008/07/19/building-to-serve-others-part-1/

31   Keel, T. (2007). *Intuitive Leadership: Embracing a Paradigm of Narrative, Metaphor, and Chaos.* (p. 138). Grand Rapids, MI: Baker Books.